GOOD TO GREAT

ALSO BY JIM COLLINS

Built to Last

(with Jerry I. Porras)

GOOD TO GREAT

Why Some Companies Make the Leap . . . and Others Don't

JIM COLLINS

RANDOM HOUSE
BUSINESS BOOKS

First published in the US in 2001 by Collins Business

Random House Business Books,
Random House, 20 Vauxhall Bridge Road, London SW1V 2SA

Random House Australia (Pty) Limited
20 Alfred Street, Milsons Point
Sydney, New South Wales 2061, Australia

Random House New Zealand Limited
18 Poland Road, Glenfield
Auckland 10, New Zealand

Random House (Pty) Limited
Isle of Houghton, Corner of Boundary Road & Carse O'Gowrie,
Houghton 2198, South Africa

Random House Publishers India Private Limited
301 World Trade Tower, Hotel Intercontinental Grand Complex,
Barakhamba Lane, New Delhi 110 001, India

The Random House Group Limited Reg. No. 954009

Papers used by Random House are natural, recyclable products made from wood grown in sustainable forests. The manufacturing processes conform to the environmental regulations of the country of origin.

ISBN 9780712676090

Companies, institutions and other organizations wishing to make bulk purchases of books published by Random House should contact their local bookstore or Random House direct:
Special Sales Director
Random House, 20 Vauxhall Bridge Road, London SW1V 2SA

Tel 020 7840 8470 Fax 020 7828 6681

www.randomhouse.co.uk
businessbooks@randomhouse.co.uk

Printed and bound in India by Replika Press Private Limited

This book is dedicated to the Chimps.

I love you all, each and every one.

CONTENTS

MEMBERS OF THE *GOOD-TO-GREAT* RESEARCH TEAM ASSEMBLED FOR TEAM MEETING, JANUARY 2000

First row: Vicki Mosur Osgood, Alyson Sinclair, Stefanie A. Judd, Christine Jones

Second row: Eric Hagen, Duane C. Duffy, Paul Weissman, Scott Jones, Weijia (Eve) Li

Third row: Nicholas M. Osgood, Jenni Cooper, Leigh Wilbanks, Anthony J. Chirikos

Fourth row: Brian J. Bagley, Jim Collins, Brian C. Larsen, Peter Van Genderen, Lane Hornung

Not pictured: Scott Cederberg, Morten T. Hansen, Amber L. Young

Photo credit: JIM COLLINS COLLECTION.

ACKNOWLEDGMENTS

To say this book is "by Jim Collins" overstates the case. Without the significant contributions made by other people, this book would certainly not exist.

At the top of the list are members of the research team. I was truly blessed to have an extraordinary group of people dedicated to the project. In aggregate, they contributed something on the order of 15,000 hours of work to the project, and the standard they set for themselves in the quality of their work set a high standard for me to try to live up to. As I struggled with writing the book, I pictured all the hardworking members of the team who dedicated months (in some cases, years) to this effort looking over my shoulder and holding me accountable, challenging me to create a final manuscript that met their standards, worthy of their toil and contribution. I hope this effort meets with their approval. Any failure to reach that standard rests entirely with me.

Members of the Research Team for
Good to Great

Brian J. Bagley	*Lane Hornung*	*Vicki Mosur Osgood*
Scott Cederberg	*Christine Jones*	*Alyson Sinclair*
Anthony J. Chirikos	*Scott Jones*	*Peter Van Genderen*
Jenni Cooper	*Stefanie A. Judd*	*Paul Weissman*
Duane C. Duffy	*Brian C. Larsen*	*Leigh Wilbanks*
Eric Hagen	*Weijia (Eve) Li*	*Amber L. Young*
Morten T. Hansen	*Nicholas M. Osgood*	

In addition, I would like to thank Denis B. Nock at the University of Colorado Graduate School of Business, who was instrumental in helping me identify and recruit the very best graduate students to join the research team. Getting the right research team members on the bus was *the* single most important step in making the project successful, and Denis played a singularly important role in getting a whole busload of great people. Also at the University of Colorado, I am indebted to Carol Krismann and her dedicated staff at the William M. White Business Library, who patiently worked with members of the research team to locate all sorts of arcane information. In addition to Carol, I would like to acknowledge Betty Grebe, Lynnette Leiker, Dinah McKay, Martha Jo Sani, and Jean Whelan.

I am particularly indebted to a large number of critical readers who invested hours in reading drafts of the manuscript and feeding me the brutal facts about what needed to be improved. Yet despite sometimes searing (and always helpful) feedback, they continually reinforced my faith in the potential of the project. For their frankness and insight, I would like to thank Kirk Arnold, R. Wayne Boss, Natalia Cherney-Roca, Paul M. Cohen, Nicole Toomey Davis, Andrew Fenniman, Christopher Forman, William C. Garriock, Terry Gold, Ed Greenberg, Martha Greenberg, Wayne H. Gross, George H. Hagen, Becky Hall, Liz Heron, John G. Hill, Ann H. Judd, Rob Kaufman, Joe Kennedy, Keith Kennedy, Butch Kerzner, Alan Khazei, Anne Knapp, Betina Koski, Ken Krechmer, Barbara B. Lawton, Ph.D., Kyle Lefkoff, Kevin Maney, Bill Miller, Joseph P. Modica, Thomas W. Morris, Robert Mrlik, John T. Myser, Peter Nosler, Antonia Ozeroff, Jerry Peterson, Jim Reid, James J. Robb, John Rogers, Kevin Rumon, Heather Reynolds Sagar, Victor Sanvido, Mason D. Schumacher, Jeffrey L. Seglin, Sina Simantob, Orin Smith, Peter Staudhammer, Rick Sterling, Ted Stolberg, Jeff Tarr, Jean Taylor, Kim Hollingsworth Taylor, Tom Tierney, John Vitale, Dan Wardrop, Mark H. Willes, David L. Witherow, and Anthony R. Yue.

We were very fortunate to have the participation of executives instrumental in the transformation at the good-to-great companies who patiently endured our questions during one- to two-hour interviews and, at times, follow-up conversations. To each of the following people, I would express my hopes that this book captures the best of what you accomplished. Truly, you are the unsung heroes of American business: Robert Aders, William F. Aldinger, III, Richard J. Appert, Charles J. Aschauer, Jr., Dick Auchter, H. David Aycock, James D. Bernd, Douglas M. Bibby, Roger E. Birk, Marc C. Breslawsky, Eli Broad, Dr. Charles S. Brown, Walter Bruckart, Vernon A. Brunner, James E. Campbell, Fred Canning, Joseph J. Cisco, Richard Cooley, Michael J. Critelli, Joseph F. Cullman 3rd, John A. Doherty, Douglas D. Drysdale, Lyle Everingham,

Meredith B. Fischer, Paul N. Fruitt, Andreas Gembler, Milton L. Glass, James G. Grosklaus, Jack Grundhofer, George B. Harvey, James Herring, James D. Hlavacek, Gene D. Hoffman, J. Timothy Howard, Charles D. Hunter, F. Kenneth Iverson, James A. Johnson, L. Daniel Jorndt, Robert L. Joss, Arthur Juergens, William E. Kelvie, Linda K. Knight, Glenn S. Kraiss, Robert J. Levin, Edmund Wattis Littlefield, David O. Maxwell, Hamish Maxwell, Ellen Merlo, Hyman Meyers, Arjay Miller, John N. D. Moody, David Nassef, Frank Newman, Arthur C. Nielsen, Jr., John D. Ong, Dr. Emanuel M. Papper, Richard D. Parsons, Derwyn Phillips, Marvin A. Pohlman, William D. Pratt, Fred Purdue, Michael J. Quigley, George Rathmann, Carl E. Reichardt, Daniel M. Rexinger, Bill Rivas, Dennis Roney, Francis C. Rooney, Jr., Wayne R. Sanders, Robert A. Schoellhorn, Bernard H. Semler, Samuel Siegel, Thomas F. Skelly, Joseph P. Stiglich, Joseph F. Turley, Glenn S. Utt Jr., Edward Villanueva, Charles R. Walgreen, Jr., Charles R. Walgreen, III, William H. Webb, George Weissman, Blair White, William Wilson, Alan L. Wurtzel, and William E. Zierden.

Numerous people from the companies in our research were enormously helpful with arranging interviews and providing us key documents and information. In particular, I would like to note Catherine Babington, David A. Baldwin, Ann Fahey-Widman, and Miriam Welty Trangsrud at Abbott Laboratories; Ann M. Collier at Circuit City; John P. DiQuollo at Fannie Mae; David A. Fausch and Danielle M. Frizzi at Gillette; Tina Barry for her assistance at Kimberly-Clark and her insights about Darwin Smith; Lisa Crouch and Angie McCoy at Kimberly-Clark; Jack Cornett at Kroger; Terry S. Lisenby and Cornelia Wells at Nucor; Steven C. Parrish and Timothy A. Sompolski at Philip Morris; Sheryl Y. Battles and Diana L. Russo at Pitney Bowes, Thomas L. Mammoser and Laurie L. Meyer at Walgreens; and Naomi S. Ishida at Wells Fargo.

I would like to give special thanks to Diane Compagno Miller for her help in opening doors at Wells Fargo, John S. Reed for his help in opening doors at Philip Morris, Sharon L. Wurtzel for her help in opening doors at Circuit City, Carl M. Brauer for his insights on Circuit City and generous sharing of his manuscript, James G. Clawson for his Circuit City cases and insights, Karen Lewis for her assistance with Hewlett-Packard Company Archives, Tracy Russell and her colleagues at The Center for Research in Security Prices for their diligence in ensuring that we had the most current data available, Virginia A. Smith for her helpful guidance, Nick Sagar for key beta, Marvin Bressler for his insight and wisdom, Bruce

Woolpert for helping me to understand the concept of mechanisms (and for his ongoing support), Ruth Ann Bagley for her diligent proofreading, Dr. Jeffrey T. Luftig for access to his remarkable brain, Professor William Briggs for his ability to break a complex problem into useful simplicity, Admiral Jim Stockdale for his invaluable teaching, Jennifer Futernick for her inspiration in creating the McKinsey salon that ignited this project, and Bill Meehan for the initial spark.

I would like to make special note of Jerry Porras as my research mentor; James J. Robb as my talented graphics consultant, Peter Ginsberg as my trusted agent and fellow council member in the publishing world; Lisa Berkowitz, who makes magic happen; and Adrian Zackheim, who has enthusiastically believed in and supported this book from the moment he learned of it.

Finally, I am deeply thankful for my great good fortune to be married to Joanne Ernst. After twenty years of marriage, she continues to put up with my somewhat neurotic nature and propensity to become consumed with projects such as this one. Not only is she my most helpful critic, but she is also my deepest and most enduring support. The ultimate definition of success in life is that your spouse likes and respects you ever more as the years go by. By that measure, more than any other, I hope to be as successful as she is.

PREFACE

As I was finishing this manuscript, I went for a run up a steep, rocky trail in Eldorado Springs Canyon, just south of my home in Boulder, Colorado. I had stopped on top at one of my favorite sitting places with a view of the high country still covered in its winter coat of snow, when an odd question popped into my mind: How much would someone have to pay me *not* to publish *Good to Great*?

It was an interesting thought experiment, given that I'd just spent the previous five years working on the research project and writing this book. Not that there isn't *some* number that might entice me to bury it, but by the time I crossed the hundred-million-dollar threshold, it was time to head back down the trail. Even that much couldn't convince me to abandon the project. I am a teacher at heart. As such, it is impossible for me to imagine not sharing what we've learned with students around the world. And it is in the spirit of learning and teaching that I bring forth this work.

After many months of hiding away like a hermit in what I call monk mode, I would very much enjoy hearing from people about what works for them and what does not. I hope you will find much of value in these pages and will commit to applying what you learn to whatever you do, if not to your company, then to your social sector work, and if not there, then at least to your own life.

—Jim Collins
jimcollins@aol.com
www.jimcollins.com
Boulder, Colorado
March 27, 2001

GOOD TO GREAT

CHAPTER 1

GOOD IS THE ENEMY OF GREAT

That's what makes death so hard—unsatisfied curiosity.

—BERYL MARKHAM,
West with the Night[1]

Good is the enemy of great.

And that is one of the key reasons why we have so little that becomes great.

We don't have great schools, principally because we have good schools. We don't have great government, principally because we have good government. Few people attain great lives, in large part because it is just so easy to settle for a good life. The vast majority of companies never become great, precisely because the vast majority become quite good—and that is their main problem.

This point became piercingly clear to me in 1996, when I was having dinner with a group of thought leaders gathered for a discussion about organizational performance. Bill Meehan, the managing director of the San Francisco office of McKinsey & Company, leaned over and casually confided, "You know, Jim, we love *Built to Last* around here. You and your coauthor did a very fine job on the research and writing. Unfortunately, it's useless."

Curious, I asked him to explain.

"The companies you wrote about were, for the most part, always great," he said. "They never had to turn themselves from good companies into great companies. They had parents like David Packard and George Merck, who shaped the character of greatness from early on. But what about the vast majority of companies that wake up partway through life and realize that they're good, but not great?"

I now realize that Meehan was exaggerating for effect with his "useless" comment, but his essential observation was correct—that truly great com-

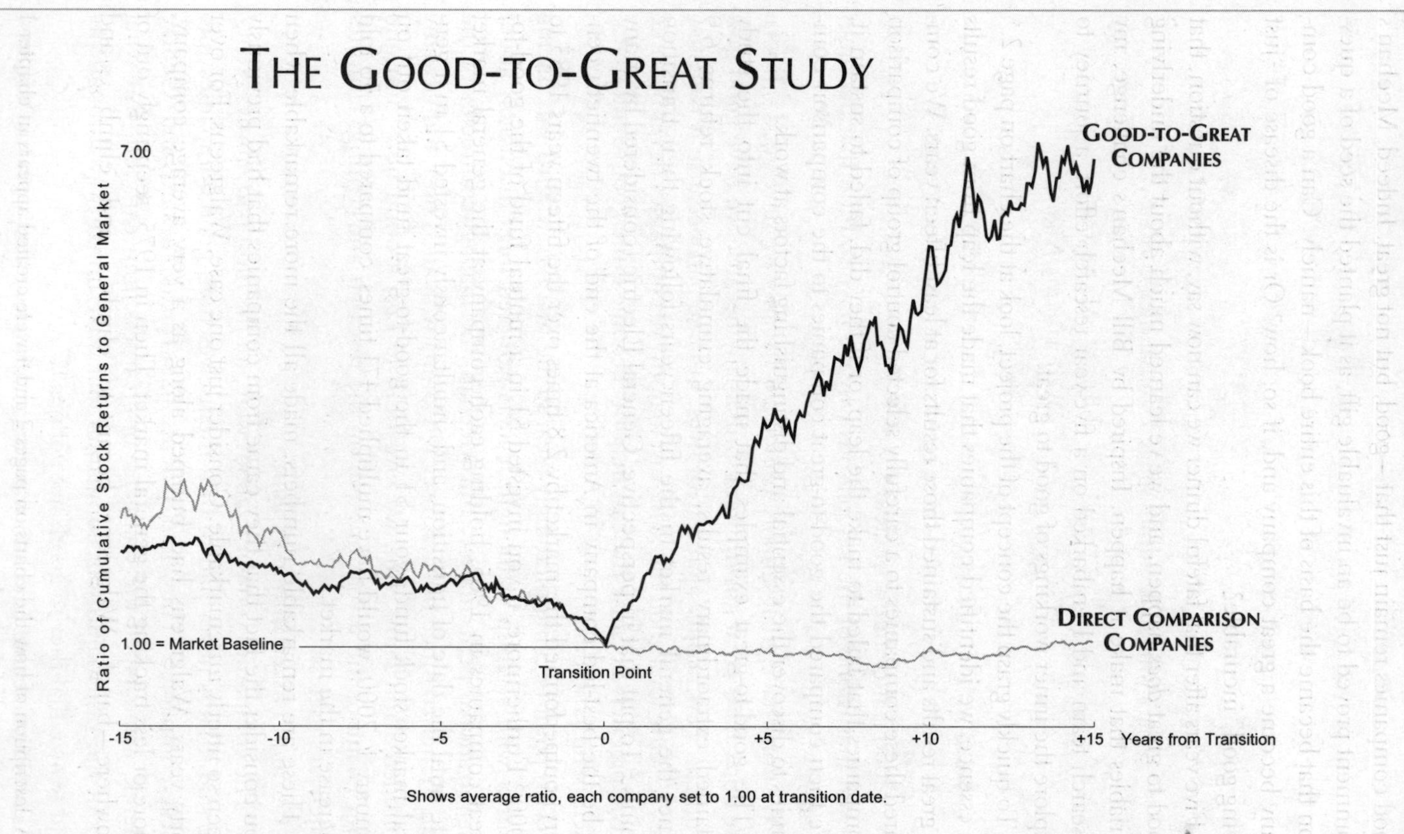

THE GOOD-TO-GREAT STUDY
7.00
GOOD-TO-GREAT COMPANIES
Ratio of Cumulative Stock Returns to General Market
1.00 = Market Baseline
Transition Point
DIRECT COMPARISON COMPANIES
-15
-10
-5
0
+5
+10
+15 Years from Transition
Shows average ratio, each company set to 1.00 at transition date.

panies, for the most part, have always been great. And the vast majority of good companies remain just that—good, but not great. Indeed, Meehan's comment proved to be an invaluable gift, as it planted the seed of a question that became the basis of this entire book—namely, Can a good company become a great company and, if so, how? Or is the disease of "just being good" incurable?

Five years after that fateful dinner we can now say, without question, that good to great *does* happen, and we've learned much about the underlying variables that make it happen. Inspired by Bill Meehan's challenge, my research team and I embarked on a five-year research effort, a journey to explore the inner workings of good to great.

To quickly grasp the concept of the project, look at the chart on page 2.* In essence, we identified companies that made the leap from good results to great results and sustained those results for at least fifteen years. We compared these companies to a carefully selected control group of comparison companies that failed to make the leap, or if they did, failed to sustain it. We then compared the good-to-great companies to the comparison companies to discover the essential and distinguishing factors at work.

The good-to-great examples that made the final cut into the study attained extraordinary results, averaging cumulative stock returns 6.9 times the general market in the fifteen years following their transition points.[2] To put that in perspective, General Electric (considered by many to be the best-led company in America at the end of the twentieth century) outperformed the market by 2.8 times over the fifteen years 1985 to 2000.[3] Furthermore, if you invested $1 in a mutual fund of the good-to-great companies in 1965, holding each company at the general market rate until the date of transition, and simultaneously invested $1 in a general market stock fund, your $1 in the good-to-great fund taken out on January 1, 2000, would have multiplied 471 times, compared to a 56 fold increase in the market.[4]

These are remarkable numbers, made all the more remarkable when you consider the fact that they came from companies that had previously been so utterly *un*remarkable. Consider just one case, Walgreens. For over forty years, Walgreens had bumped along as a very average company, more or less tracking the general market. Then in 1975, seemingly out of nowhere—bang!—Walgreens began to climb . . . and climb . . . and

*A description of how the charts on pages 2 and 4 were created appears in chapter 1 notes at the end of the book.

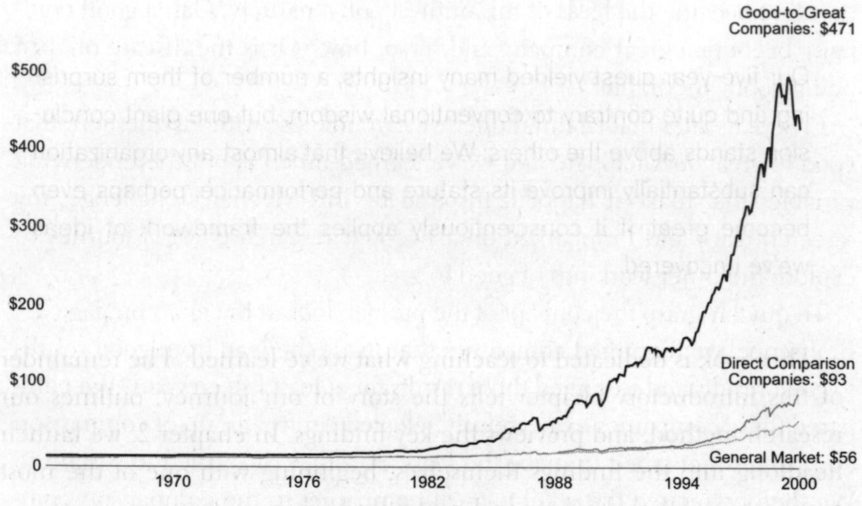

climb . . . and climb . . . and it just kept climbing. From December 31, 1975, to January 1, 2000, $1 invested in Walgreens beat $1 invested in technology superstar Intel by nearly two times, General Electric by nearly five times, Coca-Cola by nearly eight times, and the general stock market (including the NASDAQ stock run-up at the end of 1999) by over *fifteen* times.*

How on earth did a company with such a long history of being nothing special transform itself into an enterprise that outperformed some of the best-led organizations in the world? And why was Walgreens able to make the leap when other companies in the same industry with the same opportunities and similar resources, such as Eckerd, did *not* make the leap? This single case captures the essence of our quest.

This book is not about Walgreens per se, or any of the specific compa-

*Calculations of stock returns used throughout this book reflect the total cumulative return to an investor, dividends reinvested and adjusted for stock splits. The "general stock market" (often referred to as simply "the market") reflects the totality of stocks traded on the New York Exchange, American Stock Exchange, and NASDAQ. See the notes to chapter 1 for details on data sources and calculations.

nies we studied. It is about *the question*—Can a good company become a great company and, if so, how?—and our search for timeless, universal answers that can be applied by any organization.

> Our five-year quest yielded many insights, a number of them surprising and quite contrary to conventional wisdom, but one giant conclusion stands above the others: We believe that almost *any* organization can substantially improve its stature and performance, perhaps even become great, if it conscientiously applies the framework of ideas we've uncovered.

This book is dedicated to teaching what we've learned. The remainder of this introductory chapter tells the story of our journey, outlines our research method, and previews the key findings. In chapter 2, we launch headlong into the findings themselves, beginning with one of the most provocative of the whole study: Level 5 leadership.

UNDAUNTED CURIOSITY

People often ask, "What motivates you to undertake these huge research projects?" It's a good question. The answer is, "Curiosity." There is nothing I find more exciting than picking a question that I don't know the answer to and embarking on a quest for answers. It's deeply satisfying to climb into the boat, like Lewis and Clark, and head west, saying, "We don't know what we'll find when we get there, but we'll be sure to let you know when we get back."

Here is the abbreviated story of this particular odyssey of curiosity.

Phase 1: The Search

With the question in hand, I began to assemble a team of researchers. (When I use "we" throughout this book, I am referring to the research team. In all, twenty-one people worked on the project at key points, usually in teams of four to six at a time.)

Our first task was to find companies that showed the good-to-great pattern exemplified in the chart on page 2. We launched a six-month "death march of financial analysis," looking for companies that showed the following basic pattern: fifteen-year cumulative stock returns at or below the general stock market, punctuated by a transition point, then cumulative returns at least three times the market over the next fifteen years. We picked fifteen years because it would transcend one-hit wonders and lucky breaks (you can't just be lucky for fifteen years) and would exceed the average tenure of most chief executive officers (helping us to separate great companies from companies that just happened to have a single great leader). We picked three times the market because it exceeds the performance of most widely acknowledged great companies. For perspective, a mutual fund of the following "marquis set" of companies beat the market by only 2.5 times over the years 1985 to 2000: 3M, Boeing, Coca-Cola, GE, Hewlett-Packard, Intel, Johnson & Johnson, Merck, Motorola, Pepsi, Procter & Gamble, Wal-Mart, and Walt Disney. Not a bad set to beat.

From an initial universe of companies that appeared on the Fortune 500 in the years 1965 to 1995, we systematically searched and sifted, eventually finding eleven good-to-great examples. (I've put a detailed description of our search in Appendix 1.A.) However, a couple of points deserve brief mention here. First, a company had to demonstrate the good-to-great pattern *independent of its industry*; if the whole industry showed the same pattern, we dropped the company. Second, we debated whether we should use additional selection criteria beyond cumulative stock returns, such as impact on society and employee welfare. We eventually decided to limit our selection to the good-to-great *results* pattern, as we could not conceive of any legitimate and consistent method for selecting on these other variables without introducing our own biases. In the last chapter, however, I address the relationship between corporate values and *enduring* great companies, but the focus of this particular research effort is on the very specific question of how to turn a good organization into one that produces sustained great results.

At first glance, we were surprised by the list. Who would have thought that Fannie Mae would beat companies like GE and Coca-Cola? Or that Walgreens could beat Intel? The surprising list—a dowdier group would be hard to find—taught us a key lesson right up front. It is possible to turn good into great in the most unlikely of situations. This became the first of many surprises that led us to reevaluate our thinking about corporate greatness.

GOOD-TO-GREAT CASES

Company	Results from Transition Point to 15 Years beyond Transition Point*	T Year to T Year + 15
Abbott	3.98 times the market	1974–1989
Circuit City	18.50 times the market	1982–1997
Fannie Mae	7.56 times the market	1984–1999
Gillette	7.39 times the market	1980–1995
Kimberly-Clark	3.42 times the market	1972–1987
Kroger	4.17 times the market	1973–1988
Nucor	5.16 times the market	1975–1990
Philip Morris	7.06 times the market	1964–1979
Pitney Bowes	7.16 times the market	1973–1988
Walgreens	7.34 times the market	1975–1990
Wells Fargo	3.99 times the market	1983–1998

*Ratio of cumulative stock returns relative to the general stock market.

Phase 2: Compared to What?

Next, we took perhaps the most important step in the entire research effort: contrasting the good-to-great companies to a carefully selected set of "comparison companies." The crucial question in our study is *not*, What did the good-to-great companies share in common? Rather, the crucial question is, What did the good-to-great companies share in common that *distinguished* them from the comparison companies? Think of it this way: Suppose you wanted to study what makes gold medal winners in the Olympic Games. If you only studied the gold medal winners by themselves, you'd find that they all had coaches. But if you looked at the athletes that made the Olympic team, but never won a medal, you'd find that they *also* had coaches! The key question is, What systematically *distinguishes* gold medal winners from those who never won a medal?

We selected two sets of comparison companies. The first set consisted of "direct comparisons"—companies that were in the same industry as the good-to-great companies with the same opportunities and similar resources at the time of transition, but that showed no leap from good to great. (See Appendix 1.B for details of our selection process.) The second consisted of "unsustained comparisons"—companies that made a short-term shift from good to great but failed to maintain the trajectory—to address the question of sustainability. (See Appendix 1.C.) In all, this gave us a total study set of twenty-eight companies: eleven good-to-great companies, eleven direct comparisons, and six unsustained comparisons.

THE ENTIRE STUDY SET

Good-to-Great Companies	*Direct Comparisons*
Abbott	Upjohn
Circuit City	Silo
Fannie Mae	Great Western
Gillette	Warner-Lambert
Kimberly-Clark	Scott Paper
Kroger	A&P
Nucor	Bethlehem Steel
Philip Morris	R. J. Reynolds
Pitney Bowes	Addressograph
Walgreens	Eckerd
Wells Fargo	Bank of America

Unsustained Comparisons
Burroughs
Chrysler
Harris
Hasbro
Rubbermaid
Teledyne

Phase 3: Inside the Black Box

We then turned our attention to a deep analysis of each case. We collected all articles published on the twenty-eight companies, dating back fifty years or more. We systematically coded all the material into categories, such as strategy, technology, leadership, and so forth. Then we interviewed most of the good-to-great executives who held key positions of responsibility during the transition era. We also initiated a wide range of qualitative and quantitative analyses, looking at everything from acquisitions to executive compensation, from business strategy to corporate culture, from layoffs to leadership style, from financial ratios to management turnover. When all was said and done, the total project consumed 10.5 people years of effort. We read and systematically coded nearly 6,000 articles, generated more than 2,000 pages of interview transcripts, and created 384 million bytes of computer data. (See Appendix 1.D for a detailed list of all our analyses and activities.)

We came to think of our research effort as akin to looking inside a black box. Each step along the way was like installing another lightbulb to shed light on the inner workings of the good-to-great process.

With data in hand, we began a series of weekly research-team debates. For each of the twenty-eight companies, members of the research team and I would systematically read all the articles, analyses, interviews, and the research coding. I would make a presentation to the team on that specific company, drawing potential conclusions and asking questions. Then we would debate, disagree, pound on tables, raise our voices, pause and reflect, debate some more, pause and think, discuss, resolve, question, and debate yet again about "what it all means."

> It is important to understand that we developed all of the concepts in this book by making *empirical* deductions *directly from the data*. We did not begin this project with a theory to test or prove. We sought to build a theory from the ground up, derived directly from the evidence.

The core of our method was a systematic process of contrasting the good-to-great examples to the comparisons, always asking, "What's different?"

We also made particular note of "dogs that did not bark." In the Sherlock Holmes classic *"The Adventure of Silver Blaze,"* Holmes identified "the curious incident of the dog in the night-time" as the key clue. It turns out that the dog did nothing in the nighttime and *that*, according to Holmes, was the curious incident, which led him to the conclusion that the prime suspect must have been someone who knew the dog well.

In our study, what we *didn't* find—dogs that we might have expected to bark but didn't—turned out to be some of the best clues to the inner workings of good to great. When we stepped inside the black box and turned on the lightbulbs, we were frequently just as astonished at what we did *not* see as what we did. For example:

- Larger-than-life, celebrity leaders who ride in from the outside are *negatively* correlated with taking a company from good to great. Ten of eleven good-to-great CEOs came from inside the company, whereas the comparison companies tried outside CEOs six times more often.
- We found no systematic pattern linking specific forms of executive compensation to the process of going from good to great. The idea that the structure of executive compensation is a key driver in corporate performance is simply not supported by the data.
- Strategy per se did not separate the good-to-great companies from the comparison companies. Both sets of companies had well-defined strategies, and there is no evidence that the good-to-great companies spent more time on long-range strategic planning than the comparison companies.

- The good-to-great companies did not focus principally on what to *do* to become great; they focused equally on what *not* to do and what to *stop* doing.
- Technology and technology-driven change has virtually nothing to do with igniting a transformation from good to great. Technology can *accelerate* a transformation, but technology cannot *cause* a transformation.
- Mergers and acquisitions play virtually no role in igniting a transformation from good to great; two big mediocrities joined together never make one great company.
- The good-to-great companies paid scant attention to managing change, motivating people, or creating alignment. Under the right conditions, the problems of commitment, alignment, motivation, and change largely melt away.
- The good-to-great companies had no name, tag line, launch event, or program to signify their transformations. Indeed, some reported being unaware of the magnitude of the transformation at the time; only later, in retrospect, did it become clear. Yes, they produced a truly revolutionary leap in results, but *not* by a revolutionary process.
- The good-to-great companies were not, by and large, in great industries, and some were in terrible industries. In no case do we have a company that just happened to be sitting on the nose cone of a rocket when it took off. Greatness is not a function of circumstance. Greatness, it turns out, is largely a matter of conscious choice.

Phase 4: Chaos to Concept

I've tried to come up with a simple way to convey what was required to go from all the data, analyses, debates, and "dogs that did not bark" to the final findings in this book. The best answer I can give is that it was an iterative process of looping back and forth, developing ideas and testing them against the data, revising the ideas, building a framework, seeing it break under the weight of evidence, and rebuilding it yet again. That process was repeated over and over, until everything hung together in a coherent framework of concepts. We all have a strength or two in life, and I suppose mine is the ability to take a lump of unorganized information, see patterns, and extract order from the mess—to go from chaos to concept.

That said, however, I wish to underscore again that the concepts in the final framework are not my "opinions." While I cannot extract my own psychology and biases entirely from the research, each finding in the final framework met a rigorous standard before the research team would deem it significant. Every primary concept in the final framework showed up as a change variable in 100 percent of the good-to-great companies and in less than 30 percent of the comparison companies during the pivotal years. Any insight that failed this test did not make it into the book as a chapter-level concept.

Here, then, is an overview of the framework of concepts and a preview of what's to come in the rest of the book. (See the diagram below.) Think of the transformation as a process of buildup followed by breakthrough, broken into three broad stages: disciplined people, disciplined thought, and disciplined action. Within each of these three stages, there are two key concepts, shown in the framework and described below. Wrapping around this entire framework is a concept we came to call the flywheel, which captures the gestalt of the entire process of going from good to great.

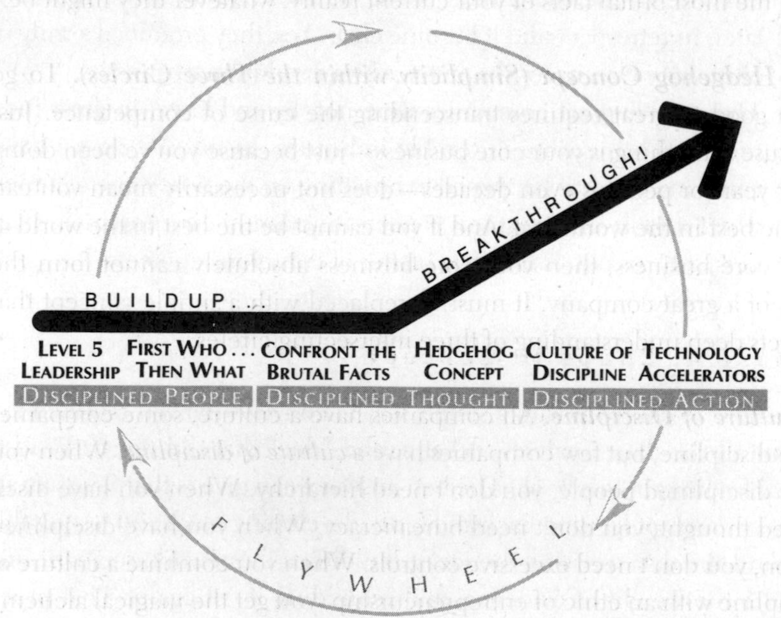

Level 5 Leadership. We were surprised, shocked really, to discover the type of leadership required for turning a good company into a great one. Compared to high-profile leaders with big personalities who make headlines and become celebrities, the good-to-great leaders seem to have come from Mars. Self-effacing, quiet, reserved, even shy—these leaders are a

paradoxical blend of personal humility and professional will. They are more like Lincoln and Socrates than Patton or Caesar.

First Who . . . Then What. We expected that good-to-great leaders would begin by setting a new vision and strategy. We found instead that they *first* got the right people on the bus, the wrong people off the bus, and the right people in the right seats—and *then* they figured out where to drive it. The old adage "People are your most important asset" turns out to be wrong. People are *not* your most important asset. The *right* people are.

Confront the Brutal Facts (Yet Never Lose Faith). We learned that a former prisoner of war had more to teach us about what it takes to find a path to greatness than most books on corporate strategy. Every good-to-great company embraced what we came to call the Stockdale Paradox: You must maintain unwavering faith that you can and will prevail in the end, regardless of the difficulties, AND *at the same time* have the discipline to confront the most brutal facts of your current reality, whatever they might be.

The Hedgehog Concept (Simplicity within the Three Circles). To go from good to great requires transcending the curse of competence. Just because something is your core business—just because you've been doing it for years or perhaps even decades—does not necessarily mean you can be the best in the world at it. And if you cannot be the best in the world at your core business, then your core business absolutely cannot form the basis of a great company. It must be replaced with a simple concept that reflects deep understanding of three intersecting circles.

A Culture of Discipline. All companies have a culture, some companies have discipline, but few companies have a *culture of discipline.* When you have disciplined people, you don't need hierarchy. When you have disciplined thought, you don't need bureaucracy. When you have disciplined action, you don't need excessive controls. When you combine a culture of discipline with an ethic of entrepreneurship, you get the magical alchemy of great performance.

Technology Accelerators. Good-to-great companies *think* differently about the role of technology. They never use technology as the primary means of igniting a transformation. Yet, paradoxically, they are pioneers in the application of *carefully selected* technologies. We learned that technology by itself is never a primary, root cause of either greatness or decline.

The Flywheel and the Doom Loop. Those who launch revolutions, dramatic change programs, and wrenching restructurings will almost certainly fail to make the leap from good to great. No matter how dramatic the end result, the good-to-great transformations never happened in one fell swoop. There was no single defining action, no grand program, no one killer innovation, no solitary lucky break, no miracle moment. Rather, the process resembled relentlessly pushing a giant heavy flywheel in one direction, turn upon turn, building momentum until a point of breakthrough, and beyond.

From Good to Great to Built to Last. In an ironic twist, I now see *Good to Great* not as a sequel to *Built to Last*, but as more of a *prequel*. This book is about how to turn a good organization into one that produces sustained great results. *Built to Last* is about how you take a company with great results and turn it into an *enduring* great company of iconic stature. To make that final shift requires core values and a purpose beyond just making money combined with the key dynamic of preserve the core / stimulate progress.

Good to Great Concepts	→	Sustained Great Results	+	*Built to Last* Concepts	→	Enduring Great Company

If you are already a student of *Built to Last*, please set aside your questions about the precise links between the two studies as you embark upon the findings in *Good to Great*. In the last chapter, I return to this question and link the two studies together.

THE TIMELESS "PHYSICS" OF GOOD TO GREAT

I had just finished presenting my research to a set of Internet executives gathered at a conference, when a hand shot up. "Will your findings continue to apply in the new economy? Don't we need to throw out all the old ideas and start from scratch?" It's a legitimate question, as we do live in a time of dramatic change, and it comes up so often that I'd like to dispense with it right up front, before heading into the meat of the book.

Yes, the world is changing, and will continue to do so. But that does not mean we should stop the search for timeless principles. Think of it this way: While the practices of engineering continually evolve and change, the laws of physics remain relatively fixed. I like to think of our work as a search for timeless principles—the enduring physics of great organizations—that will remain true and relevant no matter how the world changes around us. Yes, the specific application will change (the engineering), but certain immutable laws of organized human performance (the physics) will endure.

The truth is, there's nothing new about being in a new economy. Those who faced the invention of electricity, the telephone, the automobile, the radio, or the transistor—did they feel it was any less of a new economy than we feel today? And in each rendition of the new economy, the best leaders have adhered to certain basic principles, with rigor and discipline.

Some people will point out that the scale and pace of change is greater today than anytime in the past. Perhaps. Even so, some of the companies in our good-to-great study faced rates of change that rival anything in the new economy. For example, during the early 1980s, the banking industry was completely transformed in about three years, as the full weight of deregulation came crashing down. It was certainly a new economy for the banking industry! Yet Wells Fargo applied every single finding in this book to produce great results, right smack in the middle of the fast-paced change triggered by deregulation.

As you immerse yourself in the coming chapters, keep one key point in mind. This book is not about the old economy. Nor is it about the new economy. It is not even about the companies you're reading about, or even about business per se. It is ultimately about one thing: the timeless principles of good to great. It's about how you take a good organization and turn it into one that produces sustained great results, using whatever definition of results best applies to your organization.

This might come as a surprise, but I don't primarily think of my work as about the study of business, nor do I see this as fundamentally a business book. Rather, I see my work as being about discovering what creates enduring great organizations of *any* type. I'm curious to understand the fundamental differences between great and good, between excellent and mediocre. I just happen to use corporations as a means of getting inside the black box. I do this because publicly traded corporations, unlike other types of organizations, have two huge advantages for research: a widely agreed upon definition of results (so we can rigorously select a study set) and a plethora of easily accessible data.

That good is the enemy of great is not just a business problem. It is a *human* problem. If we have cracked the code on the question of good to great, we should have something of value to any type of organization. Good schools might become great schools. Good newspapers might become great newspapers. Good churches might become great churches. Good government agencies might become great agencies. And good companies might become great companies.

So, I invite you to join me on an intellectual adventure to discover what it takes to turn good into great. I also encourage you to question and challenge what you learn. As one of my favorite professors once said, "The best students are those who never quite believe their professors." True enough. But he also said, "One ought not to reject the data merely because one does not like what the data implies." I offer everything herein for your thoughtful consideration, not blind acceptance. You're the judge and jury. Let the evidence speak.

CHAPTER 2

LEVEL 5 LEADERSHIP

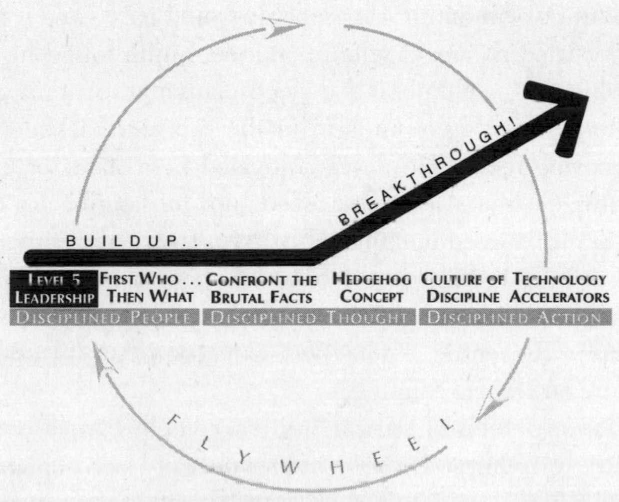

You can accomplish anything in life, provided that you do not mind who gets the credit.

—HARRY S. TRUMAN[1]

In 1971, a seemingly ordinary man named Darwin E. Smith became chief executive of Kimberly-Clark, a stodgy old paper company whose stock had fallen 36 percent behind the general market over the previous twenty years.

Smith, the company's mild-mannered in-house lawyer, wasn't so sure the board had made the right choice—a feeling further reinforced when a director pulled Smith aside and reminded him that he lacked some of the qualifications for the position.[2] But CEO he was, and CEO he remained for twenty years.

What a twenty years it was. In that period, Smith created a stunning transformation, turning Kimberly-Clark into the leading paper-based consumer products company in the world. Under his stewardship, Kimberly-Clark generated cumulative stock returns 4.1 times the general market, handily beating its direct rivals Scott Paper and Procter & Gamble and outperforming such venerable companies as Coca-Cola, Hewlett-Packard, 3M, and General Electric.

It was an impressive performance, one of the best examples in the twentieth century of taking a good company and making it great. Yet few people—even ardent students of management and corporate history—know anything about Darwin Smith. He probably would have liked it that way. A man who carried no airs of self-importance, Smith found his favorite companionship among plumbers and electricians and spent his vacations rumbling around his Wisconsin farm in the cab of a backhoe, digging holes and moving rocks.[3] He never cultivated hero status or executive celebrity status.[4] When a journalist asked him to describe his management style, Smith, dressed unfashionably like a farm boy wearing his first suit bought at J. C. Penney, just stared back from the other side of his nerdy-looking black-rimmed glasses. After a long, uncomfortable silence, he said simply: "Eccentric."[5] The *Wall Street Journal* did not write a splashy feature on Darwin Smith.

But if you were to think of Darwin Smith as somehow meek or soft, you would be terribly mistaken. His awkward shyness and lack of pretense was coupled with a fierce, even stoic, resolve toward life. Smith grew up as a poor Indiana farm-town boy, putting himself through college by working the day shift at International Harvester and attending Indiana University at night. One day, he lost part of a finger on the job. The story goes that he went to class that evening and returned to work the next day. While that might be a bit of an exaggeration, he clearly did not let a lost finger slow down his progress toward graduation. He kept working full-time, he kept going to class at night, and he earned admission to Harvard Law School.[6] Later in life, two months after becoming CEO, doctors diagnosed Smith with nose and throat cancer, predicting he had less than a year to live. He informed the board but made it clear that he was not dead yet and had no plans to die anytime soon. Smith held fully to his demanding work schedule while commuting weekly from Wisconsin to Houston for radiation therapy and lived twenty-five more years, most of them as CEO.[7]

Smith brought that same ferocious resolve to rebuilding Kimberly-Clark, especially when he made the most dramatic decision in the company's history: Sell the mills.[8] Shortly after he became CEO, Smith and his team had concluded that the traditional core business—coated paper—was doomed to mediocrity. Its economics were bad and the competition weak.[9] But, they reasoned, if Kimberly-Clark thrust itself into the

BEFORE DARWIN SMITH

Kimberly-Clark, Cumulative Value of $1 Invested, 1951 – 1971

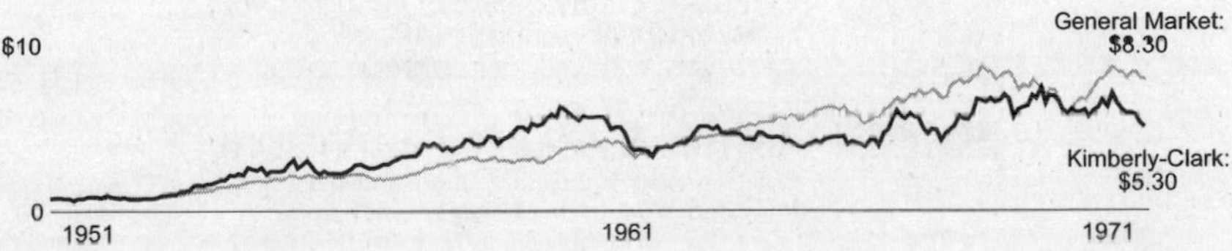

DARWIN SMITH TENURE

Kimberly-Clark, Cumulative Value of $1 Invested, 1971 – 1991

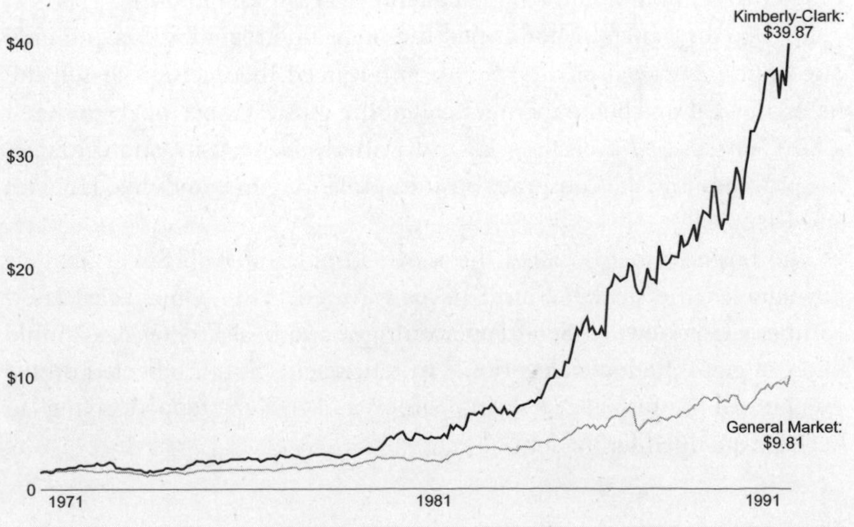

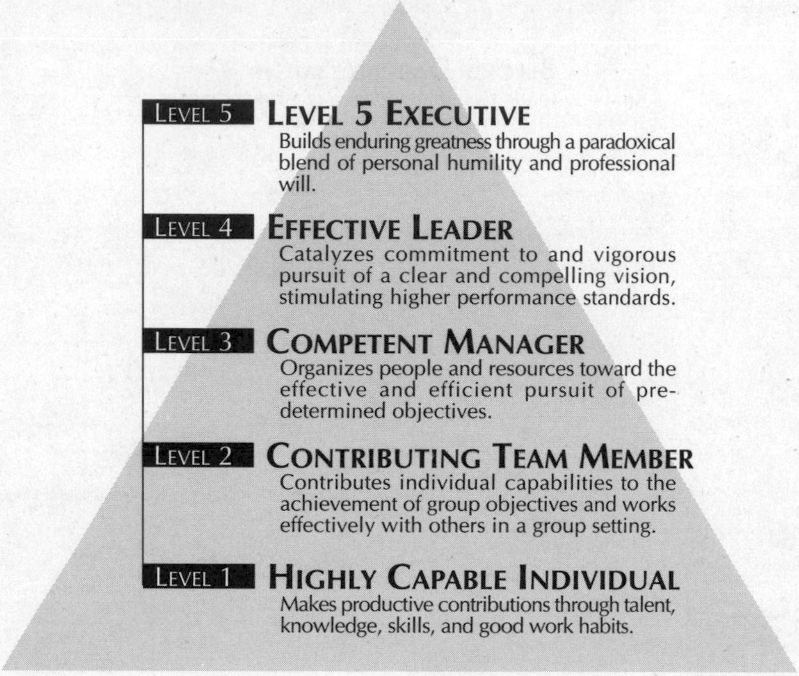

LEVEL 5 **LEVEL 5 EXECUTIVE**
Builds enduring greatness through a paradoxical blend of personal humility and professional will.

LEVEL 4 **EFFECTIVE LEADER**
Catalyzes commitment to and vigorous pursuit of a clear and compelling vision, stimulating higher performance standards.

LEVEL 3 **COMPETENT MANAGER**
Organizes people and resources toward the effective and efficient pursuit of predetermined objectives.

LEVEL 2 **CONTRIBUTING TEAM MEMBER**
Contributes individual capabilities to the achievement of group objectives and works effectively with others in a group setting.

LEVEL 1 **HIGHLY CAPABLE INDIVIDUAL**
Makes productive contributions through talent, knowledge, skills, and good work habits.

LEVEL 5 HIERARCHY

fire of the *consumer* paper-products industry, world-class competition like Procter & Gamble would force it to achieve greatness or perish.

So, like the general who burned the boats upon landing, leaving only one option (succeed or die), Smith announced the decision to sell the mills, in what one board member called the gutsiest move he'd ever seen a CEO make. Sell even the mill in Kimberly, Wisconsin, and throw all the proceeds into the consumer business, investing in brands like Huggies and Kleenex.[10]

The business media called the move stupid and Wall Street analysts downgraded the stock.[11] Smith never wavered. Twenty-five years later, Kimberly-Clark owned Scott Paper outright and beat Procter & Gamble in six of eight product categories.[12] In retirement, Smith reflected on his exceptional performance, saying simply, "I never stopped trying to become qualified for the job."[13]

NOT WHAT WE EXPECTED

Darwin Smith stands as a classic example of what we came to call a Level 5 leader—an individual who blends extreme personal humility with intense professional will. We found leaders of this type at the helm of every good-to-great company during the transition era. Like Smith, they were self-effacing individuals who displayed the fierce resolve to do whatever needed to be done to make the company great.

> Level 5 leaders channel their ego needs away from themselves and into the larger goal of building a great company. It's not that Level 5 leaders have no ego or self-interest. Indeed, they are incredibly ambitious—*but their ambition is first and foremost for the institution, not themselves.*

The term *Level* 5 refers to the highest level in a hierarchy of executive capabilities that we identified in our research. (See the diagram on page 20.) While you don't need to move in sequence from Level 1 to Level 5—it might be possible to fill in some of the lower levels later—fully developed Level 5 leaders embody all five layers of the pyramid. I am not going to belabor all five levels here, as Levels 1 through 4 are somewhat self-explanatory and are discussed extensively by other authors. This chapter will focus instead on the distinguishing traits of the good-to-great leaders—namely level 5 traits—in contrast to the comparison leaders in our study.

But first, please permit a brief digression to set an important context. We were not looking for Level 5 leadership or anything like it. In fact, I gave the research team explicit instructions to *downplay* the role of top executives so that we could avoid the simplistic "credit the leader" or "blame the leader" thinking common today.

To use an analogy, the "Leadership is the answer to everything" perspective is the modern equivalent of the "God is the answer to everything" perspective that held back our scientific understanding of the physical world in the Dark Ages. In the 1500s, people ascribed all events they didn't understand to God. Why did the crops fail? God did it. Why did we have an earthquake? God did it. What holds the planets in place? God. But with the Enlightenment, we began the search for a more scientific understanding—physics, chemistry, biology, and so forth. Not that we became atheists, but we gained deeper understanding about how the universe ticks.

Similarly, every time we attribute everything to "Leadership," we're no different from people in the 1500s. We're simply admitting our ignorance. Not that we should become leadership atheists (leadership *does* matter), but every time we throw our hands up in frustration—reverting back to "Well, the answer must be Leadership!"—we prevent ourselves from gaining deeper, more scientific understanding about what makes great companies tick.

So, early in the project, I kept insisting, "Ignore the executives." But the research team kept pushing back, "No! There is something consistently unusual about them. We can't ignore them." And I'd respond, "But the comparison companies also had leaders, even some great leaders. So, what's different?" Back and forth the debate raged.

Finally—as should always be the case—the data won.

The good-to-great executives were all cut from the same cloth. It didn't matter whether the company was consumer or industrial, in crisis or steady state, offered services or products. It didn't matter when the transition took place or how big the company. All the good-to-great companies had Level 5 leadership at the time of transition. Furthermore, the absence of Level 5 leadership showed up as a consistent pattern in the comparison companies. Given that Level 5 leadership cuts against the grain of conventional wisdom, especially the belief that we need larger-than-life saviors with big personalities to transform companies, it is important to note that Level 5 is an empirical finding, not an ideological one.

HUMILITY + WILL = LEVEL 5

Level 5 leaders are a study in duality: modest and willful, humble and fearless. To quickly grasp this concept, think of United States President Abraham Lincoln (one of the few Level 5 presidents in United States history), who never let his ego get in the way of his primary ambition for the larger cause of an enduring great nation. Yet those who mistook Mr. Lincoln's personal modesty, shy nature, and awkward manner as signs of weakness found themselves terribly mistaken, to the scale of 250,000 Confederate and 360,000 Union lives, including Lincoln's own.[14]

While it might be a bit of a stretch to compare the good-to-great CEOs to Abraham Lincoln, they did display the same duality. Consider the case of Colman Mockler, CEO of Gillette from 1975 to 1991. During Mockler's tenure, Gillette faced three attacks that threatened to destroy the company's opportunity for greatness. Two attacks came as hostile takeover bids from Revlon, led by Ronald Perelman, a cigar-chomping raider with a reputation for breaking apart companies to pay down junk bonds and finance more hostile raids.[15] The third attack came from Coniston Partners, an investment group that bought 5.9 percent of Gillette stock and initiated a proxy battle to seize control of the board, hoping to sell the company to the highest bidder and pocket a quick gain on their shares.[16] Had Gillette been flipped to Perelman at the price he offered, shareowners would have reaped an instantaneous 44 percent gain on their stock.[17] Looking at a $2.3 billion short-term stock profit across 116 million shares, most executives would have capitulated, pocketing millions from flipping their own stock and cashing in on generous golden parachutes.[18]

Colman Mockler did not capitulate, choosing instead to fight for the future greatness of Gillette, even though he himself would have pocketed a substantial sum on his own shares. A quiet and reserved man, always courteous, Mockler had the reputation of a gracious, almost patrician gentleman. Yet those who mistook Mockler's reserved nature for weakness found themselves beaten in the end. In the proxy fight, senior Gillette executives reached out to thousands of individual investors—person by person, phone call by phone call—and won the battle.

Now, you might be thinking, "But that just sounds like self-serving entrenched management fighting for their interests at the expense of shareholder interests." On the surface, it might look that way, but consider two key facts.

First, Mockler and his team staked the company's future on huge investments in radically new and technologically advanced systems (later known as Sensor and Mach3). Had the takeover been successful, these projects would almost certainly have been curtailed or eliminated, and none of us would be shaving with Sensor, Sensor for Women, or the Mach3—leaving hundreds of millions of people to a more painful daily battle with stubble.[19]

Second, at the time of the takeover battle, Sensor promised significant future profits that were not reflected in the stock price because it was in secret development. With Sensor in mind, the board and Mockler believed that the future value of the shares far exceeded the current price,

Cumulative Value of $1 Invested, 1976 – 1996
Gillette versus Takeover Bid and Market

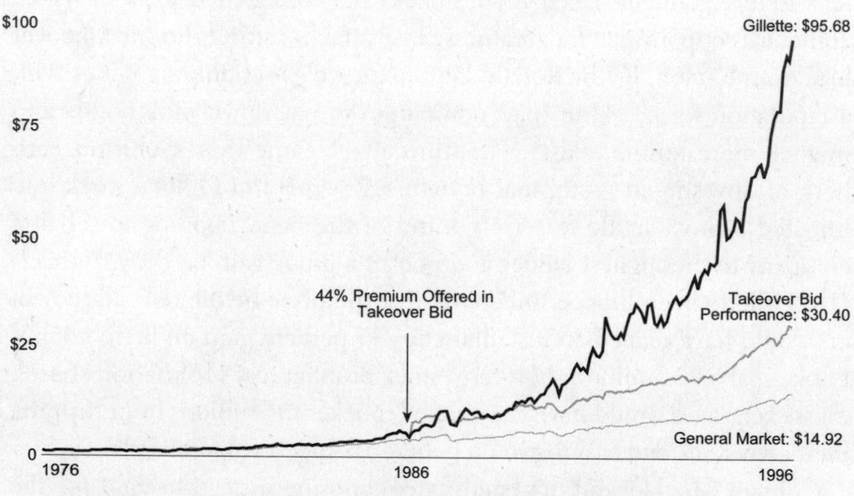

This chart shows how an investor would have fared under the following scenarios:

1. $1 invested in Gillette, held from December 31, 1976 through December 31, 1996.
2. $1 invested in Gillette, held from December 31, 1976 *but then sold* to Ronald Perelman for a 44.44% premium on October 31, 1986, the proceeds then invested in the general stock market.
3. $1 invested in General Market held from December 31, 1976 through December 31, 1996.

even with the price premium offered by the raiders. To sell out would have made short-term shareflippers happy but would have been utterly irresponsible to long-term shareholders.

In the end, Mockler and the board were proved right, stunningly so. If a shareflipper had accepted the 44 percent price premium offered by Ronald Perelman on October 31, 1986, and then invested the full amount in the general market for ten years, through the end of 1996, he would have come out three times *worse* off than a shareholder who had stayed with Mockler and Gillette.[20] Indeed, the company, its customers, *and* the shareholders would have been ill served had Mockler capitulated to the raiders, pocketed his millions, and retired to a life of leisure.

Sadly, Mockler was never able to enjoy the full fruits of his effort. On January 25, 1991, the Gillette team received an advance copy of the cover of *Forbes* magazine, which featured an artist's rendition of Mockler standing atop a mountain holding a giant razor above his head in a triumphal pose, while the vanquished languish on the hillsides below. The other executives razzed the publicity-shy Mockler, who had likely declined requests to be photographed for the cover in the first place, amused at seeing him portrayed as a corporate version of Conan the Triumphant. Walking back to his office, minutes after seeing this public acknowledgment of his sixteen years of struggle, Mockler crumpled to the floor, struck dead by a massive heart attack.[21]

I do not know whether Mockler would have chosen to die in harness, but I am quite confident that he would not have changed his approach as chief executive. His placid persona hid an inner intensity, a dedication to making anything he touched the best it could possibly be—not just because of what he would get, but because he simply couldn't imagine doing it any other way. It wouldn't have been an option within Colman Mockler's value system to take the easy path and turn the company over to those who would milk it like a cow, destroying its potential to become great, any more than it would have been an option for Lincoln to sue for peace and lose forever the chance of an enduring great nation.

Ambition for the Company: Setting Up Successors for Success

When David Maxwell became CEO of Fannie Mae in 1981, the company was losing $1 million every single business day. Over the next nine years, Maxwell transformed Fannie Mae into a high-performance culture that rivaled the best Wall Street firms, earning $4 million every business day and beating the general stock market 3.8 to 1. Maxwell retired while still at the top of his game, feeling that the company would be ill served if he stayed on too long, and turned the company over to an equally capable successor, Jim Johnson. Shortly thereafter, Maxwell's retirement package, which had grown to be worth $20 million based on Fannie Mae's spectacular performance, became a point of controversy in Congress (Fannie Mae operates under a government charter). Maxwell responded by writing a letter to his successor, in which he expressed concern that the controversy would trigger an adverse reaction in Washington that could jeopardize the future of the company. He then instructed Johnson not to pay him the remaining balance—$5.5 million—and asked that the entire amount be contributed to the Fannie Mae foundation for low-income housing.[22]

David Maxwell, like Darwin Smith and Colman Mockler, exemplified a key trait of Level 5 leaders: ambition first and foremost for the company and concern for *its* success rather than for one's own riches and personal renown. Level 5 leaders want to see the company even more successful in the next generation, comfortable with the idea that most people won't even know that the roots of that success trace back to their efforts. As one Level 5 leader said, "I want to look out from my porch at one of the great companies in the world someday and be able to say, 'I used to work there.' "

In contrast, the comparison leaders, concerned more with their own reputation for personal greatness, often failed to set the company up for success in the next generation. After all, what better testament to your own personal greatness than that the place falls apart after you leave?

> In over three quarters of the comparison companies, we found executives who set their successors up for failure or chose weak successors, or both.

Some had the "biggest dog" syndrome—they didn't mind other dogs in the kennel, as long as they remained the biggest one. One comparison CEO was said to have treated successor candidates "the way Henry the VIII treated wives."[23]

Consider the case of Rubbermaid, an unsustained comparison company that grew from obscurity to number one on *Fortune*'s annual list of America's Most Admired Companies and then, just as quickly, disintegrated into such sorry shape that it had to be acquired by Newell to save itself. The architect of this remarkable story, a charismatic and brilliant leader named Stanley Gault, became synonymous in the late 1980s with the success of the company. In 312 articles collected on Rubbermaid, Gault comes through as a hard-driving, egocentric executive. In one article, he responds to the accusation of being a tyrant with the statement, "Yes, but I'm a sincere tyrant."[24] In another, drawn directly from his own comments on leading change, the word *I* appears forty-four times ("I could lead the charge"; "I wrote the twelve objectives"; "I presented and explained the objectives"), whereas the word *we* appears just sixteen times.[25] Gault had every reason to be proud of his executive success. Rubbermaid generated forty consecutive quarters of earnings growth under his leadership—an impressive performance, and one that deserves respect.

But—and this is the key point—Gault did not leave behind a company that would be great without *him*. His chosen successor lasted only one year on the job and the next in line faced a management team so shallow that he had to temporarily shoulder four jobs while scrambling to identify a new number two executive.[26] Gault's successors found themselves struggling not only with a management void, but also with strategic voids that would eventually bring the company to its knees.[27]

Of course, you might say, "Yes, Rubbermaid fell apart after Gault, but that just proves his personal greatness as a leader." Exactly! Gault was indeed a tremendous Level 4 leader, perhaps one of the best in the last fifty years. But he was not a Level 5 leader, and that is one key reason why Rubbermaid went from good to great for a brief shining moment and then, just as quickly, went from great to irrelevant.

A Compelling Modesty

In contrast to the very *I*-centric style of the comparison leaders, we were struck by how the good-to-great leaders *didn't* talk about themselves. During interviews with the good-to-great leaders, they'd talk about the company and the contributions of other executives as long as we'd like but would deflect discussion about their own contributions. When pressed to talk about themselves, they'd say things like, "I hope I'm not sounding like a big shot." Or, "If the board hadn't picked such great successors, you probably wouldn't be talking with me today." Or, "Did I have a lot to do with it? Oh, that sounds so self-serving. I don't think I can take much credit. We were blessed with marvelous people." Or, "There are plenty of people in this company who could do my job better than I do."

It wasn't just false modesty. Those who worked with or wrote about the good-to-great leaders continually used words like *quiet, humble, modest, reserved, shy, gracious, mild-mannered, self-effacing, understated, did not believe his own clippings;* and so forth. Board member Jim Hlavacek described Ken Iverson, the CEO who oversaw Nucor's transformation from near bankruptcy to one of the most successful steel companies in the world:

> Ken is a very modest and humble man. I've never known a person as successful in doing what he's done that's as modest. And, I work for a lot of CEOs of large companies. And that's true in his private life as well. The simplicity of him. I mean little things like he always gets his dogs at the local pound. He has a simple house that's he's lived in for ages. He only has a carport and he complained to me one day about how he had to use

his credit card to scrape the frost off his windows and he broke the credit card. "You know, Ken, there's a solution for it; enclose your carport." And he said, "Ah, heck, it isn't that big of a deal. . . ." He's that humble and simple.[28]

The eleven good-to-great CEOs are some of the most remarkable CEOs of the century, given that only eleven companies from the Fortune 500 met the exacting standards for entry into this study. Yet, despite their remarkable results, almost no one ever remarked about them! George Cain, Alan Wurtzel, David Maxwell, Colman Mockler, Darwin Smith, Jim Herring, Lyle Everingham, Joe Cullman, Fred Allen, Cork Walgreen, Carl Reichardt—how many of these extraordinary executives had you heard of?

When we systematically tabulated all 5,979 articles in the study, we found fewer articles surrounding the transition date for the good-to-great companies than for the comparisons, by a factor of two.[29] Furthermore, we rarely found articles that focused on the good-to-great CEOs.

The good-to-great leaders never wanted to become larger-than-life heroes. They never aspired to be put on a pedestal or become unreachable icons. They were seemingly ordinary people quietly producing extraordinary results.

Some of the comparison leaders provide a striking contrast. Scott Paper, the comparison company to Kimberly-Clark, hired a CEO named Al Dunlap, a man cut from a very different cloth than Darwin Smith. Dunlap loudly beat on his own chest, telling anyone who would listen (and many who would prefer not to) about what he had accomplished. Quoted in *Business Week* about his nineteen months atop Scott Paper, he boasted, "The Scott story will go down in the annals of American business history as one of the most successful, quickest turnarounds ever, [making] other turnarounds pale by comparison."[30]

According to *Business Week*, Dunlap personally accrued $100 million for 603 days of work at Scott Paper (that's $165,000 *per day*), largely by slashing the workforce, cutting the R&D budget in half, and putting the company on growth steroids in preparation for sale.[31] After selling off the company and pocketing his quick millions, Dunlap wrote a book about himself, in which he trumpeted his nickname Rambo in Pinstripes. "I love the Rambo movies," he wrote. "Here's a guy who has zero chance of success and always wins. Rambo goes into situations against all odds, expecting to get his brains blown out. But he doesn't. At the end of the day he succeeds, he gets rid of the bad guys. He creates peace out of war. That's what I do, too."[32] Darwin Smith may have enjoyed the mindless Rambo movies as well, but I suspect he never walked out of a theater and said to his wife, "You know, I really relate to this Rambo character; he reminds me of me."

Granted, the Scott Paper story is one of the more dramatic in our study, but it's not an isolated case. In over two thirds of the comparison cases, we noted the presence of a gargantuan personal ego that contributed to the demise or continued mediocrity of the company.[33]

We found this pattern particularly strong in the unsustained comparisons—cases where the company would show a leap in performance under a talented yet egocentric leader, only to decline in later years. Lee Iacocca, for example, saved Chrysler from the brink of catastrophe, performing one of the most celebrated (and deservedly so) turnarounds in American business history. Chrysler rose to a height of 2.9 times the market at a point about halfway through his tenure. Then, however, he diverted his attention to making himself one of the most celebrated CEOs in American business history. *Investor's Business Daily* and the *Wall Street Journal* chronicled how Iacocca appeared regularly on talk shows like the *Today* show and *Larry King Live*, personally starred in over eighty commercials, entertained the idea of running for president of the United States (quoted at one point, "Running Chrysler has been a bigger job than running the country. . . . I could handle the national economy in six months"), and widely promoted his autobiography. The book, *Iacocca*, sold seven million copies and elevated him to rock star status, leading him to be mobbed by thousands of cheering fans upon his arrival in Japan.[34] Iacocca's personal stock soared, but in the second half of his tenure, Chrysler's stock fell 31 percent behind the general market.

Sadly, Iacocca had trouble leaving center stage and letting go of the perks of executive kingship. He postponed his retirement so many times that insiders at Chrysler began to joke that Iacocca stood for "I Am Chairman of Chrysler Corporation Always."[35] And when he did finally retire, he demanded that the board continue to provide a private jet and stock options.[36] Later, he joined forces with noted takeover artist Kirk Kerkorian to launch a hostile takeover bid for Chrysler.[37]

Chrysler experienced a brief return to glory in the five years after Iacocca's retirement, but the company's underlying weaknesses eventually led to a buyout by German carmaker Daimler-Benz.[38] Certainly, the demise of Chrysler as a stand-alone company does not rest entirely on Iacocca's shoulders (the next generation of management made the fateful decision to sell the company to the Germans), but the fact remains: Iacocca's brilliant turnaround in the early 1980s did not prove to be sustained and Chrysler failed to become an enduring great company.

Unwavering Resolve . . . to Do What Must Be Done

It is very important to grasp that Level 5 leadership is not just about humility and modesty. It is equally about ferocious resolve, an almost stoic determination to do whatever needs to be done to make the company great.

Indeed, we debated for a long time on the research team about how to describe the good-to-great leaders. Initially, we penciled in terms like "selfless executive" and "servant leader." But members of the team violently objected to these characterizations.

"Those labels don't ring true," said Anthony Chirikos. "It makes them sound weak or meek, but that's not at all the way I think of Darwin Smith or Colman Mockler. They would do almost anything to make the company great."

Then Eve Li suggested, "Why don't we just call them Level 5 leaders? If we put a label like 'selfless' or 'servant' on them, people will get entirely the wrong idea. We need to get people to engage with the whole concept, to see *both* sides of the coin. If you only get the humility side, you miss the whole idea."

Level 5 leaders are fanatically driven, infected with an incurable need to produce *results*. They will sell the mills or fire their brother, if that's what it takes to make the company great.

When George Cain became CEO of Abbott Laboratories, it sat in the bottom quartile of the pharmaceutical industry, a drowsy enterprise that had lived for years off its cash cow, erythromycin. Cain didn't have an inspiring personality to galvanize the company, but he had something much more powerful: inspired standards. He could not stand mediocrity in any form and was utterly intolerant of anyone who would accept the idea that good is good enough. Cain then set out to destroy one of the key causes of Abbott's mediocrity: nepotism. Systematically rebuilding both the board and the executive team with the best people he could find, Cain made it clear that neither family ties nor length of tenure would have anything to do with whether you held a key position in the company. If you didn't have the capacity to become the best executive in the industry in your span of responsibility, then you would lose your paycheck.[39]

Such rigorous rebuilding might be expected from an outsider brought in to turn the company around, but Cain was an eighteen-year veteran insider *and* a family member, the son of a previous Abbott president. Holiday gatherings were probably tense for a few years in the Cain clan. ("Sorry I had to fire you. Want another slice of turkey?") In the end, though, family members were quite pleased with the performance of their stock, for Cain set in motion a profitable growth machine that, from its transition date in 1974 to 2000, created shareholder returns that beat the market 4.5 to 1, handily outperforming industry superstars Merck and Pfizer.

Upjohn, the direct comparison company to Abbott, also had family leadership during the same era as George Cain. Unlike George Cain, Upjohn's CEO never showed the same resolve to break the mediocrity of nepotism. By the time Abbott had filled all key seats with the best people, regardless of family background, Upjohn still had B level family members holding key positions.[40] Virtually identical companies with identical stock charts up to the point of transition, Upjohn then fell 89 percent behind Abbott over the next twenty-one years before capitulating in a merger to Pharmacia in 1995.

As an interesting aside, Darwin Smith, Colman Mockler, and George Cain came from inside the company. Stanley Gault, Al Dunlap, and Lee Iacocca rode in as saviors from the outside, trumpets blaring. This reflects a more systematic finding from our study. The evidence does not support the idea that you need an outside leader to come in and shake up the place to go from good to great. In fact, going for a high-profile outside change agent is *negatively correlated* with a sustained transformation from good to great. (See Appendix 2.A.)

Ten out of eleven good-to-great CEOs came from *inside* the company, three of them by family inheritance. The comparison companies turned to outsiders with *six times* greater frequency—yet they failed to produce sustained great results.[41]

A superb example of insider-driven change comes from Charles R. "Cork" Walgreen 3d, who transformed dowdy Walgreens into a company that outperformed the stock market by over fifteen times from the end of 1975 to January 1, 2000.[42] After years of dialogue and debate within his executive team about Walgreens' food-service operations, Cork sensed that the team had finally reached a watershed point of clarity and understanding: Walgreens' brightest future lay in convenient drugstores, not food service. Dan Jorndt, who succeeded Walgreen as CEO in 1998, described what happened next:

> Cork said at one of our planning committee meetings, "Okay, now I am going to draw the line in the sand. We are going to be out of the restaurant business completely in five years." At the time, we had over five hundred restaurants. You could have heard a pin drop. He said, "I want to let everybody know the clock is ticking. . . ." Six months later, we were at our next planning committee meeting and someone mentioned just in passing that we only had five years to be out of the restaurant business. Cork was not a real vociferous fellow. He sort of tapped on the table and said, "Listen, you have four and a half years. I said you had five years six months ago. Now you've got four and a half years." Well, that next day, things really clicked into gear to winding down our restaurant business. He never wavered. He never doubted; he never second-guessed.[43]

Like Darwin Smith selling the mills at Kimberly-Clark, Cork Walgreen's decision required stoic resolve. Not that food service was the largest part of the business (although it did add substantial profits to the bottom line). The real problem was more emotional. Walgreens had, after all, invented the malted milkshake and food service was a long-standing family tradition dating back to his grandfather. Some food-service outlets were even named after the CEO himself—a restaurant chain named Corky's. But no matter, if Walgreens had to fly in the face of long-standing family tradition in order to focus its resources where it could be the best in the world (convenient drugstores), Cork would do it. Quietly, doggedly, simply.[44]

The quiet, dogged nature of Level 5 leaders showed up not only in big decisions, like selling off the food-service operations or fighting corporate raiders, but also in a personal style of sheer workmanlike diligence. Alan Wurtzel, a second-generation family member who took over his family's small company and turned it into Circuit City, perfectly captured the gestalt of this trait. When asked about differences between himself and his counterpart CEO at Circuit City's comparison company, Wurtzel summed up: "The show horse and the plow horse—he was more of a show horse, whereas I was more of a plow horse."[45]

The Window and the Mirror

Alan Wurtzel's plow horse comment is fascinating in light of two other facts. First, he holds a doctor of jurisprudence degree from Yale—clearly, his plow horse nature had nothing to do with a lack of intelligence. Second, his plow horse approach set the stage for truly *best in show* results. Let me put it this way: If you had to choose between $1 invested in Circuit City or $1 invested in General Electric on the day that the legendary Jack Welch took over GE in 1981 and held to January 1, 2000, you would have been better off with Circuit City—by six times.[46] Not a bad performance, for a plow horse.

You might expect that extraordinary results like these would lead Alan Wurtzel to discuss the brilliant decisions he made. But when we asked him to list the top five factors in his company's transformation, ranked by importance, Wurtzel gave a surprising answer: The number one factor was *luck*. "We were in a great industry, with the wind at our backs."

We pushed back, pointing out that we selected the good-to-great companies based on performance that surpassed their industry's average. Furthermore, the comparison company (Silo) was in the same industry, with the same wind and probably bigger sails! We debated the point for a few minutes, with Wurtzel continuing his preference for attributing much of his success to just being in the right place at the right time. Later, when asked to discuss the factors behind the enduring nature of the transformation, he said, "The first thing that comes to mind is luck. . . . I was lucky to find the right successor."[47]

Luck. What an odd factor to talk about. Yet the good-to-great executives talked a lot about luck in our interviews. In one interview with a

Nucor executive, we asked why the company had such a remarkable track record of good decisions; he responded: "I guess we were just lucky."[48] Joseph F. Cullman 3d, the Level 5 transition CEO of Philip Morris, flat-out refused to take credit for his company's success, attributing his good fortune to having great colleagues, successors, and predecessors.[49] Even the book he wrote—a book he undertook at the urging of his colleagues, which he never intended to distribute widely outside the company—had the unusual title *I'm a Lucky Guy*. The opening paragraph reads: "I was a very lucky guy from the very beginning of my life: marvelous parents, good genes, lucky in love, lucky in business, and lucky when a Yale classmate had my orders changed to report to Washington, D.C., in early 1941, instead of to a ship that was sunk with all hands lost in the North Atlantic, lucky to be in the Navy, and lucky to be alive at eighty-five."[50]

We were at first puzzled by this emphasis on good luck. After all, we found no evidence that the good-to-great companies were blessed with more good luck (or more bad luck, for that matter) than the comparison companies. Then we began to notice a contrasting pattern in the comparison executives: They credited substantial blame to *bad* luck, frequently bemoaning the difficulties of the environment they faced.

Compare Bethlehem Steel to Nucor. Both companies operated in the steel industry and produced hard-to-differentiate products. Both companies faced the competitive challenge of cheap imported steel. Yet executives at the two companies had completely different views of the same environment. Bethlehem Steel's CEO summed up the company's problems in 1983 by blaming imports: "Our first, second, and third problems are imports."[51] Ken Iverson and his crew at Nucor considered the same challenge from imports a *blessing*, a stroke of good fortune ("Aren't we lucky; steel is heavy, and they have to ship it all the way across the ocean, giving us a huge advantage!"). Iverson saw the first, second, and third problems facing the American steel industry not to be imports, but *management*.[52] He even went so far as to speak out publicly against government protection against imports, telling a stunned gathering of fellow steel executives in 1977 that the real problems facing the American steel industry lay in the fact that management had failed to keep pace with innovation.[53]

The emphasis on luck turns out to be part of a pattern that we came to call *the window and the mirror*.

> Level 5 leaders look out the window to apportion credit to factors outside themselves when things go well (and if they cannot find a specific person or event to give credit to, they credit good luck). At the same time, they look in the mirror to apportion responsibility, never blaming bad luck when things go poorly.

The comparison leaders did just the opposite. They'd look out the window for something or someone outside themselves to blame for poor results, but would preen in front of the mirror and credit themselves when things went well. Strangely, the window and the mirror do not reflect objective reality. Everyone outside the window points inside, directly at the Level 5 leader, saying, "He was the key; without his guidance and leadership, we would not have become a great company." And the Level 5 leader points right back out the window and says, "Look at all the great people and good fortune that made this possible; I'm a lucky guy." They're both right, of course. But the Level 5s would never admit that fact.

CULTIVATING LEVEL 5 LEADERSHIP

Not long ago, I shared the Level 5 finding with a gathering of senior executives. A woman who had recently become chief executive of her company raised her hand and said, "I believe what you say about the good-to-great leaders. But I'm disturbed because when I look in the mirror, I know that I'm not Level 5, not yet anyway. Part of the reason I got this job is because of my ego drives. Are you telling me that I can't make this a great company if I'm not Level 5?"

"I don't know for certain that you absolutely must be a Level 5 leader to make your company great," I replied. "I will simply point back to the data: Of 1,435 companies that appeared on the Fortune 500 in our initial candidate list, only eleven made the very tough cut into our study. In those eleven, all of them had Level 5 leadership in key positions, including the CEO, at the pivotal time of transition."

She sat there, quiet for moment, and you could tell everyone in the room was mentally urging her to ask *the question.* Finally, she said, "Can you learn to become Level 5?"

Summary: The Two Sides of Level 5 Leadership

Professional Will	Personal Humility
Creates superb results, a clear catalyst in the transition from good to great.	Demonstrates a compelling modesty, shunning public adulation; never boastful.
Demonstrates an unwavering resolve to do whatever must be done to produce the best long-term results, no matter how difficult.	Acts with quiet, calm determination; relies principally on inspired standards, not inspiring charisma, to motivate.
Sets the standard of building an enduring great company; will settle for nothing less.	Channels ambition into the company, not the self; sets up successors for even greater success in the next generation.
Looks in the mirror, not out the window, to apportion responsibility for poor results, never blaming other people, external factors, or bad luck.	Looks out the window, not in the mirror, to apportion credit for the success of the company—to other people, external factors, and good luck.

My hypothesis is that there are two categories of people: those who do not have the seed of Level 5 and those who do. The first category consists of people who could never in a million years bring themselves to subjugate their egoistic needs to the greater ambition of building something larger and more lasting than themselves. For these people, work will always be first and foremost about what they *get*—fame, fortune, adulation, power, whatever—not what they *build*, create, and contribute.

The great irony is that the animus and personal ambition that often drive people to positions of power stand at odds with the humility required for Level 5 leadership. When you combine that irony with the fact that boards of directors frequently operate under the false belief that they need to hire a larger-than-life, egocentric leader to make an organization great, you can quickly see why Level 5 leaders rarely appear at the top of our institutions.

The second category of people—and I suspect the larger group—consists of those who have the potential to evolve to Level 5; the capability resides within them, perhaps buried or ignored, but there nonetheless. And under the right circumstances—self-reflection, conscious personal development, a mentor, a great teacher, loving parents, a significant life experience, a Level 5 boss, or any number of other factors—they begin to develop.

In looking at the data, we noticed that some of the leaders in our study had significant life experiences that might have sparked or furthered their maturation. Darwin Smith fully blossomed after his experience with cancer. Joe Cullman was profoundly affected by his World War II experiences, particularly the last-minute change of orders that took him off a doomed ship on which he surely would have died.[54] A strong religious belief or conversion might also nurture development of Level 5 traits. Colman Mockler, for example, converted to evangelical Christianity while getting his MBA at Harvard, and later, according to the book *Cutting Edge*, became a prime mover in a group of Boston business executives who met frequently over breakfast to discuss the carryover of religious values to corporate life.[55] Other leaders in our study, however, had no obvious catalytic event; they just led normal lives and somehow ended up atop the Level 5 hierarchy.

I believe—although I cannot prove—that potential Level 5 leaders are highly prevalent in our society. *The problem is not, in my estimation, a dearth of potential Level 5 leaders. They exist all around us, if we just know what to look for.* And what is that? Look for situations where extraordinary results exist but where no individual steps forth to claim excess credit. You will likely find a potential Level 5 leader at work.

For your own development, I would love to be able to give you a list of steps for becoming Level 5, but we have no solid research data that would support a credible list. Our research exposed Level 5 as a key component inside the black box of what it takes to shift a *company* from good to great. Yet inside that black box is yet another black box—namely, the inner development of a *person* to Level 5. We could speculate on what might be inside that inner black box, but it would mostly be just that—speculation. So, in short, Level 5 is a very satisfying idea, a powerful idea, and, to produce the best transitions from good to great, perhaps an essential idea. A "Ten-Step List to Level 5" would trivialize the concept.

My best advice, based on the research, is to begin practicing the other good-to-great disciplines we discovered. We found a symbiotic relationship between Level 5 and the remaining findings. On the one hand, Level 5 traits enable you to implement the other findings; on the other hand, practicing the other findings helps you to become Level 5. Think of it this way: This chapter is about what Level 5s *are*; the rest of the book describes what they *do*. Leading with the other disciplines can help you move in the right direction. There is no guarantee that doing so will turn you into a full-fledged Level 5, but it gives you a tangible place to begin.

We cannot say for sure what percentage of people have the seed within, or how many of those can nurture it. Even those of us who discovered Level 5 on the research team do not know for ourselves whether we will succeed in fully evolving to Level 5. And yet, all of us who worked on the finding have been deeply affected and inspired by the idea. Darwin Smith, Colman Mockler, Alan Wurtzel, and all the other Level 5s we learned about have become models for us, something worthy to aspire toward. Whether or not we make it all the way to Level 5, it is worth the effort. For like all basic truths about what is best in human beings, when we catch a glimpse of that truth, we know that our own lives and all that we touch will be the better for the effort.

CHAPTER SUMMARY

LEVEL 5 LEADERSHIP

KEY POINTS

- Every good-to-great company had Level 5 leadership during the pivotal transition years.
- "Level 5" refers to a five-level hierarchy of executive capabilities, with Level 5 at the top. Level 5 leaders embody a paradoxical mix of personal humility and professional will. They are ambitious, to be sure, but ambitious first and foremost for the company, not themselves.
- Level 5 leaders set up their successors for even greater success in the next generation, whereas egocentric Level 4 leaders often set up their successors for failure.
- Level 5 leaders display a compelling modesty, are self-effacing and understated. In contrast, two thirds of the comparison companies had leaders with gargantuan personal egos that contributed to the demise or continued mediocrity of the company.
- Level 5 leaders are fanatically driven, infected with an incurable need to produce sustained *results*. They are resolved to do whatever it takes to make the company great, no matter how big or hard the decisions.
- Level 5 leaders display a workmanlike diligence—more plow horse than show horse.
- Level 5 leaders look out the window to attribute success to factors other than themselves. When things go poorly, however, they look in the mirror and blame themselves, taking full responsibility. The comparison CEOs often did just the opposite—they looked in the mirror to take credit for success, but out the window to assign blame for disappointing results.
- One of the most damaging trends in recent history is the tendency (especially by boards of directors) to select dazzling, celebrity leaders and to de-select potential Level 5 leaders.
- I believe that potential Level 5 leaders exist all around us, if we just know what to look for, and that many people have the potential to evolve into Level 5.

UNEXPECTED FINDINGS

- Larger-than-life, celebrity leaders who ride in from the outside are negatively correlated with going from good to great. Ten of eleven good-to-great CEOs came from *inside* the company, whereas the comparison companies tried outside CEOs six times more often.
- Level 5 leaders attribute much of their success to good luck, rather than personal greatness.
- We were not looking for Level 5 leadership in our research, or anything like it, but the data was overwhelming and convincing. It is an empirical, not an ideological, finding.

CHAPTER 3

FIRST WHO . . . THEN WHAT

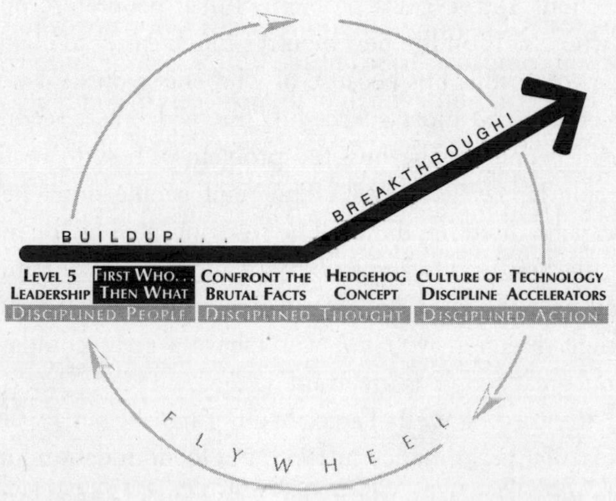

There are going to be times when we can't wait for somebody.
Now, you're either on the bus or off the bus.

—KEN KESEY,
from *The Electric Kool-Aid Acid Test*
by Tom Wolfe[1]

When we began the research project, we expected to find that the first step in taking a company from good to great would be to set a new direction, a new vision and strategy for the company, and then to get people committed and aligned behind that new direction.

We found something quite the opposite.

The executives who ignited the transformations from good to great did not first figure out where to drive the bus and then get people to take it there. No, they *first* got the right people on the bus (and the wrong people off the bus) and *then* figured out where to drive it. They said, in essence, "Look, I don't really know where we should take this bus. But I know this much: If we get the right people on the bus, the right people in the right seats, and the wrong people off the bus, then we'll figure out how to take it someplace great."

The good-to-great leaders understood three simple truths. First, if you begin with "who," rather than "what," you can more easily adapt to a changing world. If people join the bus primarily because of where it is going, what happens if you get ten miles down the road and you need to change direction? You've got a problem. But if people are on the bus because of who else is on the bus, then it's much easier to change direction: "Hey, I got on this bus because of who else is on it; if we need to change direction to be more successful, fine with me." Second, if you have the right people on the bus, the problem of how to motivate and manage people largely goes away. The right people don't need to be tightly managed or fired up; they will be self-motivated by the inner drive to produce the best results and to be part of creating something great. Third, if you have the wrong people, it doesn't matter whether you discover the right direction; you *still* won't have a great company. Great vision without great people is irrelevant.

Consider the case of Wells Fargo. Wells Fargo began its fifteen-year stint of spectacular performance in 1983, but the foundation for the shift dates back to the early 1970s, when then-CEO Dick Cooley began building one of the most talented management teams in the industry (*the* best team, according to investor Warren Buffett).[2] Cooley foresaw that the banking industry would eventually undergo wrenching change, but he did not pretend to know what form that change would take. So instead of mapping out a strategy for change, he and chairman Ernie Arbuckle focused on "injecting an endless stream of talent" directly into the veins of the company. They hired outstanding people whenever and wherever they found them, often without any specific job in mind. "That's how you build the future," he said. "If I'm not smart enough to see the changes that are coming, they will. And they'll be flexible enough to deal with them."[3]

Cooley's approach proved prescient. No one could predict all the changes that would be wrought by banking deregulation. Yet when these changes came, no bank handled those challenges better than Wells Fargo. At a time when its sector of the banking industry fell 59 percent behind the general stock market, Wells Fargo outperformed the market by over three times.[4]

Carl Reichardt, who became CEO in 1983, attributed the bank's success largely to the people around him, most of whom he inherited from Cooley.[5] As he listed members of the Wells Fargo executive team that had joined the company during the Cooley-Reichardt era, we were stunned. Nearly every person had gone on to become CEO of a major company:

Bill Aldinger became the CEO of Household Finance, Jack Grundhofer became CEO of U.S. Bancorp, Frank Newman became CEO of Bankers Trust, Richard Rosenberg became CEO of Bank of America, Bob Joss became CEO of Westpac Banking (one of the largest banks in Australia) and later became dean of the Graduate School of Business at Stanford University—not exactly your garden variety executive team! Arjay Miller, an active Wells Fargo board member for seventeen years, told us that the Wells Fargo team reminded him of the famed "Whiz Kids" recruited to Ford Motor Company in the late 1940s (of which Miller was a member, eventually becoming president of Ford).[6] Wells Fargo's approach was simple: You get the best people, you build them into the best managers in the industry, and you accept the fact that some of them will be recruited to become CEOs of other companies.[7]

Bank of America took a very different approach. While Dick Cooley systematically recruited the best people he could get his hands on, Bank of America, according to the book *Breaking the Bank,* followed something called the "weak generals, strong lieutenants" model.[8] If you pick strong generals for key positions, their competitors will leave. But if you pick weak generals—placeholders, rather than highly capable executives—then the strong lieutenants are more likely to stick around.

The weak generals model produced a climate very different at Bank of America than the one at Wells Fargo. Whereas the Wells Fargo crew acted as a strong team of equal partners, ferociously debating eyeball-to-eyeball in search of the best answers, the Bank of America weak generals would wait for directions from above. Sam Armacost, who inherited the weak generals model, described the management climate: "I came away quite distressed from my first couple of management meetings. Not only couldn't I get conflict, I couldn't even get comment. They were all waiting to see which way the wind blew."[9]

A retired Bank of America executive described senior managers in the 1970s as "Plastic People" who'd been trained to quietly submit to the dictates of a domineering CEO.[10] Later, after losing over $1 billion in the mid-1980s, Bank of America recruited a gang of strong generals to turn the bank around. And where did it find those strong generals? From right across the street at Wells Fargo. In fact, Bank of America recruited so many Wells Fargo executives during its turnaround that people inside began to refer to themselves as "Wells of America."[11] At that point, Bank of America began to climb upward again, but it was too little too late. From 1973 to 1998, while

Wells Fargo went from buildup to breakthrough results, Bank of America's cumulative stock returns didn't even keep pace with the general market.

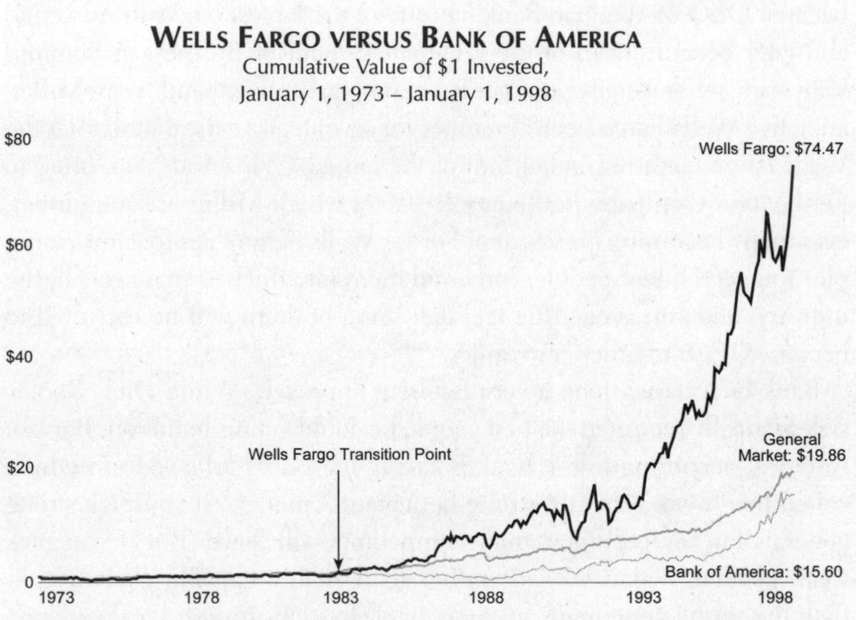

Now, you might be thinking, "That's just good management—the idea of getting the right people around you. What's new about that?" On one level, we have to agree; it is just plain old-fashioned good management. But what stands out with such distinction in the good-to-great companies are two key points that made them quite different.

> To be clear, the main point of this chapter is not just about assembling the right team—that's nothing new. The main point is to *first* get the right people on the bus (and the wrong people off the bus) *before* you figure out where to drive it. The second key point is the degree of *sheer rigor* needed in people decisions in order to take a company from good to great.

"First who" is a very simple idea to grasp, and a very difficult idea to *do*—and most don't do it well. It's easy to *talk about* paying attention to people decisions, but how many executives have the discipline of David Maxwell, who held off on developing a strategy until he got the right people in place, *while the company was losing $1 million every single business day* with $56 billion of loans underwater? When Maxwell became CEO of Fannie Mae during its darkest days, the board desperately wanted to know how he was going to rescue the company. Despite the immense pressure to act, to do something dramatic, to seize the wheel and start driving, Maxwell focused first on getting the right people on the Fannie Mae management team. His first act was to interview all the officers. He sat them down and said, "Look, this is going to be a very hard challenge. I want you to think about how demanding this is going to be. If you don't think you're going to like it, that's fine. Nobody's going to hate you."[12]

Maxwell made it absolutely clear that there would only be seats for A players who were going to put forth an A+ effort, and if you weren't up for it, you had better get off the bus, and get off *now*.[13] One executive who had just uprooted his life and career to join Fannie Mae came to Maxwell and said, "I listened to you very carefully, and I don't want to do this." He left and went back to where he came from.[14] In all, fourteen of twenty-six executives left the company, replaced by some of the best, smartest, and hardest-working executives in the entire world of finance.[15] The same standard applied up and down the Fannie Mae ranks as managers at every level increased the caliber of their teams and put immense peer pressure upon each other, creating high turnover at first, when some people just didn't pan out.[16] "We had a saying, 'You can't fake it at Fannie Mae,' " said one executive team member. "Either you knew your stuff or you didn't, and if you didn't, you'd just blow out of here."[17]

Wells Fargo and Fannie Mae both illustrate the idea that "who" questions come before "what" questions—before vision, before strategy, before tactics, before organizational structure, before technology. Dick Cooley and David Maxwell both exemplified a classic Level 5 style when they said, "I don't know where we should take this company, but I do know that if I start with the right people, ask them the right questions, and engage them in vigorous debate, we will find a way to make this company great."

NOT A "GENIUS WITH A THOUSAND HELPERS"

In contrast to the good-to-great companies, which built deep and strong executive teams, many of the comparison companies followed a "genius with a thousand helpers" model. In this model, the company is a platform for the talents of an extraordinary individual. In these cases, the towering genius, the primary driving force in the company's success, is a great asset—as long as the genius sticks around. The geniuses seldom build great management teams, for the simple reason that they don't need one, and often don't want one. If you're a genius, you don't need a Wells Fargo–caliber management team of people who could run their own shows elsewhere. No, you just need an army of good soldiers who can help implement your great ideas. However, when the genius leaves, the helpers are often lost. Or, worse, they try to mimic their predecessor with bold, visionary moves (trying to act like a genius, without being a genius) that prove unsuccessful.

Eckerd Corporation suffered the liability of a leader who had an uncanny genius for figuring out "what" to do but little ability to assemble the right "who" on the executive team. Jack Eckerd, blessed with monumental personal energy (he campaigned for governor of Florida while running his company) and a genetic gift for market insight and shrewd deal making, acquired his way from two little stores in Wilmington, Delaware, to a drugstore empire of over a thousand stores spread across the southeastern United States. By the late 1970s, Eckerd's revenues equaled Walgreens', and it looked like Eckerd might triumph as the great company in the industry. But then Jack Eckerd left to pursue his passion for politics, running for senator and joining the Ford administration in Washington. Without his guiding genius, Eckerd's company began a long decline, eventually being acquired by J. C. Penney.[18]

The contrast between Jack Eckerd and Cork Walgreen is striking. Whereas Jack Eckerd had a genius for picking the right stores to buy, Cork Walgreen had a genius for picking the right people to hire.[19] Whereas Jack Eckerd had a gift for seeing which stores should go in what locations, Cork Walgreen had a gift for seeing which people should go in what seats. Whereas Jack Eckerd failed utterly at the single most important decision facing any executive—the selection of a successor—Cork Walgreen developed multiple outstanding candidates and selected a superstar successor, who may prove to be even better than Cork himself.[20] Whereas Jack Eckerd had no executive team, but instead a bunch of capable helpers assembled to assist the great genius, Cork Walgreen built the best executive team in the industry. Whereas the primary guidance mechanism for Eckerd Corporation's strategy lay inside Jack Eckerd's head, the primary guidance mechanism for Walgreens' corporate

Level 5 + Management Team (Good-to-Great Companies)	**A "Genius with a Thousand Helpers"** (Comparison Companies)
Level 5 Leader	**Level 4 Leader**

First Who Get the right people on the bus. Build a superior executive team.	**First What** Set a vision for where to drive the bus. Develop a road map for driving the bus.

Then What Once you have the right people in place, figure out the best path to greatness.	**Then Who** Enlist a crew of highly capable "helpers" to make the vision happen.

strategy lay in the group dialogue and shared insights of the talented executive team.

The "genius with a thousand helpers" model is particularly prevalent in the unsustained comparison companies. The most classic case comes from a man known as the Sphinx, Henry Singleton of Teledyne. Singleton grew up on a Texas ranch, with the childhood dream of becoming a great businessman in the model of the rugged individualist. Armed with a Ph.D. from MIT, he founded Teledyne.[21] The name Teledyne derives from Greek and means "force applied at a distance"—an apt name, as the central force holding the far-flung empire together was Henry Singleton himself.

Through acquisitions, Singleton built the company from a small enterprise to number 293 on the Fortune 500 list in six years.[22] Within ten years, he'd completed more than 100 acquisitions, eventually creating a far-flung enterprise with 130 profit centers in everything from exotic metals to insurance.[23] Amazingly, the whole system worked, with Singleton

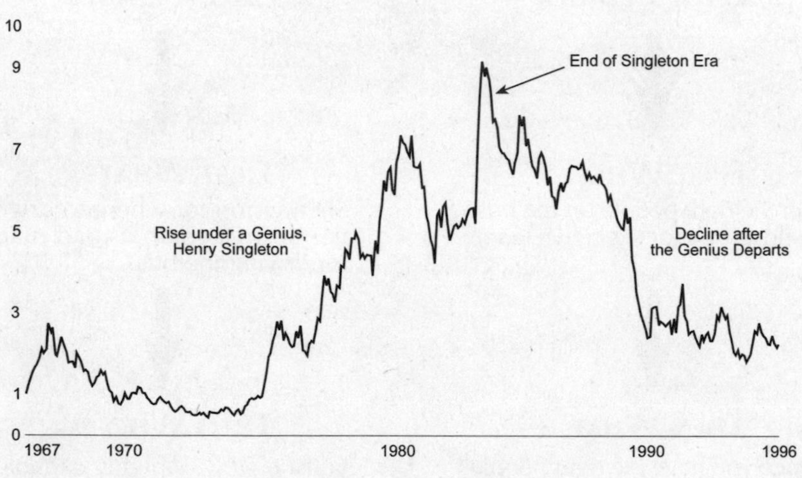

himself acting as the glue that connected all the moving parts together. At one point, he said, "I define my job as having the freedom to do what seems to me to be in the best interest of the company at any time."[24] A 1978 *Forbes* feature story maintained, "Singleton will win no awards for humility, but who can avoid standing in awe of his impressive record?" Singleton continued to run the company well into his seventies, with no serious thought given to succession. After all, why worry about succession when the very point of the whole thing is to serve as a platform to leverage the talents of your remarkable genius? "If there is a single weakness in this otherwise brilliant picture," the article continued, "it is this: Teledyne is not so much a system as it is the reflection of one man's singular discipline."[25]

What a weakness it turned out to be. Once Singleton stepped away from day-to-day management in the mid-1980s, the far-flung empire began to crumble. From the end of 1986 until its merger with Allegheny in 1995, Teledyne's cumulative stock returns imploded, falling 66 percent behind the general stock market. Singleton achieved his childhood dream of becoming a great businessman, but he failed utterly at the task of building a great company.

IT'S WHO YOU PAY, NOT HOW YOU PAY THEM

We expected to find that changes in incentive systems, especially executive incentives, would be highly correlated with making the leap from good to great. With all the attention paid to executive compensation—the shift to stock options and the huge packages that have become commonplace—surely, we thought, the amount and structure of compensation must play a key role in going from good to great. How else do you get people to do the right things that create great results?

We were dead wrong in our expectations.

> We found no systematic pattern linking executive compensation to the process of going from good to great. The evidence simply does not support the idea that the specific structure of executive compensation acts as a key lever in taking a company from good to great.

We spent weeks inputting compensation data from proxy statements and performed 112 separate analyses looking for patterns and correlations. We examined everything we could quantify for the top five officers—cash versus stock, long-term versus short-term incentives, salary versus bonus, and so forth. Some companies used stock extensively; others didn't. Some had high salaries; others didn't. Some made significant use of bonus incentives; others didn't. Most importantly, when we analyzed executive compensation patterns *relative to comparison companies, we found no systematic differences* on the use of stock (or not), high salaries (or not), bonus incentives (or not), or long-term compensation (or not). The only significant difference we found was that the good-to-great executives received slightly *less* total cash compensation ten years after the transition than their counterparts at the still-mediocre comparison companies![26]

Not that executive compensation is irrelevant. You have to be basically rational and reasonable (I doubt that Colman Mockler, David Maxwell, or Darwin Smith would have worked for free), and the good-to-great companies did spend time thinking about the issue. But once you've structured something that makes basic sense, executive compensation falls away as a distinguishing variable in moving an organization from good to great.

Why might that be? It is simply a manifestation of the "first who" principle: *It's not how you compensate your executives, it's which executives you have to compensate in the first place.* If you have the right executives on the bus, they will do everything within their power to build a great company, not because of what they will "get" for it, but because they simply cannot imagine settling for anything less. Their moral code requires building excellence for its own sake, and you're no more likely to change that with a compensation package than you're likely to affect whether they breathe. The good-to-great companies understood a simple truth: The right people will do the right things and deliver the best results they're capable of, regardless of the incentive system.

Yes, compensation and incentives are important, but for very different reasons in good-to-great companies. The purpose of a compensation system should not be to get the right *behaviors* from the wrong people, but to get the right *people* on the bus in the first place, and to keep them there.

We were not able to look as rigorously at nonexecutive compensation; such data is not available in as systematic a format as proxy statements for top officers. Nonetheless, evidence from source documents and articles suggests that the same idea applies at all levels of an organization.[27]

A particularly vivid example is Nucor. Nucor built its entire system on the idea that you can teach farmers how to make steel, but you can't teach a farmer work ethic to people who don't have it in the first place. So, instead of setting up mills in traditional steel towns like Pittsburgh and Gary, it located its plants in places like Crawfordsville, Indiana; Norfolk, Nebraska; and Plymouth, Utah—places full of real farmers who go to bed early, rise at dawn, and get right to work without fanfare. "Gotta milk the cows" and "Gonna plow the north forty before noon" translated easily into "Gotta roll some sheet steel" and "Gonna cast forty tons before lunch." Nucor ejected people who did not share this work ethic, generating as high as 50 percent turnover in the first year of a plant, followed by very low turnover as the right people settled in for the long haul.[28]

To attract and keep the best workers, Nucor paid its steelworkers more than any other steel company in the world. But it built its pay system around a high-pressure team-bonus mechanism, with over 50 percent of a worker's compensation tied directly to the productivity of his work team of twenty to forty people.[29] Nucor team members would usually show up for work thirty minutes early to arrange their tools and prepare to blast off the starting line the instant the shift gun fired.[30] "We have the hardest working steel workers in the world," said one Nucor executive. "We hire five, work them like ten, and pay them like eight."[31]

The Nucor system did not aim to turn lazy people into hard workers, but to create an environment where hardworking people would thrive and lazy workers would either jump or get thrown right off the bus. In one extreme case, workers chased a lazy teammate right out of the plant with an angle iron.[32]

> Nucor rejected the old adage that people are your most important asset. In a good-to-great transformation, people are not your most important asset. The *right* people are.

Nucor illustrates a key point. In determining "the right people," the good-to-great companies placed greater weight on character attributes than on specific educational background, practical skills, specialized knowledge, or work experience. Not that specific knowledge or skills are unimportant, but they viewed these traits as more teachable (or at least learnable), whereas they believed dimensions like character, work ethic, basic intelligence, dedication to fulfilling commitments, and values are more ingrained. As Dave Nassef of Pitney Bowes put it:

> I used to be in the Marines, and the Marines get a lot of credit for building people's values. But that's not the way it really works. The Marine Corps recruits people who share the corps' values, then provides them with the training required to accomplish the organization's mission. We look at it the same way at Pitney Bowes. We have more people who want to do the right thing than most companies. We don't just look at experience. We want to know: Who are they? Why are they? We find out who they are by asking them why they made decisions in their life. The answers to these questions give us insight into their core values.[33]

One good-to-great executive said that his best hiring decisions often came from people with no industry or business experience. In one case, he hired a manager who'd been captured twice during the Second World War and escaped both times. "I thought that anyone who could do that shouldn't have trouble with business."[34]

RIGOROUS, NOT RUTHLESS

The good-to-great companies probably sound like tough places to work—and they are. If you don't have what it takes, you probably won't last long. But they're not ruthless cultures, they're rigorous cultures. And the distinction is crucial.

To be ruthless means hacking and cutting, especially in difficult times, or wantonly firing people without any thoughtful consideration. To be rigorous means consistently applying exacting standards at all times and at all levels, especially in upper management. To be rigorous, not ruthless, means that the best people need not worry about their positions and can concentrate fully on their work.

In 1986, Wells Fargo acquired Crocker Bank and planned to shed gobs of excess cost in the consolidation. There's nothing unusual about that—every bank merger in the era of deregulation aimed to cut excess cost out of a bloated and protected industry. However, what *was* unusual about the Wells-Crocker consolidation is the way Wells integrated management or, to be more accurate, the way it didn't even try to integrate most Crocker management into the Wells culture.

The Wells Fargo team concluded right up front that the vast majority of Crocker managers would be the wrong people on the bus. Crocker people had long been steeped in the traditions and perks of old-style banker culture, complete with a marbled executive dining room with its own chef and $500,000 worth of china.[35] Quite a contrast to the spartan culture at Wells Fargo, where management ate food prepared by a college dormitory food service.[36] Wells Fargo made it clear to the Crocker managers: "Look, this is not a merger of equals; it's an acquisition; we bought your branches and your customers; we didn't acquire *you*." Wells Fargo terminated most of the Crocker management team—1,600 Crocker managers gone on day one—including nearly all the top executives.[37]

A critic might say, "That's just the Wells people protecting their own." But consider the following fact: Wells Fargo also sent some of its *own* managers packing in cases where the Crocker managers were judged as better qualified. When it came to management, the Wells Fargo standards were ferocious and consistent. Like a professional sports team, only the best made the annual cut, regardless of position or tenure. Summed up one Wells Fargo executive: "The only way to deliver to the people who are achieving is to not burden them with the people who are not achieving."[38]

On the surface, this looks ruthless. But the evidence suggests that the average Crocker manager was just not the same caliber as the average Wells manager and would have failed in the Wells Fargo performance culture. If they weren't going to make it on the bus in the long term, why let them suffer in the short term? One senior Wells Fargo executive told us: "We all agreed this was an acquisition, not a merger, and there's no sense beating around the bush, not being straightforward with people. We decided it would be best to simply do it on day one. We planned our efforts so that we could say, right up front, 'Sorry, we don't see a role for you,' or 'Yes, we do see a role; you have a job, so stop worrying about it.' We were not going to subject our culture to a death by a thousand cuts.' "[39]

To let people languish in uncertainty for months or years, stealing precious time in their lives that they could use to move on to something else, when in the end they aren't going to make it anyway—*that* would be ruthless. To deal with it right up front and let people get on with their lives—that is *rigorous*.

Not that the Crocker acquisition is easy to swallow. It's never pleasant to see thousands of people lose their jobs, but the era of bank deregulation saw hundreds of thousands of lost jobs. Given that, it's interesting to note two points. First, Wells Fargo did fewer big layoffs than its comparison company, Bank of America.[40] Second, upper management, including some senior Wells Fargo upper management, suffered more on a percentage basis than lower-level workers in the consolidation.[41] Rigor in a good-to-great company applies first at the top, focused on those who hold the largest burden of responsibility.

To be rigorous in people decisions means first becoming rigorous about *top management* people decisions. Indeed, I fear that people might use "first who rigor" as an excuse for mindlessly chopping out people to improve performance. "It's hard to do, but we've got to be rigorous," I can hear them say. And I cringe. For not only will a lot of hardworking, good people get hurt in the process, but the evidence suggests that such tactics are contrary to producing sustained great results. The good-to-great companies rarely used head-count lopping as a tactic and almost never used it as a primary strategy. Even in the Wells Fargo case, the company used layoffs *half* as much as Bank of America during the transition era.

> Six of the eleven good-to-great companies recorded zero layoffs from ten years before the breakthrough date all the way through 1998, and four others reported only one or two layoffs.

In contrast, we found layoffs used five times more frequently in the comparison companies than in the good-to-great companies. Some of the comparison companies had an almost chronic addiction to layoffs and restructurings.[42]

It would be a mistake—a tragic mistake, indeed—to think that the way you ignite a transition from good to great is by wantonly swinging the ax on vast numbers of hardworking people. Endless restructuring and mindless hacking were never part of the good-to-great model.

How to Be Rigorous

We've extracted three practical disciplines from the research for being rigorous rather than ruthless.

Practical Discipline #1: When in doubt, don't hire—keep looking.
One of the immutable laws of management physics is "Packard's Law." (So called because we first learned it in a previous research project from David Packard, cofounder of the Hewlett-Packard Company.) It goes like this: No company can grow revenues consistently faster than its ability to get enough of the right people to implement that growth and still become a great company. If your growth rate in revenues consistently outpaces your growth rate in people, you simply will not—indeed cannot—build a great company.

> Those who build great companies understand that the ultimate throttle on growth for any great company is not markets, or technology, or competition, or products. It is one thing above all others: the ability to get and keep enough of the right people.

The management team at Circuit City instinctively understood Packard's Law. Driving around Santa Barbara the day after Christmas a few years ago, I noticed something different about the Circuit City store. Other stores had signs and banners reaching out to customers: "Always the Best Prices" or "Great After-Holiday Deals" or "Best After-Christmas Selection," and so forth. But not Circuit City. It had a banner that read: "Always Looking for Great People."

The sign reminded me of our interview with Walter Bruckart, vice president during the good-to-great years. When asked to name the top five factors that led to the transition from mediocrity to excellence, Bruckart said, "One would be people. Two would be people. Three would be people. Four would be people. And five would be people. A huge part of our transition can be attributed to our discipline in picking the right people." Bruckart then recalled a conversation with CEO Alan Wurtzel during a growth spurt at Circuit City: " 'Alan, I'm really wearing down trying to find the exact right person to fill this position or that position. At what point do I compromise?' Without hesitation, Alan said, 'You don't compromise. We find another way to get through until we find the right people.' "[43]

One of the key contrasts between Alan Wurtzel at Circuit City and Sidney Cooper at Silo is that Wurtzel spent the bulk of his time in the early years focused on getting the right people on the bus, whereas Cooper spent 80 percent of his time focusing on the right stores to buy.[44] Wurtzel's first goal was to build the best, most professional management team in the industry; Cooper's first goal was simply to grow as fast as possible. Circuit City put tremendous emphasis on getting the right people all up and down the line, from delivery drivers to vice presidents; Silo developed a reputation for not being able to do the basics, like making home deliveries without damaging the products.[45] According to Circuit City's Dan Rexinger, "We made the best home delivery drivers in the industry. We told them, 'You are the last contact the customer has with Circuit City. We are going to supply you with uniforms. We will require that you shave, that you don't have B.O. You're going to be professional people.' The change in the way we handled customers when making a delivery was absolutely incredible. We would get thank-you notes back on how courteous the drivers were."[46] Five years into Wurtzel's tenure, Circuit City and Silo had essentially the same business strategy (the same answers to the "what" questions), yet Circuit City took off like a rocket, beating the general stock market 18.5 to 1 in the fifteen years after its transition, while Silo bumped along until it was finally acquired by a foreign company.[47] Same strategy, different people, different results.

Practical Discipline #2: When you know you need to make a people change, act.

The moment you feel the need to tightly manage someone, you've made a hiring mistake. The best people don't need to be managed. Guided, taught, led—yes. But not tightly managed. We've all experienced or observed the following scenario. We have a wrong person on the bus and we know it. Yet we wait, we delay, we try alternatives, we give a third and fourth chance, we hope that the situation will improve, we invest time in trying to properly manage the person, we build little systems to compensate for his shortcomings, and so forth. But the situation doesn't improve. When we go home, we find our energy diverted by thinking (or talking to our spouses) about that person. Worse, all the time and energy we spend on that one person siphons energy away from developing and working with all the right people. We continue to stumble along until the person leaves on his own (to our great sense of relief) or we finally act (also to our great sense of relief). Meanwhile, our best people wonder, "What took you so long?"

Letting the wrong people hang around is unfair to all the right people, as they inevitably find themselves compensating for the inadequacies of the wrong people. Worse, it can drive away the best people. Strong performers are intrinsically motivated by performance, and when they see their efforts impeded by carrying extra weight, they eventually become frustrated.

Waiting too long before acting is equally unfair to the people who need to get off the bus. For every minute you allow a person to continue holding a seat when you know that person will not make it in the end, you're stealing a portion of his life, time that he could spend finding a better place where he could flourish. Indeed, if we're honest with ourselves, the reason we wait too long often has less to do with concern for that person and more to do with our own convenience. He's doing an okay job and it would be a huge hassle to replace him, so we avoid the issue. Or we find the whole process of dealing with the issue to be stressful and distasteful. So, to save ourselves stress and discomfort, we wait. And wait. And wait. Meanwhile, all the best people are still wondering, "When are they going to do something about this? How long is this going to go on?"

Using data from *Moody's Company Information Reports*, we were able to examine the pattern of turnover in the top management levels. We found no difference in the *amount* of "churn" (turnover within a period of time) between the good-to-great and the comparison companies. But we did find differences in the *pattern* of churn.[48]

> The good-to-great companies showed the following bipolar pattern at the top management level: People either stayed on the bus for a long time or got off the bus in a hurry. In other words, the good-to-great companies did not churn more, they churned *better.*

The good-to-great leaders did not pursue an expedient "try a lot of people and keep who works" model of management. Instead, they adopted the following approach: "Let's take the time to make rigorous A+ selections right up front. If we get it right, we'll do everything we can to try to keep them on board for a long time. If we make a mistake, then we'll confront that fact so that we can get on with our work and they can get on with their lives."

The good-to-great leaders, however, would not rush to judgment. Often, they invested substantial effort in determining whether they had someone in the wrong seat before concluding that they had the wrong person on the bus entirely. When Colman Mockler became CEO of Gillette, he didn't go on a rampage, wantonly throwing people out the windows of a moving bus. Instead, he spent fully 55 percent of his time during his first two years in office jiggering around with the management team, changing or moving thirty-eight of the top fifty people. Said Mockler, "Every minute devoted to putting the proper person in the proper slot is worth weeks of time later."[49] Similarly, Alan Wurtzel of Circuit City sent us a letter after reading an early draft of this chapter, wherein he commented:

> Your point about "getting the right people on the bus" as compared to other companies is dead on. There is one corollary that is also important. I spent a lot of time thinking and talking about who sits where on the bus. I called it "putting square pegs in square holes and round pegs in round holes." . . . Instead of firing honest and able people who are not performing well, it is important to try to move them once or even two or three times to other positions where they might blossom.

> It might take time to know for certain if someone is simply in the wrong seat or whether he needs to get off the bus altogether. Nonetheless, when the good-to-great leaders knew they had to make a people change, they would *act*.

But how do you *know* when you know? Two key questions can help. First, if it were a hiring decision (rather than a "should this person get off the bus?" decision), would you hire the person again? Second, if the person came to tell you that he or she is leaving to pursue an exciting new opportunity, would you feel terribly disappointed or secretly relieved?

Practical Discipline #3: Put your best people on your biggest opportunities, not your biggest problems.

In the early 1960s, R. J. Reynolds and Philip Morris derived the vast majority of their revenues from the domestic arena. R. J. Reynolds' approach to international business was, "If somebody out there in the world wants a Camel, let them call us."[50] Joe Cullman at Philip Morris had a different view. He identified international markets as the single best opportunity for long-term growth, despite the fact that the company derived less than 1 percent of its revenues from overseas.

Cullman puzzled over the best "strategy" for developing international operations and eventually came up with a brilliant answer: It was not a "what" answer, but a "who." He pulled his number one executive, George Weissman, off the primary domestic business, and put him in charge of international. At the time, international amounted to almost nothing—a tiny export department, a struggling investment in Venezuela, another in Australia, and a tiny operation in Canada. "When Joe put George in charge of international, a lot of people wondered what George had done wrong," quipped one of Weissman's colleagues.[51] "I didn't know whether I was being thrown sideways, downstairs or out the window," said Weissman. "Here I was running 99% of the company and the next day I'd be running 1% or less."[52]

Yet, as *Forbes* magazine observed twenty years later, Cullman's decision to move Weissman to the smallest part of the business was a stroke of genius. Urbane and sophisticated, Weissman was the perfect person to develop markets like Europe, and he built international into the largest and fastest-growing part of the company. In fact, under Weissman's stewardship, Marlboro became the best-selling cigarette *in the world* three years *before* it became number one in the United States.[53]

The RJR versus Philip Morris case illustrates a common pattern. The good-to-great companies made a habit of putting their best people on their best opportunities, not their biggest problems. The comparison companies had a penchant for doing just the opposite, failing to grasp the fact that managing your problems can only make you good, whereas building your opportunities is the only way to become great.

There is an important corollary to this discipline: *When you decide to sell off your problems, don't sell off your best people.* This is one of those little secrets of change. If you create a place where the best people always have a seat on the bus, they're more likely to support changes in direction.

For instance, when Kimberly-Clark sold the mills, Darwin Smith made it clear: The company might be getting rid of the paper business, *but it would keep its best people*. "Many of our people had come up through the paper business. Then, all of a sudden, the crown jewels are being sold off and they're asking, 'What is my future?' " explained Dick Auchter. "And Darwin would say, 'We need all the talented managers we can get. We keep them.' "[54] Despite the fact that they had little or no consumer experience, Smith moved all the best paper people to the consumer business.

We interviewed Dick Appert, a senior executive who spent the majority of his career in the papermaking division at Kimberly-Clark, the same division sold off to create funds for the company's big move into consumer products. He talked with pride and excitement about the transformation of Kimberly-Clark, how it had the guts to sell the paper mills, how it had the foresight to exit the paper business and throw the proceeds into the consumer business, and how it had taken on Procter & Gamble. "I never had any argument with our decision to dissolve the paper division of the company," he said. "We did get rid of the paper mills at that time, and I was in absolute agreement with that."[55] Stop and think about that for a moment. The right people want to be part of building something great, and Dick Appert saw that Kimberly-Clark could become great by selling the part of the company where he had spent most of his working life.

The Philip Morris and Kimberly-Clark cases illustrate a final point about "the right people." We noticed a Level 5 atmosphere at the top executive level of every good-to-great company, especially during the key transition years. Not that every executive on the team became a fully evolved Level 5 leader to the same degree as Darwin Smith or Colman Mockler, but each core member of the team transformed personal ambition into ambition for the company. This suggests that the team members had Level 5 potential—or at least they were capable of operating in a manner consistent with the Level 5 leadership style.

You might be wondering, "What's the difference between a Level 5 executive team member and just being a good soldier?" A Level 5 executive team member does not blindly acquiesce to authority and is a strong leader in her own right, so driven and talented that she builds her arena into one of the very best in the world. Yet each team member must also have the ability to meld that strength into doing whatever it takes to make the company great.

> Indeed, one of the crucial elements in taking a company from good to great is somewhat paradoxical. You need executives, on the one hand, who argue and debate—sometimes violently—in pursuit of the best answers, yet, on the other hand, who unify fully behind a decision, regardless of parochial interests.

An article on Philip Morris said of the Cullman era, "These guys never agreed on anything and they would argue about everything, and they would kill each other and involve everyone, high and low, talented people. But when they had to make a decision, the decision would emerge. This made Philip Morris."[56] No matter how much they argued, said a Philip Morris executive, "they were always in search of the best answer. In the end, everybody stood behind the decision. All of the debates were for the common good of the company, not your own interests."[57]

FIRST WHO, GREAT COMPANIES, AND A GREAT LIFE

Whenever I teach the good-to-great findings, someone almost always raises the issue of the personal cost in making a transition from good to great. In other words, is it possible to build a great company and also build a great life?

Yes.

The secret to doing so lies right in this chapter.

I spent a few short days with a senior Gillette executive and his wife at an executive conference in Hong Kong. During the course of our conversations, I asked them if they thought Colman Mockler, the CEO most responsible for Gillette's transition from good to great, had a great life. Colman's life revolved around three great loves, they told me: his family, Harvard, and Gillette. Even during the darkest and most intense times of the takeover crises of the 1980s and despite the increasingly global nature of Gillette's business, Mockler maintained remarkable balance in his life. He did not significantly reduce the amount of time he spent with his family, rarely working evenings or weekends. He maintained his disciplined worship practices. He continued his active work on the governing board of Harvard College.[58]

When I asked how Mockler accomplished all of this, the executive said, "Oh, it really wasn't that hard for him. He was so good at assembling the right people around him, and putting the right people in the right slots, that he just didn't need to be there all hours of the day and night. That was Colman's whole secret to success and balance." The executive went on to explain that he was just as likely to meet Mockler in the hardware store as at the office. "He really enjoyed puttering around the house, fixing things up. He always seemed to find time to relax that way." Then the executive's wife added, "When Colman died and we all went to the funeral, I looked around and realized how much love was in the room. This was a man who spent nearly all his waking hours with people who loved him, who loved what they were doing, and who loved one another—at work, at home, in his charitable work, wherever."

And the statement rang a bell for me, as there was something about the good-to-great executive teams that I couldn't quite describe, but that clearly set them apart. In wrapping up our interview with George Weissman of Philip Morris, I commented, "When you talk about your time at the company, it's as if you are describing a love affair." He chuckled and said, "Yes. Other than my marriage, it was *the* passionate love affair of my life. I don't think many people would understand what I'm talking about, but I suspect my colleagues would." Weissman and many of his executive colleagues kept offices at Philip Morris, coming in on a regular basis, long after retirement. A corridor at the Philip Morris world headquarters is called "the hall of the wizards of was."[59] It's the corridor where Weissman, Cullman, Maxwell, and others continue to come into the office, in large part because they simply enjoy spending time together. Similarly, Dick Appert of Kimberly-Clark said in his interview, "I never had anyone in Kimberly-Clark in all my forty-one years say anything unkind to me. I thank God the day I was hired because I've been associated with wonderful people. Good, good people who respected and admired one another."[60]

Members of the good-to-great teams tended to become and remain friends for life. In many cases, they are still in close contact with each other years or decades after working together. It was striking to hear them talk about the transition era, for no matter how dark the days or how big the tasks, these people had fun! They enjoyed each other's company and actually looked forward to meetings. A number of the executives characterized their years on the good-to-great teams as the high point of their lives. Their experiences went beyond just mutual respect (which they certainly had), to lasting comradeship.

Adherence to the idea of "first who" might be the closest link between a great company and a great life. For no matter what we achieve, if we don't spend the vast majority of our time with people we love and respect, we cannot possibly have a great life. But if we spend the vast majority of our time with people we love and respect—people we really enjoy being on the bus with and who will never disappoint us—then we will almost certainly have a great life, no matter where the bus goes. The people we interviewed from the good-to-great companies clearly loved what they did, largely because they loved who they did it with.

CHAPTER SUMMARY

FIRST WHO . . . THEN WHAT

KEY POINTS

- The good-to-great leaders began the transformation by first getting the right people on the bus (and the wrong people off the bus) and then figured out where to drive it.
- The key point of this chapter is *not* just the idea of getting the right people on the team. The key point is that "who" questions come before "what" decisions—before vision, before strategy, before organization structure, before tactics. *First* who, *then* what—as a rigorous discipline, consistently applied.
- The comparison companies frequently followed the "genius with a thousand helpers" model—a genius leader who sets a vision and then enlists a crew of highly capable "helpers" to make the vision happen. This model fails when the genius departs.
- The good-to-great leaders were rigorous, not ruthless, in people decisions. They did not rely on layoffs and restructuring as a primary strategy for improving performance. The comparison companies used layoffs to a much greater extent.
- We uncovered three practical disciplines for being rigorous in people decisions:

  1. When in doubt, don't hire—keep looking. (*Corollary:* A company should limit its growth based on its ability to attract enough of the right people.)
  2. When you know you need to make a people change, act. (*Corollary:* First be sure you don't simply have someone in the wrong seat.)
  3. Put your best people on your biggest opportunities, not your biggest problems. (*Corollary:* If you sell off your problems, don't sell off your best people.)

- Good-to-great management teams consist of people who debate vigorously in search of the best answers, yet who unify behind decisions, regardless of parochial interests.

UNEXPECTED FINDINGS

- We found no systematic pattern linking executive compensation to the shift from good to great. The purpose of compensation is not to "motivate" the right behaviors from the wrong people, but to get and keep the right people in the first place.
- The old adage "People are your most important asset" is wrong. People are not your most important asset. The *right* people are.
- Whether someone is the "right person" has more to do with character traits and innate capabilities than with specific knowledge, background, or skills.

CHAPTER 4

CONFRONT THE BRUTAL FACTS (Yet Never Lose Faith)

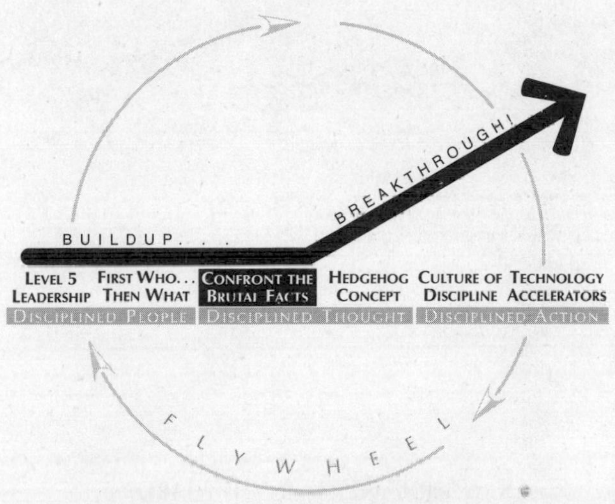

> There is no worse mistake in public leadership than to hold out false hopes soon to be swept away.
>
> —WINSTON S. CHURCHILL, *The Hinge of Fate*[1]

In the early 1950s, the Great Atlantic and Pacific Tea Company, commonly known as A&P, stood as the largest retailing organization in the world and one of the largest corporations in the United States, at one point ranking behind only General Motors in annual sales.[2] Kroger, in contrast, stood as an unspectacular grocery chain, less than half the size of A&P, with performance that barely kept pace with the general market.

Then in the 1960s, A&P began to falter while Kroger began to lay the foundations for a transition into a great company. From 1959 to 1973, both companies lagged behind the market, with Kroger pulling just a bit ahead of A&P. After that, the two companies completely diverged, and over the next twenty-five years, Kroger generated cumulative returns *ten times the market* and *eighty* times better than A&P.

How did such a dramatic reversal of fortunes happen? And how could a company as great as A&P become so awful?

Kroger, A&P, and the Market

Cumulative Value of $1 Invested,
1959 – 1973

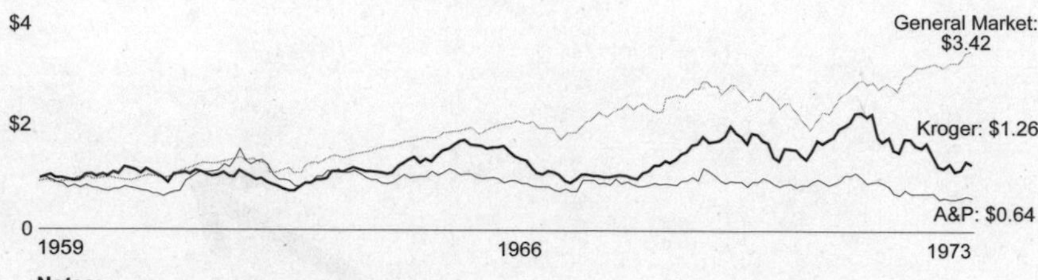

Notes:
1. Kroger transition point occurred in 1973.
2. Chart shows value of $1 invested on January 1, 1959.
3. Cumulative returns, dividends reinvested, to January 1, 1973.

Kroger, A&P, and the Market

Cumulative Value of $1 Invested,
1973 – 1998

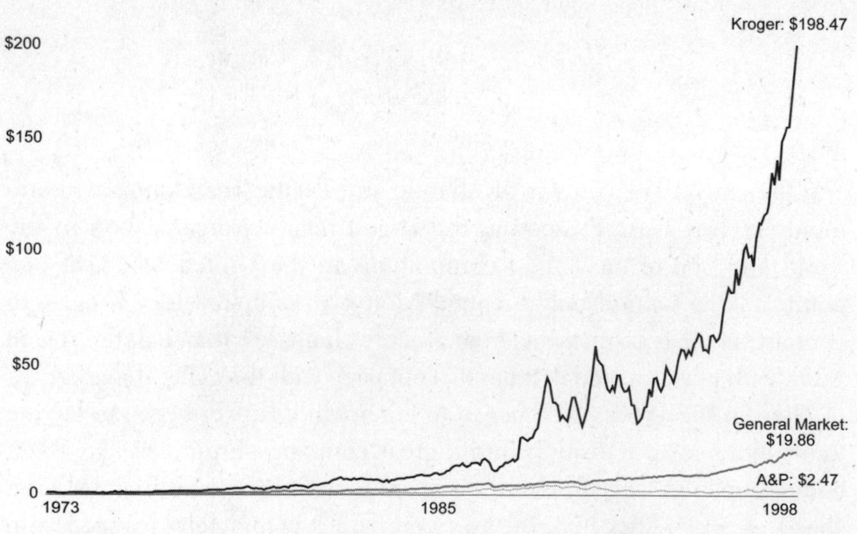

Notes:
1. Kroger transition point occurred in 1973.
2. Chart shows value of $1 invested on January 1, 1973.
3. Cumulative returns, dividends reinvested, to January 1, 1998.

A&P had a perfect model for the first half of the twentieth century, when two world wars and a depression imposed frugality upon Americans: cheap, plentiful groceries sold in utilitarian stores. But in the affluent second half of the twentieth century, Americans changed. They wanted nicer stores, bigger stores, more choices in stores. They wanted fresh-baked bread, flowers, health foods, cold medicines, fresh produce, forty-five choices of cereal, and ten types of milk. They wanted offbeat items, like five different types of expensive sprouts and various concoctions of protein powder and Chinese healing herbs. Oh, and they wanted to be able to do their banking and get their annual flu shots while shopping. In short, they no longer wanted grocery stores. They wanted Superstores, with a big block "S" on the chest—offering almost everything under one roof, with lots of parking, cheap prices, clean floors, and a gazillion checkout lines.

Now, right off the bat, you might be thinking: "Okay, so the story of A&P is one of an aging company that had a strategy that was right for the times, but the times changed and the world passed it by as younger, better-attuned companies gave customers more of what they wanted. What's so interesting about that?"

Here's what's interesting: *Both* Kroger and A&P were old companies (Kroger at 82 years, A&P at 111 years) heading into the 1970s; *both* companies had nearly all their assets invested in traditional grocery stores; *both* companies had strongholds outside the major growth areas of the United States; and *both* companies had knowledge of how the world around them was changing. Yet one of these two companies confronted the brutal facts of reality head-on and completely changed its entire system in response; the other stuck its head in the sand.

In 1958, *Forbes* magazine described A&P as "the Hermit Kingdom," run as an absolute monarchy by an aging prince.[3] Ralph Burger, the successor to the Hartford brothers who had built the A&P dynasty, sought to preserve two things above all else: cash dividends for the family foundation and the past glory of the Hartford brothers. According to one A&P director, Burger "considered himself the reincarnation of old John Hartford, even to the point of wearing a flower in his lapel every day from Hartford's greenhouse. He tried to carry out, against all opposition, what he thought Mr. John [Hartford] would have liked."[4] Burger instilled a "what would Mr. Hartford do?" approach to decisions, living by the motto "You can't argue with a hundred years of success."[5] Indeed, through

Burger, Mr. Hartford continued to be the dominant force on the board for nearly twenty years. Never mind the fact that he was already dead.[6]

As the brutal facts about the mismatch between its past model and the changing world began to pile up, A&P mounted an increasingly spirited defense against those facts. In one series of events, the company opened a new store called The Golden Key, a separate brand wherein it could experiment with new methods and models to learn what customers wanted.[7] It sold no A&P-branded products, it gave the store manager more freedom, it experimented with innovative new departments, and it began to evolve toward the modern superstore. Customers really liked it. Here, right under their noses, they began to discover the answer to the questions of why they were losing market share and what they could do about it.

What did A&P executives do with The Golden Key?

They didn't like the answers that it gave, so they closed it.[8]

A&P then began a pattern of lurching from one strategy to another, always looking for a single-stroke solution to its problems. It held pep rallies, launched programs, grabbed fads, fired CEOs, hired CEOs, and fired them yet again. It launched what one industry observer called a "scorched earth policy," a radical price-cutting strategy to build market share, but never dealt with the basic fact that customers wanted not lower prices, but *different stores*.[9] The price cutting led to cost cutting, which led to even drabber stores and poorer service, which in turn drove customers away, further driving down margins, resulting in even dirtier stores and worse service. "After a while the crud kept mounting," said one former A&P manager. "We not only had dirt, we had dirty dirt."[10]

Meanwhile, over at Kroger, a completely different pattern arose. Kroger also conducted experiments in the 1960s to test the superstore concept.[11] By 1970, the Kroger executive team came to an inescapable conclusion: The old-model grocery store (which accounted for nearly 100 percent of Kroger's business) was going to become extinct. Unlike A&P, however, Kroger confronted this brutal truth and acted on it.

The rise of Kroger is remarkably simple and straightforward, almost maddeningly so. During their interviews, Lyle Everingham and his predecessor Jim Herring (CEOs during the pivotal transition years) were polite and helpful, but a bit exasperated by our questions. To them, it just seemed so clear. When we asked Everingham to allocate one hundred points across the top five factors in the transition, he said: "I find your question a bit perplexing. Basically, we did extensive research, and the data came back loud and clear: The supercombination stores were the way of the future. We also learned that you had to be number one or number two in each market, or you had to exit.* Sure, there was some skepticism at first. But once we looked at the facts, there was really no question about what we had to do. So we just did it."[12]

Kroger decided to eliminate, change, or replace every single store and depart every region that did not fit the new realities. The whole system would be turned inside out, store by store, block by block, city by city, state by state. By the early 1990s, Kroger had rebuilt its entire system on the new model and was well on the way to becoming the number one grocery chain in America, a position it would attain in 1999.[13] Meanwhile, A&P *still* had over half its stores in the old 1950s size and had dwindled to a sad remnant of a once-great American institution.[14]

FACTS ARE BETTER THAN DREAMS

One of the dominant themes from our research is that breakthrough results come about by a series of good decisions, diligently executed and accumulated one on top of another. Of course, the good-to-great companies did not have a perfect track record. But on the whole, they made many more good decisions than bad ones, and they made many more good decisions than the comparison companies. Even more important, on the really big choices, such as Kroger's decision to throw all its resources into the task of converting its entire system to the superstore concept, they were remarkably on target.

This, of course, begs a question. Are we merely studying a set of companies that just happened by luck to stumble into the right set of decisions? Or was there something *distinctive* about their process that dramatically increased the likelihood of being right? The answer, it turns out, is that there was something quite distinctive about their process.

The good-to-great companies displayed two distinctive forms of disciplined thought. The first, and the topic of this chapter, is that they infused the entire process with the brutal facts of reality. (The second, which we

*Keep in mind, this was the early 1970s, a full decade before the "number one, number two, or exit" idea became mainstream. Kroger, like all good-to-great companies, developed its ideas by paying attention to the data right in front of it, not by following trends and fads set by others. Interestingly, over half the good-to-great companies had some version of the "number one, number two" concept in place years before it became a management fad.

will discuss in the next chapter, is that they developed a simple, yet deeply insightful, frame of reference for all decisions.) When, as in the Kroger case, you start with an honest and diligent effort to determine the truth of the situation, the right decisions often become self-evident. Not always, of course, but often. And even if all decisions do not become self-evident, one thing is certain: You absolutely cannot make a series of good decisions without first confronting the brutal facts. The good-to-great companies operated in accordance with this principle, and the comparison companies generally did not.

Consider Pitney Bowes versus Addressograph. It would be hard to find two companies in more similar positions at a specific moment in history that then diverged so dramatically. Until 1973, they had similar revenues, profits, numbers of employees, and stock charts. Both companies held near-monopoly market positions with virtually the same customer base—Pitney Bowes in postage meters and Addressograph in address-duplicating machines—and both faced the imminent reality of losing their monopolies.[15] By 2000, however, Pitney Bowes had grown to over 30,000 employees and revenues in excess of $4 billion, compared to the sorry remnants of Addressograph, which had less than $100 million and only 670 employees.[16] For the shareholder, Pitney Bowes outperformed Addressograph 3,581 to 1 (yes, *three thousand five hundred and eighty-one* times better).

In 1976, a charismatic visionary leader named Roy Ash became CEO of Addressograph. A self-described "conglomerateur," Ash had previously built Litton by stacking acquisitions together that had since faltered. According to *Fortune*, he sought to use Addressograph as a platform to reestablish his leadership prowess in the eyes of the world.[17]

Ash set forth a vision to dominate the likes of IBM, Xerox, and Kodak in the emerging field of office automation—a bold plan for a company that had previously only dominated the envelope-address-duplication business.[18] There is nothing wrong with a bold vision, but Ash became so wedded to his quixotic quest that, according to *Business Week*, he refused to confront the mounting evidence that his plan was doomed to fail and might take down the rest of the company with it.[19] He insisted on milking cash from profitable arenas, eroding the core business while throwing money after a gambit that had little chance of success.[20]

Later, after Ash was thrown out of office and the company had filed for bankruptcy (from which it did later emerge), he still refused to confront reality, saying: "We lost some battles, but we were winning the war."[21] But

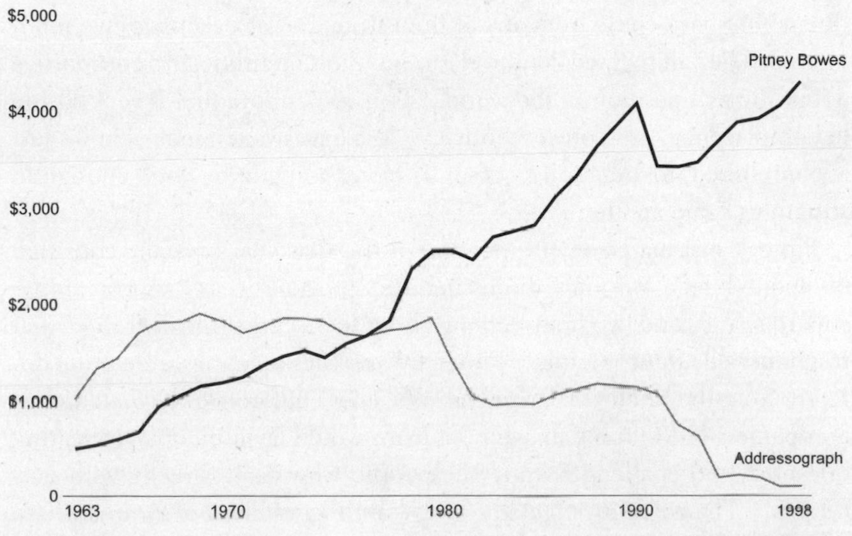

Addressograph was not even close to winning the war, and people throughout the company knew it at the time. Yet the truth went unheard until it was too late.[22] In fact, many of Addressograph's key people bailed out of the company, dispirited by their inability to get top management to deal with the facts.[23]

Perhaps we should give Mr. Ash some credit for being a visionary who tried to push his company to greater heights. (And, to be fair, the Addressograph board fired Ash before he had a chance to fully carry out his plans.)[24] But the evidence from a slew of respectable articles written at the time suggests that Ash turned a blind eye to any reality inconsistent with his own vision of the world.

> There is nothing wrong with pursuing a vision for greatness. After all, the good-to-great companies also set out to create greatness. But, unlike the comparison companies, the good-to-great companies continually refined the *path* to greatness with the brutal facts of reality.

"When you turn over rocks and look at all the squiggly things underneath, you can either put the rock down, or you can say, 'My job is to turn over rocks and look at the squiggly things,' even if what you see can scare the hell out of you."[25] That quote, from Pitney Bowes executive Fred Purdue, could have come from any of the Pitney Bowes executives we interviewed. They all seemed a bit, well, to be blunt, neurotic and compulsive about Pitney's position in the world. "This is a culture that is very hostile to complacency," said one executive.[26] "We have an itch that what we just accomplished, no matter how great, is never going to be good enough to sustain us," said another.[27]

Pitney's first management meeting of the new year typically consisted of about fifteen minutes discussing the previous year (almost always superb results) and two hours talking about the "scary squiggly things" that might impede future results.[28] Pitney Bowes sales meetings were quite different from the "aren't we great" rah-rah sales conferences typical at most companies: The entire management team would lay itself open to searing questions and challenges from salespeople who dealt directly with customers.[29] The company created a long-standing tradition of forums where people could stand up and tell senior executives what the company was doing wrong, shoving rocks with squiggly things in their faces, and saying, "Look! You'd better pay attention to this."[30]

The Addressograph case, especially in contrast to Pitney Bowes, illustrates a vital point. Strong, charismatic leaders like Roy Ash can all too easily become the de facto reality driving a company. Throughout the study, we found comparison companies where the top leader led with such force or instilled such fear that people worried more about the leader—what he would say, what he would think, what he would do—than they worried about external reality and what *it* could do to the company. Recall the climate at Bank of America, described in the previous chapter, wherein managers would not even make a comment until they knew how the CEO felt. We did not find this pattern at companies like Wells Fargo and Pitney Bowes, where people were much more worried about the scary squiggly things than about the feelings of top management.

The moment a leader allows himself to become the primary reality people worry about, rather than reality being the primary reality, you have a recipe for mediocrity, or worse. This is one of the key reasons why less charismatic leaders often produce better long-term results than their more charismatic counterparts.

Indeed, for those of you with a strong, charismatic personality, it is worthwhile to consider the idea that charisma can be as much a liability as an asset. Your strength of personality can sow the seeds of problems, when people filter the brutal facts from you. You *can* overcome the liabilities of having charisma, but it does require conscious attention.

Winston Churchill understood the liabilities of his strong personality, and he compensated for them beautifully during the Second World War. Churchill, as you know, maintained a bold and unwavering vision that Britain would not just survive, but prevail as a great nation—despite the whole world wondering not if but *when* Britain would sue for peace. During the darkest days, with nearly all of Europe and North Africa under Nazi control, the United States hoping to stay out of the conflict, and Hitler fighting a one-front war (he had not yet turned on Russia), Churchill said: "We are resolved to destroy Hitler and every vestige of the Nazi regime. From this, nothing will turn us. Nothing! We will never parley. We will never negotiate with Hitler or any of his gang. We shall fight him by land. We shall fight him by sea. We shall fight him in the air. Until, with God's help, we have rid the earth of his shadow."[31]

Armed with this bold vision, Churchill never failed, however, to confront the most brutal facts. He feared that his towering, charismatic personality might deter bad news from reaching him in its starkest form. So, early in the war, he created an entirely separate department outside the normal chain of command, called the Statistical Office, with the principal function of feeding him—continuously updated and completely unfiltered—the most brutal facts of reality.[32] He relied heavily on this special unit throughout the war, repeatedly asking for facts, just the facts. As the Nazi panzers swept across Europe, Churchill went to bed and slept soundly: "I . . . had no need for cheering dreams," he wrote. "*Facts* are better than dreams."[33]

A CLIMATE WHERE THE TRUTH IS HEARD

Now, you might be wondering, "How do you motivate people with brutal facts? Doesn't motivation flow chiefly from a compelling vision?" The answer, surprisingly, is, "*No.*" Not because vision is unimportant, but because expending energy trying to motivate people is largely a waste of time. One of the dominant themes that runs throughout this book is that if you successfully implement its findings, you will not need to spend time and energy "motivating" people. If you have the right people on the bus, they will be self-motivated. The real question then becomes: *How do you manage in such a way as not to de-motivate people?* And one of the single most de-motivating actions you can take is to hold out false hopes, soon to be swept away by events.

> Yes, leadership is about vision. But leadership is equally about creating a climate where the truth is heard and the brutal facts confronted. There's a huge difference between the opportunity to "have your say" and the opportunity to be *heard.* The good-to-great leaders understood this distinction, creating a culture wherein people had a tremendous opportunity to be heard and, ultimately, for the truth to be heard.

How do you create a climate where the truth is heard? We offer four basic practices:

1. *Lead with questions, not answers.*

In 1973, one year after he assumed CEO responsibility from his father, Alan Wurtzel's company stood at the brink of bankruptcy, dangerously close to violation of its loan agreements. At the time, the company (then named Wards, not to be confused with Montgomery Ward) was a hodgepodge of appliance and hi-fi stores with no unifying concept. Over the next ten years, Wurtzel and his team not only turned the company around, but also created the Circuit City concept and laid the foundations for a stunning record of results, beating the market twenty-two times from its transition date in 1982 to January 1, 2000.

When Alan Wurtzel started the long traverse from near bankruptcy to these stellar results, he began with a remarkable answer to the question of where to take the company: *I don't know*. Unlike leaders such as Roy Ash of Addressograph, Wurtzel resisted the urge to walk in with "the answer." Instead, once he put the right people on the bus, he began not with answers, but with *questions.* "Alan was a real spark," said a board member. "He had an ability to ask questions that were just marvelous. We had some wonderful debates in the boardroom. It was never just a dog and pony show, where you would just listen and then go to lunch."[34] Indeed, Wurtzel stands as one of the few CEOs in a large corporation who put more questions to his board members than they put to him.

He used the same approach with his executive team, constantly pushing and probing and prodding with questions. Each step along the way, Wurtzel would keep asking questions until he had a clear picture of reality and its implications. "They used to call me the prosecutor, because I would home in on a question," said Wurtzel. "You know, like a bulldog, I wouldn't let go until I understood. Why, why, why?"

Like Wurtzel, leaders in each of the good-to-great transitions operated with a somewhat Socratic style. Furthermore, they used questions for one and only one reason: to gain understanding. They didn't use questions as a form of manipulation ("Don't you agree with me on that? . . .") or as a way to blame or put down others ("Why did you mess this up? . . ."). When we asked the executives about their management team meetings during the transition era, they said that they spent much of the time "just trying to understand."

The good-to-great leaders made particularly good use of informal meetings where they'd meet with groups of managers and employees with no script, agenda, or set of action items to discuss. Instead, they would start with questions like: "So, what's on your mind?" "Can you tell me about that?" "Can you help me understand?" "What should we be worried about?" These non-agenda meetings became a forum where current realities tended to bubble to the surface.

> Leading from good to great does not mean coming up with the answers and then motivating everyone to follow your messianic vision. It means having the humility to grasp the fact that you do not yet understand enough to have the answers and then to ask the questions that will lead to the best possible insights.

2. *Engage in dialogue and debate, not coercion.*

In 1965, you could hardly find a company more awful than Nucor. It had only one division that made money. Everything else drained cash. It had no culture to be proud of. It had no consistent direction. It was on the verge of bankruptcy. At the time, Nucor was officially known as the Nuclear Corporation of America, reflecting its orientation to nuclear energy products, including the Scintillation Probe (yes, they really named it that), used for radiation measurement. It had acquired a series of unrelated businesses in such arenas as semiconductor supplies, rare earth materials, electrostatic office copiers, and roof joists. At the start of its transformation in 1965, Nucor did not manufacture one ounce of steel. Nor did it make a penny of profit. Thirty years later, Nucor stood as the fourth-largest steelmaker in the world[35] and by 1999 made greater annual profits than any other American steel company.[36]

How did Nucor transition from the utterly awful Nuclear Corporation of America into perhaps the best steel company in America? First, Nucor benefited from the emergence of a Level 5 leader, Ken Iverson, promoted to CEO from general manager of the joist division. Second, Iverson got the right people on the bus, building a remarkable team of people like Sam Siegel (described by one of his colleagues as "the best money manager in the world, a magician") and David Aycock, an operations genius.[37]

And then what?

Like Alan Wurtzel, Iverson dreamed of building a great company, but refused to begin with "the answer" for how to get there. Instead, he played the role of Socratic moderator in a series of raging debates. "We established an ongoing series of general manager meetings, and my role was more as a mediator," commented Iverson. "They were chaos. We would stay there for hours, ironing out the issues, until we came to something. . . . At times, the meetings would get so violent that people almost went across the table at each other. . . . People yelled. They waved their arms around and pounded on tables. Faces would get red and veins bulged out."[38]

Iverson's assistant tells of a scene repeated over the years, wherein colleagues would march into Iverson's office and yell and scream at each other, but then emerge with a conclusion.[39] Argue and debate, then sell the nuclear business; argue and debate, then focus on steel joists; argue and debate, then begin to manufacture their own steel; argue and debate, then invest in their own mini-mill; argue and debate, then build a second mini-mill, and so forth. Nearly all the Nucor executives we spoke with described a climate of debate, wherein the company's strategy "evolved through many agonizing arguments and fights."[40]

Like Nucor, all the good-to-great companies had a penchant for intense dialogue. Phrases like "loud debate," "heated discussions," and "healthy conflict" peppered the articles and interview transcripts from all the companies. They didn't use discussion as a sham process to let people "have their say" so that they could "buy in" to a predetermined decision. The process was more like a heated scientific debate, with people engaged in a search for the best answers.

3. *Conduct autopsies, without blame.*

In 1978, Philip Morris acquired the Seven-Up Company, only to sell it eight years later at a loss.[41] The financial loss was relatively small compared to Philip Morris's total assets, but it was a highly visible black eye that consumed thousands of hours of precious management time.

In our interviews with the Philip Morris executives, we were struck by how they all brought up the debacle on their own and discussed it openly. Instead of hiding their big, ugly mistake, they seemed to feel an almost therapeutic need to talk about it. In his book, *I'm a Lucky Guy,* Joe Cullman dedicates five pages to dissecting the 7UP disaster. He doesn't hold back the embarrassing truth about how flawed the decision was. It is a five-page clinical analysis of the mistake, its implications, and its lessons.

Hundreds, if not thousands, of people hours had been spent in autopsies of the 7UP case. Yet, as much as they talked about this conspicuous failure, no one pointed fingers to single out blame. There is only one exception to this pattern: Joe Cullman, standing in front of the mirror, pointing the finger right at himself. "[It] . . . became apparent that this was another Joe Cullman plan that didn't work," he writes.[42] He goes even further, implying that if he'd only listened better to the people who challenged his idea at the time, the disaster might have been averted. He goes out of his way to give credit to those who were right in retrospect, naming those specific individuals who were more prescient than himself.

In an era when leaders go to great lengths to preserve the image of their own track record—stepping forth to claim credit about how they were visionary when their colleagues were not, but finding others to blame when their decisions go awry—it is quite refreshing to come across Cullman. He set the tone: "*I* will take responsibility for this bad decision. But we will all take responsibility for extracting the maximum learning from the tuition we've paid."

When you conduct autopsies without blame, you go a long way toward creating a climate where the truth is heard. If you have the right people on the bus, you should almost never need to assign blame but need only to search for understanding and learning.

4. *Build "red flag" mechanisms.*

We live in an information age, when those with more and better information supposedly have an advantage. If you look across the rise and fall of organizations, however, you will rarely find companies stumbling because they lacked information.

Bethlehem Steel executives had known for years about the threat of mini-mill companies like Nucor. They paid little attention until they woke up one day to discover large chunks of market share taken away.[43]

Upjohn had plenty of information that indicated some of its forthcoming products would fail to deliver anticipated results or, worse, had potentially serious side effects. Yet it often ignored those problems. With Halcion, for example, an insider was quoted in *Newsweek* saying, "dismissing safety concerns about Halcion had become virtual company policy." In another case when Upjohn found itself under fire, it framed its problems as "adverse publicity," rather than confronting the truth of its own shortcomings.[44]

Executives at Bank of America had plenty of information about the realities of deregulation, yet they failed to confront the one big implication of those realities: In a deregulated world, banking would be a commodity, and the old perks and genteel traditions of banking would be gone forever. Not until it had lost $1.8 billion did Bank of America fully accept this fact. In contrast, Carl Reichardt of Wells Fargo, called the ultimate realist by his predecessor, hit the brutal facts of deregulation head-on.[45] Sorry, fellow bankers, but we can preserve the banker class no more. We've got to be businessmen with as much attention to costs and effectiveness as McDonald's.

Indeed, we found no evidence that the good-to-great companies had more or better information than the comparison companies. None. Both sets of companies had virtually identical access to good information. The key, then, lies not in better information, but in turning information into information *that cannot be ignored.*

One particularly powerful way to accomplish this is through red flag mechanisms. Allow me to use a personal example to illustrate the idea. When teaching by the case method at Stanford Business School, I issued to each MBA student an 8.5" × 11" bright red sheet of paper, with the following instructions: "This is your red flag for the quarter. If you raise your hand with your red flag, the classroom will stop for you. There are no restrictions on when and how to use your red flag; the decision rests entirely in your hands. You can use it to voice an observation, share a personal experience, present an analysis, disagree with the professor, challenge a CEO guest, respond to a fellow student, ask a question, make a suggestion, or whatever. There will be no penalty whatsoever for any use of a red flag. Your red flag can be used only once during the quarter. Your red flag is nontransferable; you cannot give or sell it to another student."

With the red flag, I had no idea precisely *what* would happen each day in class. In one situation, a student used her red flag to state, "Professor Collins, I think you are doing a particularly ineffective job of running class today. You are leading too much with your questions and stifling our independent thinking. Let us think for ourselves." The red flag confronted me with the brutal fact that my own questioning style stood in the way of people's learning. A student survey at the end of the quarter would have given me that same information. But the red flag—real time, in front of everyone in the classroom—turned information about the shortcomings of the class into information that I absolutely could not ignore.

I got the idea for red flag mechanisms from Bruce Woolpert, who instituted a particularly powerful device called short pay at his company Graniterock. Short pay gives the customer full discretionary power to decide whether and how much to pay on an invoice based upon his own subjective evaluation of how satisfied he feels with a product or service. Short pay is not a refund policy. The customer does not need to return the product, nor does he need to call Graniterock for permission. He simply circles the offending item on the invoice, deducts it from the total, and sends a check for the balance. When I asked Woolpert his reasons for short pay, he said, "You can get a lot of information from customer surveys, but there are always ways of explaining away the data. With short pay, you absolutely have to pay attention to the data. You often don't know that a customer is upset until you lose that customer entirely. Short pay acts as an early warning system that forces us to adjust quickly, long before we would lose that customer."

To be clear, we did not generally find red flag mechanisms as vivid and dramatic as short pay in the good-to-great companies. Nonetheless, I've decided to include this idea here, at the urging of research assistant Lane Hornung. Hornung, who helped me systematically research and collate mechanisms across companies for a different research project, makes the compelling argument that if you're a fully developed Level 5 leader, you might not need red flag mechanisms. But if you are not yet a Level 5 leader, or if you suffer the liability of charisma, red flag mechanisms give you a practical and useful tool for turning information into information that cannot be ignored and for creating a climate where the truth is heard.*

UNWAVERING FAITH AMID THE BRUTAL FACTS

When Procter & Gamble invaded the paper-based consumer business in the late 1960s, Scott Paper (then the leader) simply resigned itself to second place without a fight and began looking for ways to diversify.[46] "The company had a meeting for analysts in 1971 that was one of the most depressing I've ever attended," said one analyst. "Management essentially threw in the towel and said, 'We've been had.' "[47] The once-proud company began to look at its competition and say, "Here's how we stack up against the best," and sigh, "Oh, well . . . at least there are people in the business worse than we are."[48] Instead of figuring out how to get back on the offensive and win, Scott just tried to protect what it had. Conceding the top end of the market to P&G, Scott hoped that, by hiding away in

*For a more complete discussion of mechanisms, see the article "Turning Goals into Results: The Power of Catalytic Mechanisms," *Harvard Business Review*, July–August, 1999.

the B category, it would be left alone by the big monster that had invaded its turf.[49]

Kimberly-Clark, on the other hand, viewed competing against Procter & Gamble not as a liability, but as an *asset*. Darwin Smith and his team felt exhilarated by the idea of going up against the best, seeing it as an opportunity to make Kimberly-Clark better and stronger. They also viewed it as a way to stimulate the competitive juices of Kimberly people at all levels. At one internal gathering, Darwin Smith stood up and started his talk by saying, "Okay, I want everyone to rise in a moment of silence." Everyone looked around, wondering what Darwin was up to. Did someone die? And so, after a moment of confusion, they all stood up and stared at their shoes in reverent silence. After an appropriate pause, Smith looked out at the group and said in a somber tone, "That was a moment of silence for P&G."

The place went bananas. Blair White, a director who witnessed the incident, said, "He had everyone wound up in this thing, all up and down the company, right down to the plant floor. We were taking on Goliath!"[50] Later, Wayne Sanders (Smith's successor) described to us the incredible benefit of competing against the best: "Could we have a better adversary than P&G? Not a chance. I say that because we respect them so much. They are bigger than we are. They are very talented. They are great at marketing. They beat the hell out of every one of their competitors, except one, Kimberly-Clark. That is one of the things that makes us so proud."[51]

Scott Paper's and Kimberly-Clark's differing reactions to P&G bring us to a vital point. In confronting the brutal facts, the good-to-great companies left themselves stronger and more resilient, not weaker and more dispirited. There is a sense of exhilaration that comes in facing head-on the hard truths and saying, "We will never give up. We will never capitulate. It might take a long time, but we *will* find a way to prevail."

Robert Aders of Kroger summed this up nicely at the end of his interview, describing the psychology of the Kroger team as it faced the daunting twenty-year task of methodically turning over the entire Kroger system. "There was a certain Churchillian character to what we were doing. We had a very strong will to live, the sense that we are Kroger, Kroger was here before and will be here long after we are gone, and, by god, we are going to win this thing. *It might take us a hundred years, but we will persist for a hundred years, if that's what it takes.*"[52]

Throughout our research, we were continually reminded of the "hardiness" research studies done by the International Committee for the Study of Victimization. These studies looked at people who had suffered serious adversity—cancer patients, prisoners of war, accident victims, and so forth—and survived. They found that people fell generally into three categories: those who were permanently dispirited by the event, those who got their life back to normal, and those who used the experience as a defining event that made them stronger.[53] The good-to-great companies were like those in the third group, with the "hardiness factor."

When Fannie Mae began its transition in the early 1980s, almost no one gave it high odds for success, much less for greatness. Fannie Mae had $56 billion of loans that were losing money. It received about 9 percent interest on its mortgage portfolio but had to pay up to 15 percent on the debt it issued. Multiply that difference times $56 billion, and you get a very large negative number! Furthermore, by charter, Fannie Mae could not diversify outside the mortgage finance business. Most people viewed Fannie Mae as totally beholden to shifts in the direction of interest rates—they go up and Fannie Mae loses, they go down and Fannie Mae wins—and many believed that Fannie Mae could succeed only if the government stepped in to clamp down on interest rates.[54] "That's their only hope," said one analyst.[55]

But that's not the way David Maxwell and his newly assembled team viewed the situation. They never wavered in their faith, consistently emphasizing in their interviews with us that they never had the goal to merely survive but to *prevail* in the end as a great company. Yes, the interest spread was a brutal fact that was not going to magically disappear. Fannie Mae had no choice but to become the best capital markets player in the world at managing mortgage interest risk. Maxwell and his team set out to create a new business model that would depend much less on interest rates, involving the invention of very sophisticated mortgage finance instruments. Most analysts responded with derision. "When you've got $56 billion worth of loans in place and underwater, talking about new programs is a joke," said one. "That's like Chrysler [then asking for federal loan guarantees to stave off bankruptcy] going into the aircraft business."[56]

After completing my interview with David Maxwell, I asked how he and his team dealt with the naysayers during those dark days. "It was never an issue internally," he said. "Of course, we had to stop doing a lot of stupid things, and we had to invent a completely new set of financial devices. But we never entertained the possibility that we would fail. We were going to use the calamity as an opportunity to remake Fannie Mae into a great company."[57]

During a research meeting, a team member commented that Fannie Mae reminded her of an old television show, *The Six Million Dollar Man* with Lee Majors. The pretext of the series is that an astronaut suffers a serious crash while testing a moon landing craft over a southwestern desert. Instead of just trying to save the patient, doctors completely redesign him into a superhuman cyborg, installing atomic-powered robotic devices such as a powerful left eye and mechanical limbs.[58] Similarly, David Maxwell and his team didn't use the fact that Fannie Mae was bleeding and near death as a pretext to merely restructure the company. They used it as an opportunity to create something much stronger and more powerful. Step by step, day by day, month by month, the Fannie Mae team rebuilt the entire business model around risk management and reshaped the corporate culture into a high-performance machine that rivaled anything on Wall Street, eventually generating stock returns nearly eight times the market over fifteen years.

THE STOCKDALE PARADOX

Of course, not all good-to-great companies faced a dire crisis like Fannie Mae; fewer than half did. But every good-to-great company faced significant adversity along the way to greatness, of one sort or another—Gillette and the takeover battles, Nucor and imports, Wells Fargo and deregulation, Pitney Bowes losing its monopoly, Abbott Labs and a huge product recall, Kroger and the need to replace nearly 100 percent of its stores, and so forth. In every case, the management team responded with a powerful psychological duality. On the one hand, they stoically accepted the brutal facts of reality. On the other hand, they maintained an unwavering faith in the endgame, and a commitment to prevail as a great company despite the brutal facts. We came to call this duality the Stockdale Paradox.

The name refers to Admiral Jim Stockdale, who was the highest-ranking United States military officer in the "Hanoi Hilton" prisoner-of-war camp during the height of the Vietnam War. Tortured over twenty times during his eight-year imprisonment from 1965 to 1973, Stockdale lived out the war without any prisoner's rights, no set release date, and no certainty as to whether he would even survive to see his family again. He shouldered the burden of command, doing everything he could to create conditions that would increase the number of prisoners who would survive unbroken, while fighting an internal war against his captors and their attempts to use the prisoners for propaganda. At one point, he beat himself with a stool and cut himself with a razor, deliberately disfiguring himself, so that he could not be put on videotape as an example of a "well-treated prisoner." He exchanged secret intelligence information with his wife through their letters, knowing that discovery would mean more torture and perhaps death. He instituted rules that would help people to deal with torture (no one can resist torture indefinitely, so he created a stepwise system—after *x* minutes, you can say certain things—that gave the men milestones to survive toward). He instituted an elaborate internal communications system to reduce the sense of isolation that their captors tried to create, which used a five-by-five matrix of tap codes for alpha characters. (Tap-tap equals the letter *a*, tap-pause-tap-tap equals the letter *b*, tap-tap-pause-tap equals the letter *f*, and so forth, for twenty-five letters, *c* doubling in for *k*.) At one point, during an imposed silence, the prisoners mopped and swept the central yard using the code, swish-swashing out "We love you" to Stockdale, on the third anniversary of his being shot down. After his release, Stockdale became the first three-star officer in the history of the navy to wear both aviator wings and the Congressional Medal of Honor.[59]

You can understand, then, my anticipation at the prospect of spending part of an afternoon with Stockdale. One of my students had written his paper on Stockdale, who happened to be a senior research fellow studying the Stoic philosophers at the Hoover Institution right across the street from my office, and Stockdale invited the two of us for lunch. In preparation, I read *In Love and War*, the book Stockdale and his wife had written in alternating chapters, chronicling their experiences during those eight years.

As I moved through the book, I found myself getting depressed. It just seemed so bleak—the uncertainty of his fate, the brutality of his captors, and so forth. And then, it dawned on me: "Here I am sitting in my warm and comfortable office, looking out over the beautiful Stanford campus on a beautiful Saturday afternoon. I'm getting depressed reading this, and I know the end of the story! I know that he gets out, reunites with his family, becomes a national hero, and gets to spend the later years of his life studying philosophy on this same beautiful campus. If it feels depressing for me, how on earth did he deal with it when he was actually there and *did not know the end of the story?*"

"I never lost faith in the end of the story," he said, when I asked him. "I never doubted not only that I would get out, but also that I would prevail in the end and turn the experience into the defining event of my life, which, in retrospect, I would not trade."

* * *

I didn't say anything for many minutes, and we continued the slow walk toward the faculty club, Stockdale limping and arc-swinging his stiff leg that had never fully recovered from repeated torture. Finally, after about a hundred meters of silence, I asked, "Who didn't make it out?"

"Oh, that's easy," he said. "The optimists."

"The optimists? I don't understand," I said, now completely confused, given what he'd said a hundred meters earlier.

"The optimists. Oh, they were the ones who said, 'We're going to be out by Christmas.' And Christmas would come, and Christmas would go. Then they'd say, 'We're going to be out by Easter.' And Easter would come, and Easter would go. And then Thanksgiving, and then it would be Christmas again. And they died of a broken heart."

Another long pause, and more walking. Then he turned to me and said, "This is a very important lesson. You must never confuse faith that you will prevail in the end—which you can never afford to lose—with the discipline to confront the most brutal facts of your current reality, whatever they might be."

To this day, I carry a mental image of Stockdale admonishing the optimists: "We're not getting out by Christmas; deal with it!"

* * *

That conversation with Admiral Stockdale stayed with me, and in fact had a profound influence on my own development. Life is unfair—sometimes to our advantage, sometimes to our disadvantage. We will all experience disappointments and crushing events somewhere along the way, setbacks for which there is no "reason," no one to blame. It might be disease; it might be injury; it might be an accident; it might be losing a loved one; it might be getting swept away in a political shake-up; it might be getting shot down over Vietnam and thrown into a POW camp for eight years. What separates people, Stockdale taught me, is not the presence or absence of difficulty, but how they deal with the inevitable difficulties of life. In wrestling with life's challenges, the Stockdale Paradox (you must retain faith that you will prevail in the end *and* you must also confront the most brutal facts of your current reality) has proved powerful for coming back from difficulties not weakened, but stronger—not just for me, but for all those who've learned the lesson and tried to apply it.

The Stockdale Paradox

Retain faith that you will prevail in the end, regardless of the difficulties.	*AND at the same time*	Confront the most brutal facts of your current reality, whatever they might be.

I never really considered my walk with Stockdale as part of my research into great companies, categorizing it more as a personal rather than corporate lesson. But as we unraveled the research evidence, I kept coming back to it in my own mind. Finally, one day during a research-team meeting, I shared the Stockdale story. There was silence around the table when I finished, and I thought, "They must think I'm really out in left field."

Then Duane Duffy, a quiet and thoughtful team member who had done the A&P versus Kroger analysis, said, "That's exactly what I've been struggling with. I've been trying to get my hands around the essential difference between A&P and Kroger. And that's it. Kroger was like Stockdale, and A&P was like the optimists who always thought they'd be out by Christmas."

Then other team members began to chime in, noting the same difference between their comparison sets—Wells Fargo versus Bank of America both facing deregulation, Kimberly-Clark versus Scott Paper both facing the terrible might of Procter & Gamble, Pitney Bowes versus Addressograph both facing the loss of their monopolies, Nucor versus Bethlehem Steel both facing imports, and so forth. They all demonstrated this paradoxical psychological pattern, and we dubbed it the Stockdale Paradox.

The Stockdale Paradox is a signature of all those who create greatness, be it in leading their own lives or in leading others. Churchill had it during the Second World War. Admiral Stockdale, like Viktor Frankl before him, lived it in a prison camp. And while our good-to-great companies cannot claim to have experienced either the grandeur of saving the free world or the depth of personal experience of living in a POW camp, they all embraced the Stockdale Paradox. It didn't matter how bleak the situation or how stultifying their mediocrity, they all maintained unwavering faith that they would not just survive, but prevail as a great company. And yet, at the same time, they became relentlessly disciplined at confronting the most brutal facts of their current reality.

Like much of what we found in our research, the key elements of greatness are deceptively simple and straightforward. The good-to-great leaders were able to strip away so much noise and clutter and just focus on the few things that would have the greatest impact. They were able to do so in large part because they operated from both sides of the Stockdale Paradox, never letting one side overshadow the other. If you are able to adopt this dual pattern, you will dramatically increase the odds of making a series of good decisions and ultimately discovering a simple, yet deeply insightful, concept for making the really big choices. And once you have that simple, unifying concept, you will be very close to making a sustained transition to breakthrough results. It is to the creation of that concept that we now turn.

CHAPTER SUMMARY

CONFRONT THE BRUTAL FACTS

(YET NEVER LOSE FAITH)

KEY POINTS

- All good-to-great companies began the process of finding a path to greatness by confronting the brutal facts of their current reality.
- When you start with an honest and diligent effort to determine the truth of your situation, the right decisions often become self-evident. It is impossible to make good decisions without infusing the entire process with an honest confrontation of the brutal facts.
- A primary task in taking a company from good to great is to create a culture wherein people have a tremendous opportunity to be heard and, ultimately, for the truth to be heard.
- Creating a climate where the truth is heard involves four basic practices:

    1. Lead with questions, not answers.
    2. Engage in dialogue and debate, not coercion.
    3. Conduct autopsies, without blame.
    4. Build red flag mechanisms that turn information into information that cannot be ignored.

- The good-to-great companies faced just as much adversity as the comparison companies, but responded to that adversity differently. They hit the realities of their situation head-on. As a result, they emerged from adversity even stronger.
- A key psychology for leading from good to great is the Stockdale Paradox: Retain absolute faith that you can and will prevail in the end, regardless of the difficulties, *AND at the same time* confront the most brutal facts of your current reality, whatever they might be.

UNEXPECTED FINDINGS

- Charisma can be as much a liability as an asset, as the strength of your leadership personality can deter people from bringing you the brutal facts.
- Leadership does not begin just with vision. It begins with getting people to confront the brutal facts and to act on the implications.
- Spending time and energy trying to "motivate" people is a waste of effort. The real question is not, "How do we motivate our people?" If you have the right people, they will be self-motivated. The key is to not *de*-motivate them. One of the primary ways to de-motivate people is to ignore the brutal facts of reality.

CHAPTER 5

THE HEDGEHOG CONCEPT
(Simplicity within the Three Circles)

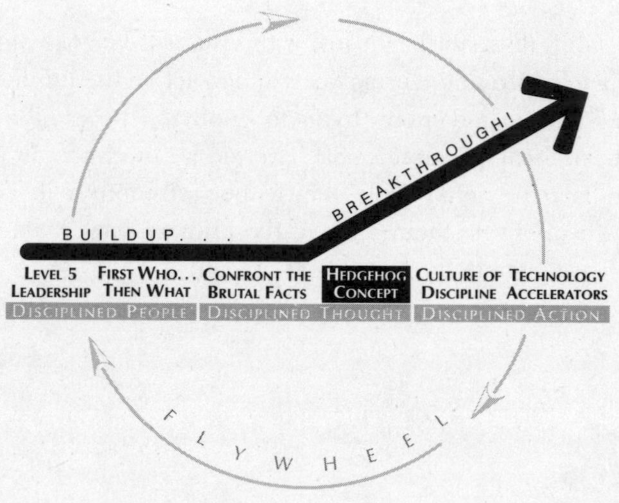

Know thyself.

—SCRIBES OF DELPHI,
via Plato[1]

Are you a hedgehog or a fox?

In his famous essay "The Hedgehog and the Fox," Isaiah Berlin divided the world into hedgehogs and foxes, based upon an ancient Greek parable: "The fox knows many things, but the hedgehog knows one big thing."[2] The fox is a cunning creature, able to devise a myriad of complex strategies for sneak attacks upon the hedgehog. Day in and day out, the fox circles around the hedgehog's den, waiting for the perfect moment to pounce. Fast, sleek, beautiful, fleet of foot, and crafty—the fox looks like the sure winner. The hedgehog, on the other hand, is a dowdier creature, looking like a genetic mix-up between a porcupine and a small armadillo. He waddles along, going about his simple day, searching for lunch and taking care of his home.

The fox waits in cunning silence at the juncture in the trail. The hedgehog, minding his own business, wanders right into the path of the fox.

"Aha, I've got you now!" thinks the fox. He leaps out, bounding across the ground, lightning fast. The little hedgehog, sensing danger, looks up and thinks, "Here we go again. Will he ever learn?" Rolling up into a perfect little ball, the hedgehog becomes a sphere of sharp spikes, pointing outward in all directions. The fox, bounding toward his prey, sees the hedgehog defense and calls off the attack. Retreating back to the forest, the fox begins to calculate a new line of attack. Each day, some version of this battle between the hedgehog and the fox takes place, and despite the greater cunning of the fox, the hedgehog always wins.

Berlin extrapolated from this little parable to divide people into two basic groups: foxes and hedgehogs. Foxes pursue many ends at the same time and see the world in all its complexity. They are "scattered or diffused, moving on many levels," says Berlin, never integrating their thinking into one overall concept or unifying vision. Hedgehogs, on the other hand, simplify a complex world into a single organizing idea, a basic principle or concept that unifies and guides everything. It doesn't matter how complex the world, a hedgehog reduces all challenges and dilemmas to simple—indeed almost simplistic—hedgehog ideas. For a hedgehog, anything that does not somehow relate to the hedgehog idea holds no relevance.

Princeton professor Marvin Bressler pointed out the power of the hedgehog during one of our long conversations: "You want to know what separates those who make the biggest impact from all the others who are just as smart? They're hedgehogs." Freud and the unconscious, Darwin and natural selection, Marx and class struggle, Einstein and relativity, Adam Smith and division of labor—they were all hedgehogs. They took a complex world and simplified it. "Those who leave the biggest footprints," said Bressler, "have thousands calling after them, 'Good idea, but you went too far!' "[3]

To be clear, hedgehogs are not stupid. Quite the contrary. They understand that the essence of profound insight is simplicity. What could be more simple than $e = mc^2$? What could be simpler than the idea of the unconscious, organized into an id, ego, and superego? What could be more elegant than Adam Smith's pin factory and "invisible hand"? No, the hedgehogs aren't simpletons; they have a piercing insight that allows them to see through complexity and discern underlying patterns. Hedgehogs see what is essential, and ignore the rest.

What does all this talk of hedgehogs and foxes have to do with good to great? Everything.

> Those who built the good-to-great companies were, to one degree or another, hedgehogs. They used their hedgehog nature to drive toward what we came to call a Hedgehog Concept for their companies. Those who led the comparison companies tended to be foxes, never gaining the clarifying advantage of a Hedgehog Concept, being instead scattered, diffused, and inconsistent.

Consider the case of Walgreens versus Eckerd. Recall how Walgreens generated cumulative stock returns from the end of 1975 to 2000 that exceeded the market by over fifteen times, handily beating such great companies as GE, Merck, Coca-Cola, and Intel. It was a remarkable performance for such an anonymous—some might even say boring—company. When interviewing Cork Walgreen, I kept asking him to go deeper, to help us understand these extraordinary results. Finally, in exasperation, he said, "Look, it just wasn't that complicated! Once we understood the concept, we just moved straight ahead."[4]

What was the concept? Simply this: the best, most convenient drugstores, with high profit per customer visit. That's it. That's the breakthrough strategy that Walgreens used to beat Intel, GE, Coca-Cola, and Merck.

In classic hedgehog style, Walgreens took this simple concept and implemented it with fanatical consistency. It embarked on a systematic program to replace all inconvenient locations with more convenient ones, preferably corner lots where customers could easily enter and exit from multiple directions. If a great corner location would open up just half a block away from a profitable Walgreens store in a good location, the company would close the good store (even at a cost of $1 million to get out of the lease) to open a great new store on the corner.[5] Walgreens pioneered drive-through pharmacies, found customers liked the idea, and built hundreds of them. In urban areas, the company clustered its stores tightly together, on the precept that no one should have to walk more than a few blocks to reach a Walgreens.[6] In downtown San Francisco, for example, Walgreens clustered nine stores within a one-mile radius. Nine stores![7] If you look closely, you will see Walgreens stores as densely packed in some cities as Starbucks coffee shops in Seattle.

Walgreens then linked its convenience concept to a simple economic idea, profit per customer visit. Tight clustering (nine stores per mile!) leads to local economies of scale, which provides the cash for more clustering, which in turn draws more customers. By adding high-margin ser-

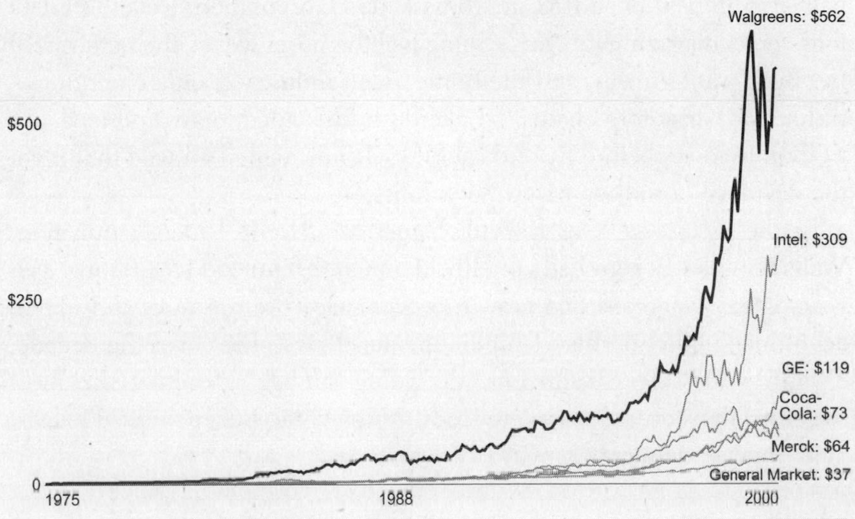

vices, like one-hour photo developing, Walgreens increased its profit per customer visit. More convenience led to more customer visits, which, when multiplied times increased profit per customer visit, threw cash back into the system to build *even more* convenient stores. Store by store, block by block, city by city, region by region, Walgreens became more and more of a hedgehog with this incredibly simple idea.

In a world overrun by management faddists, brilliant visionaries, ranting futurists, fearmongers, motivational gurus, and all the rest, it's refreshing to see a company succeed so brilliantly by taking one simple concept and just doing it with excellence and imagination. Becoming the best in the world at convenient drugstores, steadily increasing profit per customer visit—what could be more obvious and straightforward?

Yet, if it was so obvious and straightforward, why didn't Eckerd see it? While Walgreens stuck *only* to cities where it could implement the convenience/clustering concept, we found no evidence of a similarly coherent concept for growth at Eckerd. Deal makers to the core, Eckerd's executives compulsively leapt at opportunities to acquire clumps of stores—forty-two units here, thirty-six units there—in hodgepodge fashion, with no obvious unifying theme.

While Walgreens executives understood that profitable growth would come by pruning away all that did not fit with the Hedgehog Concept, Eckerd executives lurched after growth for growth's sake. In the early 1980s, just as Walgreens became religious about carrying out its convenient drugstore concept, Eckerd threw itself into the home video market with its purchase of American Home Video Corporation. Eckerd's CEO told *Forbes* magazine in 1981, "Some feel the purer we are the better we'll be. But I want growth, and the home video industry is only emerging—unlike, say, drugstore chains."[8] Eckerd's home video foray produced $31 million in losses before Eckerd sold it to Tandy, which crowed that it got the deal for $72 million below book value.[9]

In the precise year of Eckerd's American Home Video acquisition, Walgreens and Eckerd had virtually identical revenues ($1.7 billion). Ten years later, Walgreens had grown to over twice the revenues of Eckerd, accumulating net profits $1 billion greater than Eckerd over the decade. Twenty years later, Walgreens was going strong, as one of the most sustained transformations in our study. Meanwhile, Eckerd ceased to exist as an independent company.[10]

THE THREE CIRCLES

The notion of a Hedgehog Concept originated in our research team meetings when we were trying to make sense of Walgreens' spectacular returns.

"Aren't we just talking about strategy?" I asked. "Convenient drugstores, profit per customer visit—isn't that just basic strategy? What's so interesting about that?"

"But Eckerd also had strategy," said Jenni Cooper, who analyzed the contrast between the two companies. "We can't say that it's just about having strategy. They *both* had strategy." Jenni was correct in her observation. Strategy per se did not distinguish the good-to-great companies from the comparison companies. *Both* sets of companies had strategic plans, and there is absolutely no evidence that the good-to-great companies invested more time and energy in strategy development and long-range planning.

"Okay, so are we just talking about good strategy versus bad strategy?"

The team sat there for a minute, thinking. Then Leigh Wilbanks observed, "But what I find so striking is their incredible simplicity. I mean, look at Kroger with the superstore concept, or Kimberly-Clark with the move to paper-based consumer products, or Walgreens with convenient drugstores. These were simple, simple, simple ideas."

The research-team members all jumped into the fray, bantering about the companies they were studying. It soon became abundantly clear that all the good-to-great companies attained a very simple concept that they used as a frame of reference for all their decisions, and this understanding coincided with breakthrough results. Meanwhile, the comparison companies like Eckerd got all tripped up by their snazzy strategies for growth.

"Okay," I pushed back, "but is simplicity enough? Just because it's simple doesn't mean it's *right*. The world is filled with failed companies that had simple but *wrong* ideas."

Then we decided to undertake a systematic look at the concepts that guided the good-to-great companies in contrast to the comparison companies. After a few months of sifting and sorting, considering possibilities and tossing them out, we finally came to see that the Hedgehog Concept in each good-to-great company wasn't just any random simple idea.

> The essential strategic difference between the good-to-great and comparison companies lay in two fundamental distinctions. First, the good-to-great companies founded their strategies on deep understanding along three key dimensions—what we came to call the three circles. Second, the good-to-great companies translated that understanding into a simple, crystalline concept that guided all their efforts—hence the term *Hedgehog Concept*.

More precisely, a Hedgehog Concept is *a simple, crystalline concept that flows from deep understanding about the intersection of the following three circles:*

1. *What you can be the best in the world at* (and, equally important, what you *cannot* be the best in the world at). This discerning standard goes far beyond core competence. Just because you possess a core competence doesn't necessarily mean you can be the best in the world at it. Conversely, what you can be the best at might not even be something in which you are currently engaged.
2. *What drives your economic engine.* All the good-to-great companies attained piercing insight into how to most effectively generate sustained

and robust cash flow and profitability. In particular, they discovered the single denominator—profit per *x*—that had the greatest impact on their economics. (It would be cash flow per *x* in the social sector.)

3. *What you are deeply passionate about.* The good-to-great companies focused on those activities that ignited their passion. The idea here is not to stimulate passion but to discover what makes you passionate.

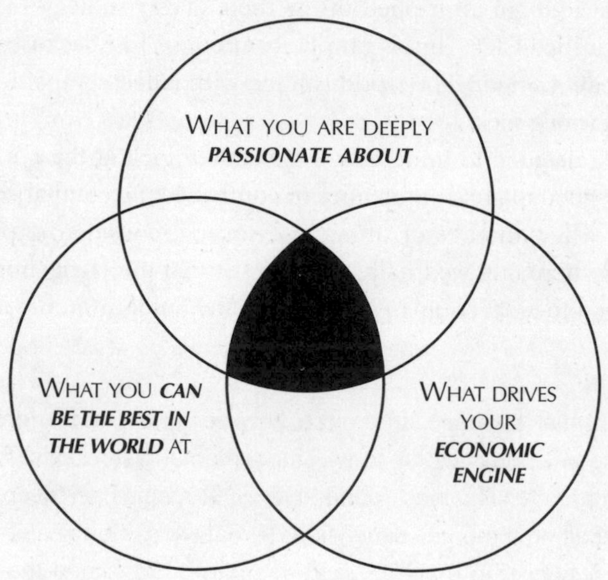

THREE CIRCLES OF THE HEDGEHOG CONCEPT

To quickly grasp the three circles, consider the following personal analogy. Suppose you were able to construct a work life that meets the following three tests. First, you are doing work for which you have a genetic or God-given talent, and perhaps you could become one of the best in the world in applying that talent. ("I feel that I was just born to be doing this.") Second, you are well paid for what you do. ("I get paid to do this? Am I dreaming?") Third, you are doing work you are passionate about and absolutely love to do, enjoying the actual process for its own sake. ("I look forward to getting up and throwing myself into my daily work, and I really believe in what I'm doing.") If you could drive toward the intersection of these three circles and translate that intersection into a simple, crystalline concept that guided your life choices, then you'd have a Hedgehog Concept for yourself.

To have a fully developed Hedgehog Concept, you need *all three* circles. If you make a lot of money doing things at which you could never be the best, you'll only build a successful company, not a great one. If you become the best at something, you'll never remain on top if you don't have intrinsic passion for what you are doing. Finally, you can be passionate all you want, but if you can't be the best at it or it doesn't make economic sense, then you might have a lot of fun, but you won't produce great results.

UNDERSTANDING WHAT YOU CAN (AND CANNOT) BE THE BEST AT

"They stick with what they understand and let their abilities, not their egos, determine what they attempt."[11] So wrote Warren Buffett about his $290 million investment in Wells Fargo despite his serious reservations about the banking industry.[12] Prior to clarifying its Hedgehog Concept, Wells Fargo had tried to be a global bank, operating like a mini-Citicorp, and a mediocre one at that. Then, at first under Dick Cooley and then under Carl Reichardt, Wells Fargo executives began to ask themselves a piercing set of questions: What can we potentially do better than any other company, and, equally important, what can we *not* do better than any other company? And if we can't be the best at it, then why are we doing it at all?

Putting aside their egos, the Wells Fargo team pulled the plug on the vast majority of its international operations, accepting the truth that it could not be better than Citicorp in global banking.[13] Wells Fargo then turned its attention to what it *could* be the best in the world at: running a bank like a business, with a focus on the western United States. That's it. That was the essence of the Hedgehog Concept that turned Wells Fargo from a mediocre Citicorp wanna-be to one of the best-performing banks in the world.

Carl Reichardt, CEO of Wells Fargo at the time of transition, stands as a consummate hedgehog. While his counterparts at Bank of America went into a reaction-revolution panic mode in response to deregulation, hiring change gurus who used sophisticated models and time-consuming encounter groups, Reichardt stripped everything down to its essential simplicity.[14] "It's not space science stuff," he told us in our interview. "What we did was so simple, and we kept it simple. It was so straightforward and obvious that it sounds almost ridiculous to talk about it. The average businessman coming from a highly competitive industry with no regulations would have jumped on this like a goose on a June bug."[15]

Reichardt kept people relentlessly focused on the simple hedgehog idea, continually reminding them that "there's more money to be made in Modesto than Tokyo."[16] Those who worked with Reichardt marveled at his genius for simplicity. "If Carl were an Olympic diver," said one of his colleagues, "he would not do a five-flip twisting thing. He would do the best swan dive in the world, and do it perfectly over and over again."[17]

The Wells Fargo focus on its Hedgehog Concept was so intense that it became, in its executives' own words, "a mantra." Throughout our interviews, Wells Fargo people echoed the same basic theme—"It wasn't that complicated. We just took a hard-nosed look at what we were doing and decided to focus entirely on those few things we knew we could do better than anyone else, not getting distracted into arenas that would feed our egos and at which we could not be the best."

This brings me to one of the most crucial points of this chapter: A Hedgehog Concept is not a goal to be the best, a strategy to be the best, an intention to be the best, a plan to be the best. It is an *understanding* of what you *can* be the best at. The distinction is absolutely crucial.

Every company would like to be the best at something, but few actually understand—with piercing insight and egoless clarity—what they actually have the potential to be the best at and, just as important, what they *cannot* be the best at. And it is this distinction that stands as one of the primary contrasts between the good-to-great companies and the comparison companies.

Consider the contrast between Abbott Laboratories and Upjohn. In 1964, the two companies were almost identical in terms of revenues, profits, and product lines. Both companies had the bulk of their business in pharmaceuticals, principally antibiotics. Both companies had family management. Both companies lagged behind the rest of the pharmaceutical industry. But then, in 1974, Abbott had a breakthrough in performance, producing cumulative returns of 4.0 times the market and 5.5 times Upjohn over the next fifteen years. One crucial difference between the two companies is that Abbott developed a Hedgehog Concept based on what it could be the best at and Upjohn did not.

Abbott began by confronting the brutal facts. By 1964, Abbott had lost the opportunity to become the best pharmaceutical company. While

Abbott had drowsily lumbered along in the 1940s and 1950s, living off its cash cow, erythromycin, companies like Merck had built research engines that rivaled Harvard and Berkeley. By 1964, George Cain and his Abbott team realized that Merck and others had such a huge research lead that trying to be the best pharmaceutical company would be like a high school football team trying to take on the Dallas Cowboys.

Even though Abbott's entire history lay in pharmaceuticals, becoming the best pharmaceutical company was no longer a viable option. So, guided by a Level 5 leader and tapping into the faith side of the Stockdale Paradox (There must be a way for us to prevail as a great company, and we will find it!), the Abbott team sought to understand what it could be the best at. Around 1967, a key insight emerged: We've lost the chance to be the best pharmaceutical company, but we have an opportunity to excel at creating products that contribute to cost-effective health care. Abbott had experimented with hospital nutritional products, designed to help patients quickly regain their strength after surgery, and diagnostic devices (one of the primary ways to reduce health care costs is through proper diagnosis). Abbott eventually became the number one company in both of these arenas, which moved it far down the path of becoming the best company in the world at creating products that make health care more cost-effective.[18]

Upjohn never confronted the same brutal reality and continued to live with the delusion that it could beat Merck.[19] Later, when it fell even further behind the pharmaceutical leaders, it diversified into arenas where it definitely could not be the best in the world, such as plastics and chemicals. As Upjohn fell even further behind, it returned to a focus on ethical drugs, yet never confronted the fact that it was just too small to win in the big-stakes pharmaceutical game.[20] Despite consistently spending nearly twice the percentage of sales on R&D as Abbott, Upjohn saw its profits dwindle to less than half those of Abbott before being acquired in 1995.[21]

The Abbott versus Upjohn case highlights the difference between a "core business" and a Hedgehog Concept. Just because something is your core business—just because you've been doing it for years or perhaps even decades—does not necessarily mean that you can be the best in the world at it. *And if you cannot be the best in the world at your core business, then your core business cannot form the basis of your Hedgehog Concept.*

Clearly, a Hedgehog Concept is not the same as a core competence. You can have competence at something but not necessarily have the potential to be the best in the world at it. To use an analogy, consider the young person who gets straight A's in high school calculus and scores high on the math part of the SAT, demonstrating a core competence at mathematics. Does that mean the person should become a mathematician? Not necessarily. Suppose now that this young person goes off to college, enrolls in math courses, and continues to earn A's, yet encounters people who are *genetically encoded* for math. As one such student said after this experience, "It would take me three hours to finish the final. Then there were those who finished the same final in thirty minutes and earned an A+. Their brains are just wired differently. I could be a very competent mathematician, but I soon realized I could never be one of the best." That young person might still get pressure from parents and friends to continue with math, saying, "But you're so good at it." Just like our young person, many people have been pulled or have fallen into careers where they can never attain complete mastery and fulfillment. Suffering from the curse of competence but lacking a clear Hedgehog Concept, they rarely become great at what they do.

The Hedgehog Concept requires a severe standard of excellence. It's not just about building on strength and competence, but about understanding what your organization truly has the potential to be the very best at and sticking to it. Like Upjohn, the comparison companies stuck to businesses at which they were "good" but could never be the best, or worse, launched off in pursuit of easy growth and profits in arenas where they had no hope of being the best. They made money but never became great.

> To go from good to great requires transcending the curse of competence. It requires the discipline to say, "Just because we are good at it—just because we're making money and generating growth—doesn't necessarily mean we can become the best at it." The good-to-great companies understood that doing what you are good at will only make you good; focusing solely on what you can potentially do better than any other organization is the only path to greatness.

Every good-to-great company eventually gained deep understanding of this principle and pinned their futures on allocating resources to those few arenas where they could potentially be the best. (See the table below.) The comparison companies rarely attained this understanding.

THE GOOD-TO-GREAT COMPANIES AND THE "BEST IN THE WORLD AT" CIRCLE OF THE HEDGEHOG CONCEPT

This table shows the understanding the good-to-great companies attained that formed the foundation of their shift from good to great. Note: This list does *not* show what the companies were already best in the world at when they began their transitions (most of these companies weren't the best at anything); rather, it shows what they came to understand they *could become* best in the world at.

Abbott Laboratories: Could become the best at creating a product portfolio that lowers the cost of health care.	**Notes:** Abbott confronted the reality that it could not become the best pharmaceutical company in the world, despite the fact that pharmaceuticals at the time accounted for 99 percent of its revenues.[22] It shifted its focus to creating a portfolio of products that contribute to lower-cost health care, principally hospital nutritionals, diagnostics, and hospital supplies.
Circuit City: Could become the best at implementing the "4-S" model (service, selection, savings, satisfaction) applied to big-ticket consumer sales.	**Notes:** Circuit City saw that it could become "the McDonald's" of big-ticket retailing, able to operate a geographically dispersed system by remote control. Its distinction lay not in the "4-S" model per se—but in the *consistent, superior execution* of the model.
Fannie Mae: Could become the best capital markets player in anything that pertains to mortgages.	**Notes:** The critical insight was to see (1) that it could be a full capital markets player as good as any on Wall Street and (2) that it could develop a unique capability to assess risk in mortgage-related securities.

Gillette: Could become the best at building premier global brands of daily necessities that require sophisticated manufacturing technology.	**Notes:** Gillette saw that it had an unusual combination of two very different skills: (1) the ability to manufacture billions of low-cost, super-high-tolerance products (e.g., razor blades) and (2) the ability to build global consumer brands—the "Coke" of blades or toothbrushes.
Kimberly-Clark: Could become the best in the world at paper-based consumer products.	**Notes:** Kimberly-Clark realized that it had a latent skill at creating "category-killer" brands—brands where the name of the product is synonymous with the name of the category (e.g., Kleenex)—in paper-based products.
Kroger: Could become the best at innovative super-combo stores.	**Notes:** Kroger always had a strength in grocery store innovation. It took this skill and applied it to the question of how to create a combination store with many innovative, high-margin "mini-stores" under one roof.
Nucor: Could become the best at harnessing culture and technology to produce low-cost steel.	**Notes:** Nucor came to see that it had tremendous skill in two activities: (1) creating a performance culture and (2) making farsighted bets on new manufacturing technologies. By combining these two, it was able to become the lowest-cost steel producer in the United States.
Philip Morris: Could become the best in the world at building brand loyalty in cigarettes and, later, other consumables.	**Notes:** Early in transition, Philip Morris saw that it could become simply the best tobacco company in the world. Later, it began to diversify into non-tobacco arenas (a step taken by all tobacco companies, as a defensive measure), but stayed close to its brand-building strengths in "sinful" products (beer, tobacco, chocolate, coffee) and food products.

Pitney Bowes: Could become the best in the world at messaging that requires sophisticated back-office equipment.	**Notes:** As Pitney wrestled with the question of how to evolve beyond postage meters, it had two key insights about its strengths: (1) that it was not a postage company, but could have a broader definition (messaging) and (2) that it had particular strength in supplying the back rooms with sophisticated machines.
Walgreens: Could become the best at convenient drugstores.	**Notes:** Walgreens saw that it was not just a drugstore but also a convenience store. It began systematically seeking the best sites for convenience—clustering many stores within a small radius and pioneering drive-through pharmacies. It also made extensive investments in technology (including recent Web site developments), linking Walgreen stores worldwide to create one giant "corner pharmacy."
Wells Fargo: Could become the best at running a bank like a business, with a focus on the western United States.	**Notes:** Wells came to two essential insights. First, most banks thought of themselves as banks, acted like banks, and protected the banker culture. Wells saw itself as a business that happened to be in banking. "Run it like a business" and "Run it like you own it" became mantras. Second, Wells recognized that it could not be the best in the world as a superglobal bank, but that it could be the best in the western United States.

INSIGHT INTO YOUR ECONOMIC ENGINE—WHAT IS YOUR DENOMINATOR?

The good-to-great companies frequently produced spectacular returns in very *un*spectacular industries. The banking industry ranked in the bottom quartile of industries (in total returns) during the same period that Wells Fargo beat the market by four times. Even more impressive, both Pitney Bowes and Nucor were in bottom 5 percent industries; yet both these companies beat the market by well over five times. Only one of the good-to-great companies had the benefit of being in a great industry (defined as a top 10 percent industry); five were in good industries; five were in bad to terrible industries. (See Appendix 5.A for a summary of industry analysis.)

> Our study clearly shows that a company does not need to be in a great industry to become a great company. Each good-to-great company built a fabulous economic engine, regardless of the industry. They were able to do this because they attained profound insights into their economics.

This is not a book on microeconomics. Each company and each industry had its own economic realities, and I'm not going to belabor them all here. The central point is that each good-to-great company attained a deep understanding of the key drivers in its economic engine and built its system in accordance with this understanding.

That said, however, we did notice one particularly provocative form of economic insight that every good-to-great company attained, the notion of a single "economic denominator." Think about it in terms of the following question: *If you could pick one and only one ratio—profit per* x *(or, in the social sector, cash flow per* x*)—to systematically increase over time, what* x *would have the greatest and most sustainable impact on your economic engine?* We learned that this single question leads to profound insight into the inner workings of an organization's economics.

Recall how Walgreens switched its focus from profit per store to profit *per customer visit.* Convenient locations are expensive, but by increasing profit per customer visit, Walgreens was able to increase convenience (nine stores in a mile!) *and* simultaneously increase profitability across its entire system. The standard metric of profit per store would have run contrary to the convenience concept. (The quickest way to increase profit per store is to decrease the number of stores and put them in less expensive locations. This would have destroyed the convenience concept.)

Or consider Wells Fargo. When the Wells team confronted the brutal fact that deregulation would transform banking into a commodity, they realized that standard banker metrics, like profit per loan and profit per deposit, would no longer be the key drivers. Instead, they grasped a new denominator: *profit per employee.* Following this logic, Wells Fargo became one of the first banks to change its distribution system to rely primarily on stripped-down branches and ATMs.

The denominator can be quite subtle, sometimes even unobvious. The key is to use the question of the denominator to gain understanding and insight into your economic model.

For example, Fannie Mae grasped the subtle denominator of profit per mortgage *risk level,* not per mortgage (which would be the "obvious" choice). It's a brilliant insight. The real driver in Fannie Mae's economics is the ability to understand risk of default in a package of mortgages better than anyone else. Then it makes money selling insurance and managing the spread on that risk. Simple, insightful, unobvious—and right.

Nucor, for example, made its mark in the ferociously price competitive steel industry with the denominator profit per ton of finished steel. At first glance, you might think that per employee or per fixed cost might be the proper denominator. But the Nucor people understood that the driving force in its economic engine was a combination of a strong-work-ethic culture *and* the application of advanced manufacturing technology. Profit per employee or per fixed cost would not capture this duality as well as profit per ton of finished steel.

Do you need to have a single denominator? No, but pushing for a single denominator tends to produce better insight than letting yourself off the hook with three or four denominators. The denominator question serves as a mechanism to force deeper understanding of the key drivers in your economic engine. As the denominator question emerged from the research, we tested the question on a number of executive teams. We found that the question always stimulated intense dialogue and debate.

Furthermore, even in cases where the team failed (or refused) to identify a single denominator, the challenge of the question drove them to deeper insight. And that is, after all, the point—to have a denominator not for the sake of having a denominator, but for the sake of gaining insight that ultimately leads to more robust and sustainable economics.

ECONOMIC DENOMINATOR

This table shows the economic denominator insight attained by the good-to-great companies during the pivotal transition years.

Abbott: *per employee*	**Key insight:** Shift from profit per product line to profit per employee fit with the idea of contributing to cost-effective health care.
Circuit City: *per geographic region*	**Key insight:** Shift from profit per single store to profit per region reflected local economies of scale. While per-store performance remained vital, regional grouping was a key insight that drove Circuit City's economics beyond Silo's.
Fannie Mae: *per mortgage risk level*	**Key insight:** Shift from profit per mortgage to profit per mortgage risk level reflected the fundamental insight that managing interest risk reduces dependence on the direction of interest rates.
Gillette: *per customer*	**Key insight:** Shift from profit per division to profit per customer reflected the economic power of repeatable purchases (e.g., razor cartridges) times high profit per purchase (e.g., Mach3, not disposable razors).
Kimberly-Clark: *per consumer brand*	**Key insight:** Shift from profit per fixed asset (the mills) to profit per consumer brand; would be less cyclical and more profitable in good times and bad.

Kroger: *per local population*	**Key insight:** Shift from profit per store to profit per local population reflected the insight that local market share drove grocery economics. If you can't attain number one or number two in local share, you should not play.
Nucor: *per ton of finished steel*	**Key insight:** Shift from profit per division to profit per ton of finished steel reflected Nucor's unique blend of high-productivity culture mixed with mini-mill technology, rather than just focusing on volume.
Philip Morris: *per global brand category*	**Key insight:** Shift from profit per sales region to profit per global brand category reflected the understanding that the real key to greatness lay in brands that could have global power, like Coke.
Pitney Bowes: *per customer*	**Key insight:** Shift from profit per postage meter to profit per customer reflected the idea that Pitney Bowes could use its postage meters as a jumping-off point to bring a range of sophisticated products into the back offices of customers.
Walgreens: *per customer visit*	**Key insight:** Shift from profit per store to profit per customer visit reflected a symbiotic relationship between convenient (and expensive) store sites and sustainable economics.
Wells Fargo: *per employee*	**Key insight:** Shift from profit per loan to profit per employee reflected understanding of the brutal fact of deregulation: Banking is a commodity.

All the good-to-great companies discovered a key economic denominator (see the table on page 106), while the comparison companies usually did not. In fact, we found only one comparison case that attained a profound insight into its economics. Hasbro built its upswing on the insight that a portfolio of classic toys and games, such as G.I. Joe and Monopoly, produces more sustainable cash flow than big onetime hits.[23] In fact, Hasbro is the one comparison company that understood all three circles of the Hedgehog Concept. It became the best in the world at acquiring and renewing tried-and-true toys, reintroducing and recycling them at just the right time to increase profit per classic brand. And its people had great passion for the business. Systematically building from all three circles, Hasbro became the best-performing comparison in our study, lending further credence to the power of the Hedgehog Concept.

Hasbro became an *unsustained* transition in part because it lost the discipline to stay within the three circles, after the unexpected death of CEO Stephen Hassenfeld. The Hasbro case reinforces a vital lesson. *If you successfully apply these ideas, but then stop doing them, you will slide backward, from great to good, or worse. The only way to remain great is to keep applying the fundamental principles that made you great.*

UNDERSTANDING YOUR PASSION

When interviewing the Philip Morris executives, we encountered an intensity and passion that surprised us. Recall from chapter 3 how George Weissman described working at the company as the great love affair of his life, second only to his marriage. Even with a most sinful collection of consumer products (Marlboro cigarettes, Miller beer, 67 percent fat-filled Velveeta, Maxwell House coffee for caffeine addicts, Toblerone for chocoholics, and so forth), we found tremendous passion for the business. Most of the top executives at Philip Morris were passionate consumers of their own products. In 1979, Ross Millhiser, then vice chairman of Philip Morris and a dedicated smoker, said, "I love cigarettes. It's one of the things that makes life really worth living."[24]

The Philip Morris people clearly loved their company and had passion for what they were doing. It's as if they viewed themselves as the lone, fiercely independent cowboy depicted in the Marlboro billboards. "We have a right to smoke, and we will protect that right!" A board member told me during my research for a previous project, "I really love being on the board of Philip Morris. It's like being part of something really special." She said this as she proudly puffed away.[25]

Now, you might say, "But that is just the defensiveness of the tobacco industry. Of course they'd feel that way. Otherwise, how could they sleep at night?" But keep in mind that R. J. Reynolds was *also* in the tobacco business and under siege from society. Yet, unlike Philip Morris, R. J. Reynolds executives began to diversify away from tobacco into any arena where it could get growth, regardless of whether they had passion for those acquisitions or whether the company could be the best in the world at them. The Philip Morris people stuck much closer to the tobacco business, in large part because they loved that business. In contrast, the R. J. Reynolds people saw tobacco as just a way to make money. As vividly portrayed in the book *Barbarians at the Gate,* R. J. Reynolds executives eventually lost passion for anything except making themselves rich through a leveraged buyout.[26]

It may seem odd to talk about something as soft and fuzzy as "passion" as an integral part of a strategic framework. But throughout the good-to-great companies, passion became a key part of the Hedgehog Concept. You can't manufacture passion or "motivate" people to feel passionate. You can only *discover* what ignites your passion and the passions of those around you.

> The good-to-great companies did not say, "Okay, folks, let's get passionate about what we do." Sensibly, they went the other way entirely: *We should only do those things that we can get passionate about.* Kimberly-Clark executives made the shift to paper-based consumer products in large part because they could get more passionate about them. As one executive put it, the traditional paper products are okay, "but they just don't have the charisma of a diaper."[27]

When Gillette executives made the choice to build sophisticated, relatively expensive shaving systems rather than fight a low-margin battle with disposables, they did so in large part because they just couldn't get excited about cheap disposable razors. "Zeien talks about shaving systems with the sort of technical gusto one expects from a Boeing or Hughes engineer," wrote one journalist about Gillette's CEO in 1996.[28] Gillette has always been at its best when it sticks to businesses that fit its Hedgehog

Concept. "People who aren't passionate about Gillette need not apply," wrote a *Wall Street Journal* reporter, who went on to describe how a top business school graduate wasn't hired because she didn't show enough passion for deodorant.[29]

Perhaps you, too, can't get passionate about deodorant. Perhaps you might find it hard to imagine being passionate about pharmacies, grocery stores, tobacco, or postage meters. You might wonder about what type of person gets all jazzed up about making a bank as efficient as McDonald's, or who considers a diaper charismatic. In the end, it doesn't really matter. The point is that *they* felt passionate about what they were doing and the passion was deep and genuine.

This doesn't mean, however, that you have to be passionate about the mechanics of the business per se (although you might be). The passion circle can be focused equally on *what the company stands for.* For example, the Fannie Mae people were not passionate about the mechanical process of packaging mortgages into market securities. But they *were* terrifically motivated by the whole idea of helping people of all classes, backgrounds, and races realize the American dream of owning their home. Linda Knight, who joined Fannie Mae in 1983, just as the company faced its darkest days, told us: "This wasn't just any old company getting into trouble; this was a company at the core of making home ownership a reality for thousands of Americans. It's a role that is far more important than just making money, and that's why we felt such depth of commitment to preserve, protect, and enhance the company."[30] As another Fannie Mae executive summed up, "I see us as a key mechanism for strengthening the whole social fabric of America. Whenever I drive through difficult neighborhoods that are coming back because more families own their homes, I return to work reenergized."

THE TRIUMPH OF UNDERSTANDING OVER BRAVADO

On the research team, we frequently found ourselves talking about the difference between "prehedgehog" and "posthedgehog" states. In the prehedgehog state, it's like groping through the fog. You're making progress on a long march, but you can't see all that well. At each juncture in the trail, you can only see a little bit ahead and must move at a deliberate, slow crawl. Then, with the Hedgehog Concept, you break into a clearing, the fog lifts, and you can see for miles. From then on, each juncture requires less deliberation, and you can shift from crawl to walk, and from walk to run. In the posthedgehog state, miles of trail move swiftly beneath your feet, forks in the road fly past as you quickly make decisions that you could not have seen so clearly in the fog.

What's so striking about the comparison companies is that—for all their change programs, frantic gesticulations, and charismatic leaders—they rarely emerged from the fog. They would try to run, making bad decisions at forks in the road, and then have to reverse course later. Or they would veer off the trail entirely, banging into trees and tumbling down ravines.(Oh, but they were sure doing it with speed and panache!)

For the comparison companies, the exact same world that had become so simple and clear to the good-to-great companies remained complex and shrouded in mist. Why? For two reasons. First, the comparison companies never asked the right questions, the questions prompted by the three circles. Second, they set their goals and strategies *more from bravado than from understanding.*

Nowhere is this more evident than in the comparison companies' mindless pursuit of growth: Over two thirds of the comparison companies displayed an obsession with growth without the benefit of a Hedgehog Concept.[31] Statements such as "We've been a growth at any price company" and "Betting that size equals success" pepper the materials on the comparison companies. In contrast, not one of the good-to-great companies focused obsessively on growth. Yet they created sustained, profitable growth far greater than the comparison companies that made growth their mantra.

Consider the case of Great Western and Fannie Mae. "Great Western is a mite unwieldy," wrote the *Wall Street Transcript.* "It wants to grow everyway it can."[32] The company found itself in finance, leasing, insurance, and manufactured houses, continually acquiring companies in an expansion binge.[33] Bigger! More! In 1985, Great Western's CEO told a gathering of analysts, "Don't worry about what you call us—a bank, an S&L, or a Zebra."[34]

Quite a contrast to Fannie Mae, which had a simple, crystalline understanding that it could be the best capital markets player in anything related to mortgages, better even than Goldman Sachs or Salomon Brothers in opening up the full capital markets to the mortgage process. It built a powerful economic machine by reframing its business model on risk management, rather than mortgage selling. And it drove the machine with great passion, the Fannie Mae people inspired by its vital role in democratizing home ownership.

Until 1984, the stock charts tracked each other like mirror images. Then in 1984, one year after it clarified its Hedgehog Concept, Fannie Mae exploded upward, while Great Western kept lollygagging along until just before its acquisition in 1997. By focusing on its simple, elegant conception—and not just focusing on "growth"—Fannie Mae grew revenues nearly threefold from its transition year in 1984 through 1996. Great Western, for all of its gobbling of growth steroids, grew revenues and earnings only 25 percent over the same period, then lost its independence in 1997.

The Fannie Mae versus Great Western case highlights an essential point: *"Growth!" is not a Hedgehog Concept.* Rather, if you have the right Hedgehog Concept and make decisions relentlessly consistent with it, you will create such momentum that your main problem will not be how to grow, but how not to grow too fast.

The Hedgehog Concept is a turning point in the journey from good to great. In most cases, the transition date follows within a few years of the Hedgehog Concept. Furthermore, everything from here on out in the book hinges upon having the Hedgehog Concept. As will become abundantly clear in the following chapters, disciplined action—the third big chunk in the framework after disciplined people and disciplined thought—only makes sense in the context of the Hedgehog Concept.

Despite its vital importance (or, rather, because of its vital importance), it would be a terrible mistake to thoughtlessly attempt to jump right to a Hedgehog Concept. You can't just go off-site for two days, pull out a bunch of flip charts, do breakout discussions, and come up with a deep understanding. Well, you can do that, but you probably won't get it right. It would be like Einstein saying, "I think it's time to become a great scientist, so I'm going to go off to the Four Seasons this weekend, pull out the flip charts, and unlock the secrets of the universe." Insight just doesn't

Fannie Mae, Great Western, and the General Market

Cumulative Value of $1 Invested,
1970 – 1984

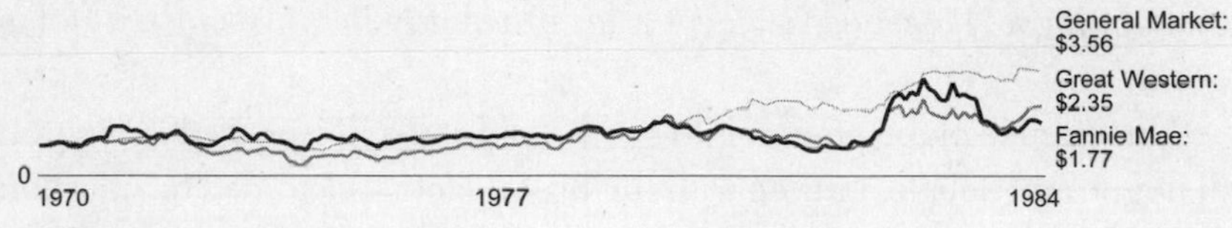

Notes:
1. Shows cumulative value of $1 invested December 31, 1970 – January 1, 1984.
2. Dividends reinvested.

Fannie Mae, Great Western, and the General Market

Cumulative Value of $1 Invested,
1984 – 2000

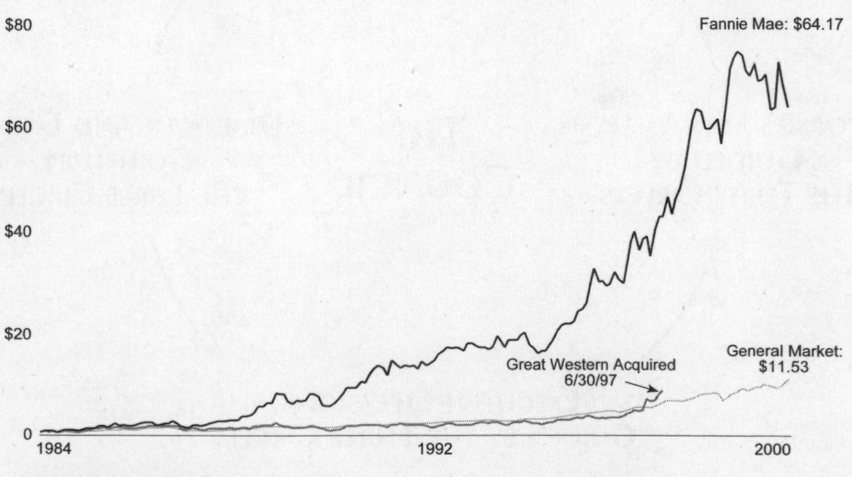

Notes:
1. Fannie Mae transition point occurred in 1984.
2. Cumulative value of $1 invested December 31, 1984 – January 1, 2000.
3. Dividends reinvested.

happen that way. It took Einstein ten years of groping through the fog to get the theory of special relativity, and he was a bright guy.[35]

It took about *four years* on average for the good-to-great companies to clarify their Hedgehog Concepts. Like scientific insight, a Hedgehog Concept simplifies a complex world and makes decisions much easier. But while it has crystalline clarity and elegant simplicity once you have it, getting the concept can be devilishly difficult and takes time. Recognize that getting a Hedgehog Concept is *an inherently iterative process*, not an event.

The essence of the process is to get the right people engaged in vigorous dialogue and debate, infused with the brutal facts and guided by questions formed by the three circles. Do we *really* understand what we can be the best in the world at, as distinct from what we can just be successful at? Do we *really* understand the drivers in our economic engine, including our economic denominator? Do we *really* understand what best ignites our passion?

One particularly useful mechanism for moving the process along is a

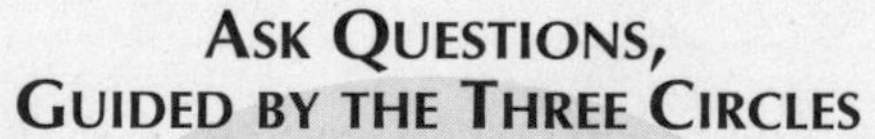

GETTING THE HEDGEHOG CONCEPT
AN ITERATIVE PROCESS

device that we came to call the Council. The Council consists of a group of the right people who participate in dialogue and debate guided by the three circles, iteratively and over time, about vital issues and decisions facing the organization. (See "Characteristics of the Council," below.)

In response to the question, "How should we go about getting our Hedgehog Concept?" I would point to the diagram on page 114 and say: "Build the Council, and use that as a model. Ask the right questions, engage in vigorous debate, make decisions, autopsy the results, and learn—all guided within the context of the three circles. Just keep going through that cycle of understanding."

When asked, "How do we accelerate the process of getting a Hedgehog Concept?" I would respond: "Increase the number of times you go around that full cycle in a given period of time." If you go through this cycle enough times, guided resolutely by the three circles, you will eventually gain the depth of understanding required for a Hedgehog Concept. It will not happen overnight, but it will eventually happen.

Characteristics of the Council

1. The council exists as a device to gain understanding about important issues facing the organization.
2. The Council is assembled and used by the leading executive and usually consists of five to twelve people.
3. Each Council member has the ability to argue and debate in search of understanding, not from the egoistic need to win a point or protect a parochial interest.
4. Each Council member retains the respect of every other Council member, *without exception.*
5. Council members come from a range of perspectives, but each member has deep knowledge about some aspect of the organization and/or the environment in which it operates.
6. The Council includes key members of the management team but is not limited to members of the management team, nor is every executive automatically a member.
7. The Council is a standing body, not an ad hoc committee assembled for a specific project.
8. The Council meets periodically, as much as once a week or as infrequently as once per quarter.

9. The Council does not seek consensus, recognizing that consensus decisions are often at odds with intelligent decisions. The responsibility for the final decision remains with the leading executive.
10. The Council is an informal body, not listed on any formal organization chart or in any formal documents.
11. The Council can have a range of possible names, usually quite innocuous. In the good-to-great companies, they had benign names like Long-Range Profit Improvement Committee, Corporate Products Committee, Strategic Thinking Group, and Executive Council.

Does every organization have a Hedgehog Concept to discover? What if you wake up, look around with brutal honesty, and conclude: "We're not the best at anything, and we never have been." Therein lies one of the most exciting aspects of the entire study. In the majority of cases, the good-to-great companies were not the best in the world at anything and showed no prospects of becoming so. Infused with the Stockdale Paradox ("There must be something we can become the best at, and *we will find it!* We must also confront the brutal facts of what we cannot be the best at, and *we will not delude ourselves!*"), every good-to-great company, no matter how awful at the start of the process, prevailed in its search for a Hedgehog Concept.

As you search for your own concept, keep in mind that when the good-to-great companies finally grasped their Hedgehog Concept, it had none of the tiresome, irritating blasts of mindless bravado typical of the comparison companies. "Yep, we could be the best at that" was stated as the recognition of a fact, no more startling than observing that the sky is blue or the grass is green. When you get your Hedgehog Concept right, it has the quiet ping of truth, like a single, clear, perfectly struck note hanging in the air in the hushed silence of a full auditorium at the end of a quiet movement of a Mozart piano concerto. There is no need to say much of anything; the quiet truth speaks for itself.

I'm reminded of a personal experience in my own family that illustrates the vital difference between bravado and understanding. My wife, Joanne, began racing marathons and triathlons in the early 1980s. As she accumulated experience—track times, swim splits, race results—she began to feel the momentum of success. One day, she entered a race with many of the best woman triathletes in the world, and—despite a weak swim where she came out of the water hundreds of places behind the top swimmers and having to push a heavy, nonaerodynamic bike up a long hill—she managed to cross the finish line in the top ten.

Then, a few weeks later while sitting at breakfast, Joanne looked up from her morning newspaper and calmly, quietly said, "I think I could win the Ironman."

The Ironman, the world championship of triathlons, involves 2.4 miles of ocean swimming and 112 miles of cycling, capped off with a 26.2-mile marathon footrace on the hot, lava-baked Kona coast of Hawaii.

"Of course, I'd have to quit my job, turn down my offers to graduate school (she had been admitted to graduate business school at a number of the top schools), and commit to full-time training. But . . ."

Her words had no bravado in them, no hype, no agitation, no pleading. She didn't try to convince me. She simply observed what she had come to understand was a fact, a truth no more shocking than stating that the walls were painted white. She had the passion. She had the genetics. And if she won races, she'd have the economics. The goal to win the Ironman flowed from early understanding of her Hedgehog Concept.

And, so, she decided to go for it. She quit her job. She turned down graduate schools. She sold the mills! (But she did keep me on her bus.) And three years later, on a hot October day in 1985, she crossed the finish line at the Hawaii Ironman in first place, world champion. When Joanne set out to win the Ironman, she did not know if she would become the world's best triathlete. But she understood that she *could*, that it was in the realm of possibility, that she was not living in a delusion. And that distinction makes all the difference. It is a distinction that those who want to go from good to great must grasp, and one that those who fail to become great so often never do.

CHAPTER SUMMARY

HEDGEHOG CONCEPT

(SIMPLICITY WITHIN THE THREE CIRCLES)

KEY POINTS

- To go from good to great requires a deep understanding of three intersecting circles translated into a simple, crystalline concept (the Hedgehog Concept):

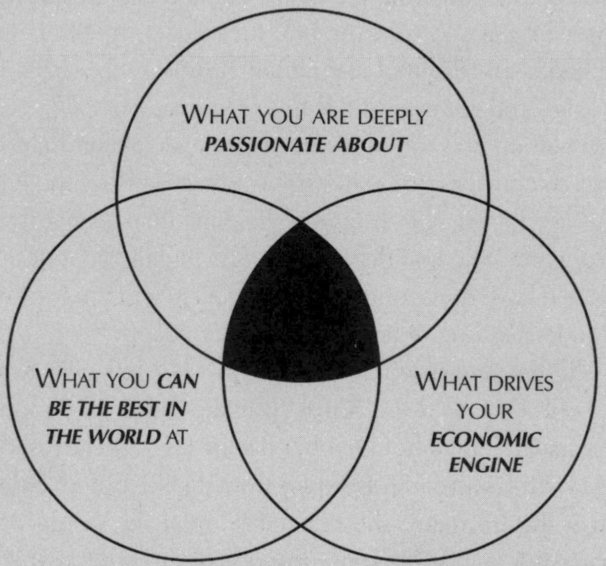

THREE CIRCLES OF THE HEDGEHOG CONCEPT

- The key is to understand what your organization *can* be the best in the world at, and equally important what it *cannot* be the best at—not what it "wants" to be the best at. The Hedgehog Concept is not a goal, strategy, or intention; it is an *understanding*.
- If you cannot be the best in the world at your core business, then your core business cannot form the basis of your Hedgehog Concept.
- The "best in the world" understanding is a much more severe standard than a core competence. You might have a competence but not necessarily have the capacity to be truly the best in the world at

that competence. Conversely, there may be activities at which you could become the best in the world, but at which you have no current competence.

- To get insight into the drivers of your economic engine, search for the one denominator (profit per *x* or, in the social sector, cash flow per *x*) that has the single greatest impact.
- Good-to-great companies set their goals and strategies based on understanding; comparison companies set their goals and strategies based on bravado.
- Getting the Hedgehog Concept is an iterative process. The Council can be a useful device.

UNEXPECTED FINDINGS

- The good-to-great companies are more like hedgehogs—simple, dowdy creatures that know "one big thing" and stick to it. The comparison companies are more like foxes—crafty, cunning creatures that know many things yet lack consistency.
- It took four years on average for the good-to-great companies to get a Hedgehog Concept.
- Strategy per se did not separate the good-to-great companies from the comparison companies. Both sets had strategies, and there is no evidence that the good-to-great companies spent more time on strategic planning than the comparison companies.
- You absolutely do not need to be in a great industry to produce sustained great results. No matter how bad the industry, every good-to-great company figured out how to produce truly superior economic returns.

CHAPTER 6

A CULTURE OF DISCIPLINE

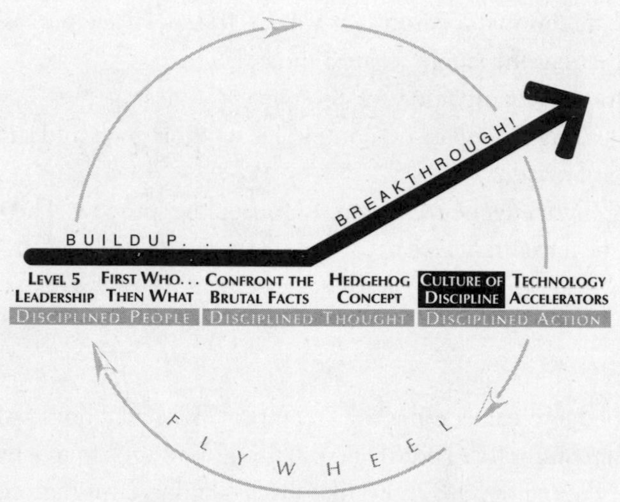

> Freedom is only part of the story and half the truth. . . . That is why I recommend that the Statue of Liberty on the East Coast be supplanted by a Statue of Responsibility on the West Coast.
>
> —VIKTOR E. FRANKL,
> *Man's Search for Meaning*[1]

In 1980, George Rathmann cofounded the biotechnology company Amgen. Over the next twenty years, Amgen grew from a struggling entrepreneurial enterprise into a $3.2 billion company with 6,400 employees, creating blood products to improve the lives of people suffering through chemotherapy and kidney dialysis.[2] Under Rathmann, Amgen became one of the few biotechnology companies that delivered consistent profitability and growth. It became so consistently profitable, in fact, that its stock price multiplied over 150 times from its public offering in June 1983 to January 2000. An investor who bought as little as $7,000 of Amgen stock would have realized a capital gain of over $1 million, thirteen times better than the same investment in the general stock market.

Few successful start-ups become great companies, in large part because they respond to growth and success in the wrong way. Entrepreneurial success is fueled by creativity, imagination, bold moves into uncharted waters, and visionary zeal. As a company grows and becomes more complex, it begins to trip over its own success—too many new people, too many new customers, too many new orders, too many new products. What was once great fun becomes an unwieldy ball of disorganized stuff. Lack of planning, lack of accounting, lack of systems, and lack of hiring constraints create friction. Problems surface—with customers, with cash flow, with schedules.

In response, someone (often a board member) says, "It's time to grow up. This place needs some professional management." The company begins to hire MBAs and seasoned executives from blue-chip companies. Processes, procedures, checklists, and all the rest begin to sprout up like weeds. What was once an egalitarian environment gets replaced with a hierarchy. Chains of command appear for the first time. Reporting relationships become clear, and an executive class with special perks begins to appear. "We" and "they" segmentations appear—just like in a real company.

The professional managers finally rein in the mess. They create order out of chaos, but they also kill the entrepreneurial spirit. Members of the founding team begin to grumble, "This isn't fun anymore. I used to be able to just get things done. Now I have to fill out these stupid forms and follow these stupid rules. Worst of all, I have to spend a horrendous amount of time in useless meetings." The creative magic begins to wane as some of the most innovative people leave, disgusted by the burgeoning bureaucracy and hierarchy. The exciting start-up transforms into just another company, with nothing special to recommend it. The cancer of mediocrity begins to grow in earnest.

George Rathmann avoided this entrepreneurial death spiral. He understood that the purpose of bureaucracy is to compensate for incompetence and lack of discipline—a problem that largely goes away if you have the right people in the first place. Most companies build their bureaucratic rules to manage the small percentage of wrong people on the bus, which in turn drives away the right people on the bus, which then increases the percentage of wrong people on the bus, which increases the need for more bureaucracy to compensate for incompetence and lack of discipline, which then further drives the right people away, and so forth. Rathmann also understood an alternative exists: Avoid bureaucracy and hierarchy and instead create a culture of discipline. When you put these two complementary forces together—a culture of discipline with an ethic of entrepreneurship—you get a magical alchemy of superior performance and sustained results.

The Good-to-Great Matrix of Creative Discipline

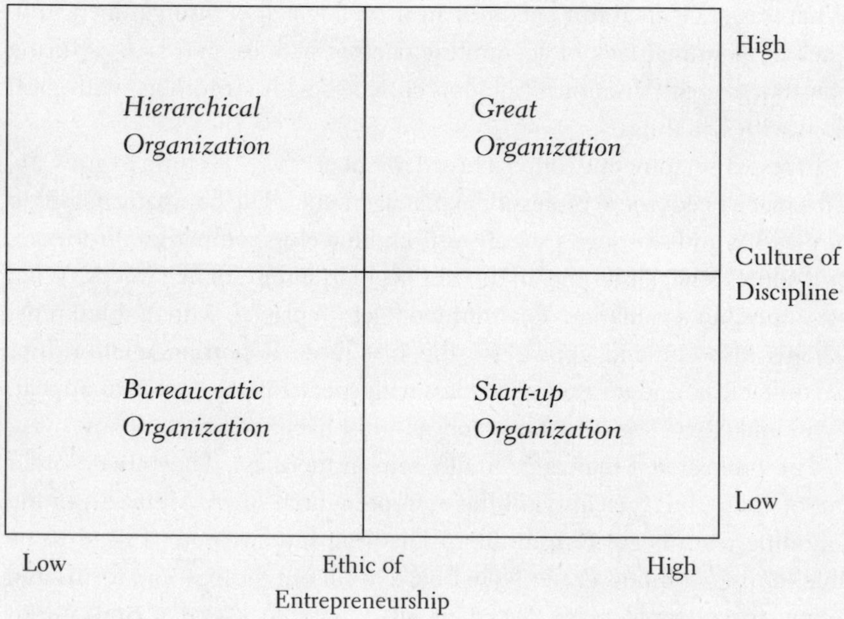

Hierarchical Organization	*Great Organization*	High
		Culture of Discipline
Bureaucratic Organization	*Start-up Organization*	Low
Low	Ethic of Entrepreneurship	High

Why start this chapter with a biotechnology entrepreneur rather than one of our good-to-great companies? Because Rathmann credits much of his entrepreneurial success to what he learned while working at Abbott Laboratories before founding Amgen:

> What I got from Abbott was the idea that when you set your objectives for the year, you record them in concrete. You can change your plans through the year, but you never change what you measure yourself against. You are rigorous at the end of the year, adhering exactly to what you said was going to happen. You don't get a chance to editorialize. You don't get a chance to adjust and finagle, and decide that you really didn't intend to do that anyway, and readjust your objectives to make yourself look better. You never just focus on what you've accomplished for the year; you focus on what you've accomplished *relative* to exactly what you said you were going to accomplish—no matter how tough the measure. That was a discipline learned at Abbott, and that we carried into Amgen.[3]

Many of the Abbott disciplines trace back to 1968, when it hired a remarkable financial officer named Bernard H. Semler. Semler did not see his job as a traditional financial controller or accountant. Rather, he set out to invent mechanisms that would drive cultural change. He created a whole new framework of accounting that he called Responsibility Accounting, wherein every item of cost, income, and investment would be clearly identified with a single individual responsible for that item.[4] The idea, radical for the 1960s, was to create a system wherein *every* Abbott manager in *every* type of job was responsible for his or her return on investment, with the same rigor that an investor holds an entrepreneur responsible. There would be no hiding behind traditional accounting allocations, no slopping funds about to cover up ineffective management, no opportunities for finger-pointing.[5]

But the beauty of the Abbott system lay not just in its rigor, but in how it used rigor and discipline to enable creativity and entrepreneurship. "Abbott developed a very disciplined organization, but not in a linear way of thinking," said George Rathmann. "[It] was exemplary at having both financial discipline and the divergent thinking of creative work. We used financial discipline as a way to provide resources for the really creative work."[6] Abbott reduced its administrative costs as a percentage of sales to the lowest in the industry (by a significant margin) *and at the same time* became a new product innovation machine like 3M, deriving up to 65 percent of revenues from new products introduced in the previous four years.[7]

This creative duality ran through every aspect of Abbott during the transition era, woven into the very fabric of the corporate culture. On the one hand, Abbott recruited entrepreneurial leaders and gave them freedom to determine the best path to achieving their objectives. On the other hand, individuals had to commit fully to the Abbott system and were held rigorously accountable for their objectives. They had freedom, but freedom within a framework. Abbott instilled the entrepreneur's zeal for opportunistic flexibility. ("We recognized that planning is priceless, but plans are useless," said one Abbott executive.)[8] But Abbott also had the discipline to say no to opportunities that failed the three circles test. While encouraging wide-ranging innovation within its divisions, Abbott simultaneously maintained fanatical adherence to its Hedgehog Concept of contributing to cost-effective health care.

Abbott Laboratories exemplifies a key finding of our study: *a culture of discipline.* By its nature, "culture" is a somewhat unwieldy topic to discuss, less prone to clean frameworks like the three circles. The main points of this chapter, however, boil down to one central idea: *Build a culture full of people who take disciplined action within the three circles, fanatically consistent with the Hedgehog Concept.*

More precisely, this means the following:

1. Build a culture around the idea of freedom and responsibility, within a framework.
2. Fill that culture with self-disciplined people who are willing to go to extreme lengths to fulfill their responsibilities. They will "rinse their cottage cheese."
3. Don't confuse a culture of discipline with a tyrannical disciplinarian.
4. Adhere with great consistency to the Hedgehog Concept, exercising an almost religious focus on the intersection of the three circles. Equally important, create a "stop doing list" and systematically unplug anything extraneous.

FREEDOM (AND RESPONSIBILITY) WITHIN A FRAMEWORK

Picture an airline pilot. She settles into the cockpit, surrounded by dozens of complicated switches and sophisticated gauges, sitting atop a massive $84 million piece of machinery. As passengers thump and stuff their bags into overhead bins and flight attendants scurry about trying to get everyone settled in, she begins her preflight checklist. Step by methodical step, she systematically moves through every required item.

Cleared for departure, she begins working with air traffic control, following precise instructions—which direction to take out of the gate, which way to taxi, which runway to use, which direction to take off. She doesn't throttle up and hurtle the jet into the air until she's cleared for takeoff. Once aloft, she communicates continually with flight-control centers and stays within the tight boundaries of the commercial air traffic system.

On approach, however, she hits a ferocious thunder-and-hail storm. Blasting winds, crossways and unpredictable, tilt the wings down to the left, then down to the right. Looking out the windows, passengers can't see the ground, only the thinning and thickening globs of gray clouds and the spatter of rain on the windows. The flight attendants announce, "Ladies and gentlemen, we've been asked to remain seated for the remainder of the flight. Please put your seats in the upright and locked position and place all your carry-on baggage under the seat in front of you. We should be on the ground shortly."

"Not *too* shortly, I hope," think the less experienced travelers, unnerved by the roiling wind and momentary flashes of lightning. But the experienced travelers just go on reading magazines, chatting with seatmates, and preparing for their meetings on the ground. "I've been through all this before," they think. "She'll only land if it's safe."

Sure enough, on final approach—wheels down as a quarter of a million pounds of steel glides down at 130 miles per hour—passengers suddenly hear the engines whine and feel themselves thrust back into their seats. The plane accelerates back into the sky. It banks around in a big arc back toward the airport. The pilot takes a moment to click on the intercom: "Sorry, folks. We were getting some bad crosswinds there. We're going to give it another try." On the next go, the winds calm just enough and she brings the plane down, safely.

Now take a step back and think about the model here. The pilot operates within a very strict system, and she does not have freedom to go outside of that system. (You don't want airline pilots saying, "Hey, I just read in a management book about the value of being empowered—freedom to experiment, to be creative, to be entrepreneurial, to try a lot of stuff and keep what works!") Yet at the same time, the crucial decisions—whether to take off, whether to land, whether to abort, whether to land elsewhere—rest with the pilot. Regardless of the strictures of the system, one central fact stands out above all others: The pilot has ultimate responsibility for the airplane and the lives of the people on it.

The point here is not that a company should have a system as strict and inflexible as the air traffic system. After all, if a corporate system fails, people don't die by the hundreds in burning, twisted hunks of steel. Customer service at the airlines might be terrible, but you are almost certain to get where you are going in one piece. The point of this analogy is that when we looked inside the good-to-great companies, we were reminded of the best part of the airline pilot model: freedom and responsibility within the framework of a highly developed system.

> The good-to-great companies built a consistent system with clear constraints, but they also gave people freedom and responsibility within the framework of that system. They hired self-disciplined people who didn't need to be managed, and then managed the system, not the people.

"This was the secret to how we were able to run stores from a great distance, by remote control," said Bill Rivas of Circuit City. "It was the combination of great store managers who had ultimate responsibility for their individual stores, operating within a great system. You've got to have management and people who believe in the system and who do whatever is necessary to make the system work. But within the boundaries of that system, store managers had a lot of leeway, to coincide with their responsibility."[9] In a sense, Circuit City became to consumer electronics retailing what McDonald's became to restaurants—not the most exquisite experience, but an enormously consistent one. The system evolved over time as Circuit City experimented by adding new items like computers and video players (just like McDonald's added breakfast Egg McMuffins). But at any given moment, everyone operated within the framework of the system. "That's one of the major differences between us and all the others who were in this same business in the early 1980s," said Bill Zierden. "They just couldn't roll it out further, and we could. We could stamp these stores out all over the country, with great consistency."[10] Therein lies one of the key reasons why Circuit City took off in the early 1980s and beat the general stock market by more than eighteen times over the next fifteen years.

In a sense, much of this book is about creating a culture of discipline. It all starts with disciplined *people*. The transition begins not by trying to discipline the wrong people into the right behaviors, but by getting *self*-disciplined people on the bus in the first place. Next we have disciplined *thought*. You need the discipline to confront the brutal facts of reality, while retaining resolute faith that you can and will create a path to greatness. Most importantly, you need the discipline to persist in the search for understanding until you get your Hedgehog Concept. Finally, we have disciplined *action*, the primary subject of this chapter. This order is important. The comparison companies often tried to jump right to disciplined action. But disciplined action without self-disciplined people is impossible to sustain, and disciplined action without disciplined thought is a recipe for disaster.

Indeed, discipline by itself will not produce great results. We find plenty of organizations in history that had tremendous discipline and that marched right into disaster, with precision and in nicely formed lines. No, the point is to first get self-disciplined people who engage in very rigorous thinking, who *then* take disciplined action within the framework of a consistent system designed around the Hedgehog Concept.

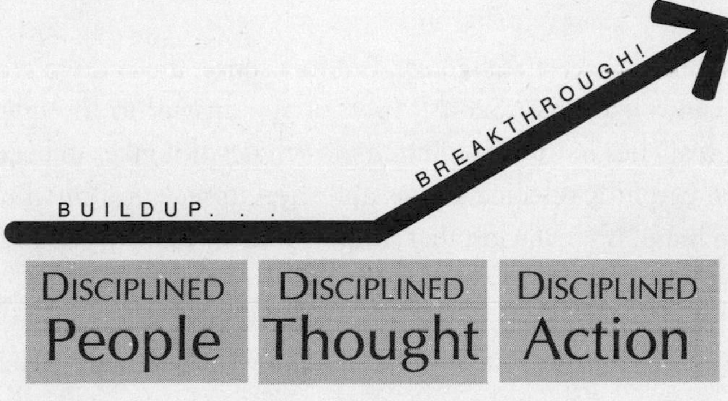

RINSING YOUR COTTAGE CHEESE

Throughout our research, we were struck by the continual use of words like *disciplined, rigorous, dogged, determined, diligent, precise, fastidious, systematic, methodical, workmanlike, demanding, consistent, focused, accountable,* and *responsible.* They peppered articles, interviews, and source materials on the good-to-great companies, and were strikingly absent from the materials on the direct comparison companies. People in the good-to-great companies became somewhat extreme in the fulfillment of their responsibilities, bordering in some cases on fanaticism.

We came to call this the "rinsing your cottage cheese" factor. The analogy comes from a disciplined world-class athlete named Dave Scott, who won the Hawaii Ironman Triathlon six times. In training, Scott would ride his bike 75 miles, swim 20,000 meters, and run 17 miles—on average, *every single day.* Dave Scott did not have a weight problem! Yet he believed that a low-fat, high-carbohydrate diet would give him an extra edge. So, Dave Scott—a man who burned at least 5,000 calories a day in training—would literally rinse his cottage cheese to get the extra fat off. Now, there is no evidence that he absolutely needed to rinse his cottage cheese to win the Ironman; that's not the point of the story. The point is that rinsing his cottage cheese was simply one more small step that he believed would make him just that much better, one more small step added to all the other small steps to create a consistent program of superdiscipline. I've always pictured Dave Scott running the 26 miles of the marathon—hammering away in hundred-degree heat on the black, baked lava fields of the Kona coast after swimming 2.4 miles in the ocean and cycling 112 miles against ferocious crosswinds—and thinking to himself: "Compared to rinsing my cottage cheese every day, this just isn't that bad."

I realize that it's a bizarre analogy. But in a sense, the good-to-great companies became like Dave Scott. Much of the answer to the question of "good to great" lies in the discipline to do whatever it takes to become the best within carefully selected arenas and then to seek continual improvement from there. It's really just that simple. And it's really just that difficult.

Everyone would like to be the best, but most organizations lack the discipline to figure out with egoless clarity what they *can* be the best at and the will to do whatever it takes to turn that potential into reality. They lack the discipline to rinse their cottage cheese.

Consider Wells Fargo in contrast to Bank of America. Carl Reichardt never doubted that Wells Fargo could emerge from bank deregulation as a stronger company, not a weaker one. He saw that the key to becoming a great company rested not with brilliant new strategies but with the sheer determination to rip a hundred years of banker mentality out of the system. "There's too much waste in banking," said Reichardt. "Getting rid of it takes tenacity, not brilliance."[11]

Reichardt set a clear tone at the top: We're not going to ask everyone else to suffer while we sit on high. We will start by rinsing our *own* cottage cheese, right here in the executive suite. He froze executive salaries for two years (despite the fact that Wells Fargo was enjoying some of the most profitable years in its history).[12] He shut the executive dining room and replaced it with a college dorm food-service caterer.[13] He closed the executive elevator, sold the corporate jets, and banned green plants from the executive suite as too expensive to water.[14] He removed free coffee from the executive suite. He eliminated Christmas trees for management.[15] He threw reports back at people who'd submitted them in fancy binders, with the admonishment: "Would you spend your *own* money this way? What does a binder add to anything?"[16] Reichardt would sit through meetings with fellow executives, in a beat-up old chair with the stuffing hanging out. Sometimes he would just sit there and pick at the stuffing while listening to proposals to spend money, said one article, "[and] a lot of must-do projects just melted away."[17]

Across the street at Bank of America, executives also faced deregulation and recognized the need to eliminate waste. However, unlike Wells Fargo,

B of A executives didn't have the discipline to rinse their own cottage cheese. They preserved their posh executive kingdom in its imposing tower in downtown San Francisco, the CEO's office described in the book *Breaking the Bank* as "a northeast corner suite with a large attached conference room, oriental rugs, and floor-to-ceiling windows that offered a sweeping panorama of the San Francisco Bay from the Golden Gate to the Bay Bridge."[18] (We found no evidence of executive chairs with the stuffing hanging out.) The elevator made its last stop at the executive floor and descended all the way to the ground in one quiet whoosh, unfettered by the intrusions of lesser beings. The vast open space in the executive suite made the windows look even taller than they actually were, creating a sense of floating above the fog in an elevated city of alien elites who ruled the world from above.[19] Why rinse our cottage cheese when life is so good?

After losing $1.8 billion across three years in the mid-1980s, B of A eventually made the necessary changes in response to deregulation (largely by hiring ex-Wells executives).[20] But even in the darkest days, B of A could not bring itself to get rid of the perks that shielded its executives from the real world. At one board meeting during Bank of America's crisis period, one member made sensible suggestions like "Sell the corporate jet." Other directors listened to the recommendations, then passed them by.[21]

A CULTURE, NOT A TYRANT

We almost didn't include this chapter in the book. On the one hand, the good-to-great companies became more disciplined than the direct comparison companies, as with Wells Fargo in contrast to Bank of America. On the other hand, the *unsustained* comparisons showed themselves to be just as disciplined as the good-to-great companies.

"Based on my analysis, I don't think we can put discipline in the book as a finding," said Eric Hagen, after he completed a special analysis unit looking at the leadership cultures across the companies. "It is absolutely clear that the unsustained comparison CEOs brought tremendous discipline to their companies, and that is why they got such great initial results. So, discipline just doesn't pass muster as a *distinguishing* variable."

Curious, we decided to look further into the issue, and Eric undertook a more in-depth analysis. As we further examined the evidence, it became clear that—despite surface appearances—there was indeed a huge difference between the two sets of companies in their approach to discipline.

> Whereas the good-to-great companies had Level 5 leaders who built an enduring *culture* of discipline, the unsustained comparisons had Level 4 leaders who *personally* disciplined the organization through sheer force.

Consider Ray MacDonald, who took command of Burroughs in 1964. A brilliant but abrasive man, MacDonald controlled the conversations, told all the jokes, and criticized those not as smart as he (which was pretty much everyone around him). He got things done through sheer force of personality, using a form of pressure that came to be known as "The MacDonald Vise."[22] MacDonald produced remarkable results during his reign. Every dollar invested in 1964, the year he became president, and taken out at the end of 1977, when he retired, produced returns 6.6 times better than the general market.[23] However, the company had no culture of discipline to endure beyond him. After he retired, his helper minions were frozen by indecision, leaving the company, according to *Business Week*, "with an inability to do anything."[24] Burroughs then began a long slide, with cumulative returns falling 93 percent below the market from the end of the MacDonald era to 2000.

We found a similar story at Rubbermaid under Stanley Gault. Recall

BURROUGHS CORPORATION, A CLASSIC UNSUSTAINED TRANSITION

Ratio of Cumulative Stock Returns to General Market, Set to 1.0 at Start of Ray MacDonald Reign

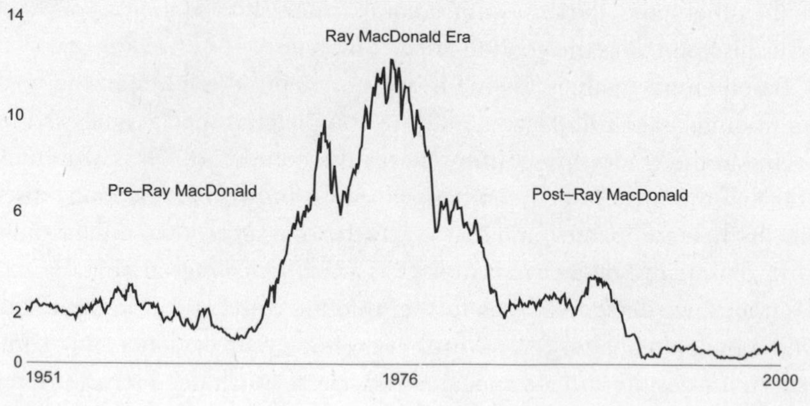

from the Level 5 chapter that Gault quipped in response to the accusation of being a tyrant, "Yes, but I'm a sincere tyrant." Gault brought strict disciplines to Rubbermaid—rigorous planning and competitor analysis, systematic market research, profit analysis, hard-nosed cost control, and so on. "This is an incredibly disciplined organization," wrote one analyst. "There is an incredible thoroughness in Rubbermaid's approach to life."[25] Precise and methodical, Gault arrived at work by 6:30 and routinely worked eighty-hour weeks, expecting his managers to do the same.[26]

As chief disciplinarian, Gault personally acted as the company's number one quality control mechanism. Walking down the street in Manhattan, he noticed a doorman muttering and swearing as he swept dirt into a Rubbermaid dustpan. "Stan whirled around and starting grilling the man on why he was unhappy," said Richard Gates, who told the story to *Fortune*. Gault, convinced that the lip of the dustpan was too thick, promptly issued a dictate to his engineers to redesign the product. "On quality, I'm a sonofabitch," said Gault. His chief operating officer concurred: "He gets livid."[27]

Rubbermaid rose dramatically under the tyranny of this singularly disciplined leader but then just as dramatically declined when he departed. Under Gault, Rubbermaid beat the market 3.6 to 1. After Gault, Rubbermaid lost 59 percent of its value relative to the market, before being bought out by Newell.

One particularly fascinating example of the disciplinarian syndrome was Chrysler under Lee Iacocca, whom *Business Week* described simply as, "The Man. The Dictator. Lee."[28] Iacocca became president of Chrysler in 1979 and imposed his towering personality to discipline the organization into shape. "Right away I knew the place was in a state of anarchy [and] needed a dose of order and discipline—and quick," wrote Iacocca of his early days.[29] In his first year, he entirely overhauled the management structure, instituted strict financial controls, improved quality control measures, rationalized the production schedule, and conducted mass layoffs to preserve cash.[30] "I felt like an Army Surgeon. . . . We had to do radical surgery, saving what we could."[31] In dealing with the unions, he said, "If you don't help me out, I'm going to blow your brains out. I'll declare bankruptcy in the morning, and you'll all be out of work."[32] Iacocca produced spectacular results and Chrysler became one of the most celebrated turnarounds in industrial history.

About midway through his tenure, however, Iacocca seemed to lose focus and the company began to decline once again. The *Wall Street Journal* wrote: "Mr. Iacocca headed the Statue of Liberty renovation, joined a

RUBBERMAID CORPORATION, A CLASSIC UNSUSTAINED TRANSITION

Ratio of Cumulative Stock Returns to General Market,
Set to 1.0 at Start of Stanley Gault Reign

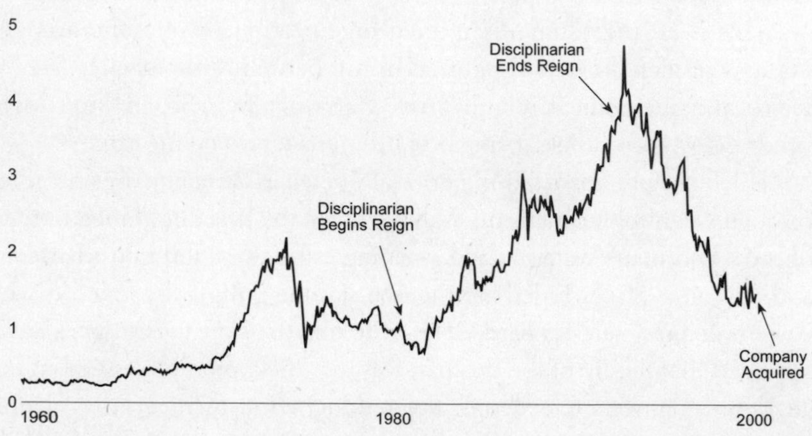

congressional commission on budget reduction and wrote a second book. He began a syndicated newspaper column, bought an Italian villa where he started bottling his own wine and olive oil. . . . Critics contend it all distracted him, and was a root cause of Chrysler's current problems. . . . Distracting or not, it's clear that being a folk hero is a demanding sideline."[33]

Worse than his moonlight career as a national hero, his lack of discipline to stay within the arenas in which Chrysler could be the best in the world led to a binge of highly undisciplined diversifications. In 1985, he was lured into the sexy aerospace business. Whereas most CEOs would be content with a single Gulfstream jet, Iacocca decided to buy the whole Gulfstream company![34] Also in the mid-1980s, he embarked on a costly and ultimately unsuccessful joint venture with Italian sports car maker Maserati. "Iacocca had a soft spot for Italians," said one retired Chrysler executive. "Iacocca, who owns a modest estate in Tuscany, was so intent on an Italian alliance that commercial realities were ignored, suggest industry insiders," wrote *Business Week*.[35] Some estimates put the loss of the failed Maserati venture at $200 million, which, according to *Forbes*, was "an enormous sum to lose on a high-price, low-volume roadster. After all, no more than a few thousand will ever be built."[36]

During the first half of his tenure, Iacocca produced remarkable results, taking the company from near bankruptcy to nearly three times the general market. During the second half of Iacocca's tenure, the company slid

31 percent behind the market and faced another potential bankruptcy.[37] "Like so many patients with a heart condition," wrote a Chrysler executive, "we'd survived surgery several years before only to revert to our unhealthy lifestyle."[38]

The above cases illustrate a pattern we found in *every* unsustained comparison: a spectacular rise under a tyrannical disciplinarian, followed by an equally spectacular decline when the disciplinarian stepped away, leaving behind no enduring culture of discipline, or when the disciplinarian himself became undisciplined and strayed wantonly outside the three circles. Yes, discipline is essential for great results, but disciplined action without disciplined understanding of the three circles cannot produce sustained great results.

FANATICAL ADHERENCE TO THE HEDGEHOG CONCEPT

For nearly forty years, Pitney Bowes lived inside the warm and protective cocoon of a monopoly. With its close relationship to the U.S. Postal Service and its patents on postage meter machines, Pitney attained 100 percent of the metered mail market.[39] By the end of the 1950s, nearly half of *all* U.S. mail passed through Pitney Bowes machines.[40] With gross profit margins in excess of 80 percent, no competition, a huge market, and a recession-proof business, Pitney Bowes wasn't so much a great company as it was a company with a great monopoly.

Then, as almost always happens to monopolies when the protective cocoon is ripped away, Pitney Bowes began a long slide. First came a consent decree that required Pitney Bowes to license its patents to competitors, royalty free.[41] Within six years, Pitney Bowes had sixteen competitors.[42] Pitney fell into a reactionary "Chicken Little/the sky is falling" diversification frenzy, throwing cash after ill-fated acquisitions and joint ventures, including a $70 million bloodbath (54 percent of net stockholders' equity at the time) from a computer retail foray. In 1973, the company lost money for the first time in its history. It was shaping up to be just another typical case of a monopoly-protected company gradually falling apart once confronted with the harsh reality of competition.

Fortunately, a Level 5 leader named Fred Allen stepped in and asked hard questions that led to deeper understanding of Pitney's role in the world. Instead of viewing itself as a "postage meter" company, Pitney came to see that it could be the best in the world at servicing the back rooms of businesses within the broader concept of "messaging." It also came to see that sophisticated back-office products, like high-end faxes and specialized copiers, played right into its economic engine of profit per customer, building off its extensive sales and service network.

Allen and his successor, George Harvey, instituted a model of disciplined diversification. For example, Pitney eventually attained 45 percent of the high-end fax market for large companies, a hugely profitable cash machine.[43] Harvey began a systematic process of investment in new technologies and products, such as the Paragon mail processor that seals and sends letters, and by the late 1980s, Pitney consistently derived over half its revenues from products introduced in the previous three years.[44] Later, Pitney Bowes became a pioneer at linking backroom machines to the Internet, yet another opportunity for disciplined diversification. The key point is that every step of diversification and innovation stayed *within the three circles.*

After falling 77 percent behind the market from the consent decree to its darkest days in 1973, Pitney Bowes reversed course, eventually rising to over eleven times the market by the start of 1999. From 1973 to 2000, Pitney Bowes outperformed Coca-Cola, 3M, Johnson & Johnson, Merck, Motorola, Procter & Gamble, Hewlett-Packard, Walt Disney, and even General Electric. Can you think of any other company that emerged from the protective comfort of a monopoly cocoon to deliver this level of results? AT&T didn't. Xerox didn't. Even IBM didn't.

Pitney Bowes illustrates what can happen when a company lacks the discipline to stay within the three circles and, conversely, what can happen when it regains that discipline.

> The good-to-great companies at their best followed a simple mantra: "*Anything that does not fit with our Hedgehog Concept, we will not do.* We will not launch unrelated businesses. We will not make unrelated acquisitions. We will not do unrelated joint ventures. If it doesn't fit, we don't do it. Period."

In contrast, we found a lack of discipline to stay within the three circles as a key factor in the demise of nearly all the comparison companies. Every comparison either (1) lacked the discipline to understand its three circles or (2) lacked the discipline to stay within the three circles.

R. J. Reynolds is a classic case. Until the 1960s, R. J. Reynolds had a simple and clear concept, built around being the best tobacco company in the United States—a position it had held for at least twenty-five years.[45] Then in 1964, the Surgeon General's Office issued its report that linked cigarettes with cancer, and R. J. Reynolds began to diversify away from tobacco as a defensive measure. Of course, all tobacco companies began to diversify at that time for the same reason, including Philip Morris. But R. J. Reynolds' wanderings outside its three circles defied all logic.

R. J. Reynolds spent nearly a third of total corporate assets in 1970 to buy a shipping container company and an oil company (Sea-Land and Aminoil), the idea being to make money by shipping its own oil.[46] Okay, not a terrible idea on its own. But what on earth did it have to do with R. J. Reynolds' Hedgehog Concept? It was a wholly undisciplined acquisition that came about in part because Sea-Land's founder was a close friend of R. J. Reynolds' chairman.[47]

After pouring more than $2 billion into Sea-Land, the total investment nearly equaled the entire amount of net stockholders' equity.[48] Finally, after years of starving the tobacco business to funnel funds into the sinking ship business, RJR acknowledged failure and sold Sea-Land.[49] One Reynolds grandson complained: "Look, these guys are the world's best at making and selling tobacco products, but what do they know about ships or oil? I'm not worried about them going broke, but they look like country boys with too much cash in their pockets."[50]

To be fair, Philip Morris did not have a perfect diversification record either, as evidenced by its failed purchase of 7UP. However, in stark contrast to R. J. Reynolds, Philip Morris displayed greater discipline in response to the 1964 surgeon general's report. Instead of abandoning its Hedgehog Concept, Philip Morris *redefined* its Hedgehog Concept in terms of building global brands in not-so-healthy consumables (tobacco, beer, soft drinks, coffee, chocolate, processed cheese, etc.). Philip Morris' superior discipline to stay within the three circles is one key reason why the results of the two companies diverged so dramatically after the 1964 report, despite the fact that they both faced the *exact* same industry opportunities and threats. From 1964 to 1989 (when R. J. Reynolds disappeared from public trading in a leveraged buyout), $1 invested in Philip Morris beat $1 invested in R. J. Reynolds by over four times.

Few companies have the discipline to discover their Hedgehog Concept, much less the discipline to build consistently within it. They fail to grasp a simple paradox: The more an organization has the discipline to stay within its three circles, the more it will have attractive opportunities for growth. Indeed, a great company *is much more likely to die of indigestion from too much opportunity than starvation from too little.* The challenge becomes not opportunity creation, but opportunity *selection.*

> It takes discipline to say "No, thank you" to big opportunities. The fact that something is a "once-in-a-lifetime opportunity" is irrelevant if it doesn't fit within the three circles.

This notion of fanatical consistency relative to the Hedgehog Concept doesn't just concern the portfolio of strategic activities. It can relate to the entire way you manage and build an organization. Nucor built its success around the Hedgehog Concept of harnessing culture and technology to produce steel. Central to the Nucor concept was the idea of aligning worker interests with management and shareholder interests through an egalitarian meritocracy largely devoid of class distinctions. Wrote Ken Iverson, in his 1998 book *Plain Talk:*

> Inequality still runs rampant in most business corporations. I'm referring now to *hierarchical* inequality which legitimizes and institutionalizes the principle of "We" vs. "They." . . . The people at the top of the corporate hierarchy grant themselves privilege after privilege, flaunt those privileges before the men and women who do the real work, then wonder why employees are unmoved by management's invocations to cut costs and boost profitability. . . . When I think of the millions of dollars spent by people at the top of the management hierarchy on efforts to motivate people who are continually put down *by* that hierarchy, I can only shake my head in wonder.[51]

When we interviewed Ken Iverson, he told us that nearly 100 percent of the success of Nucor was due to its ability to translate its simple concept into disciplined action consistent with that concept. It grew into a $3.5 billion Fortune 500 company with only four layers of management and a corporate headquarters staff of fewer than twenty-five people—executive, financial, secretarial, the whole shebang—crammed into a rented office the size of a small dental practice.[52] Cheap veneer furniture adorned the

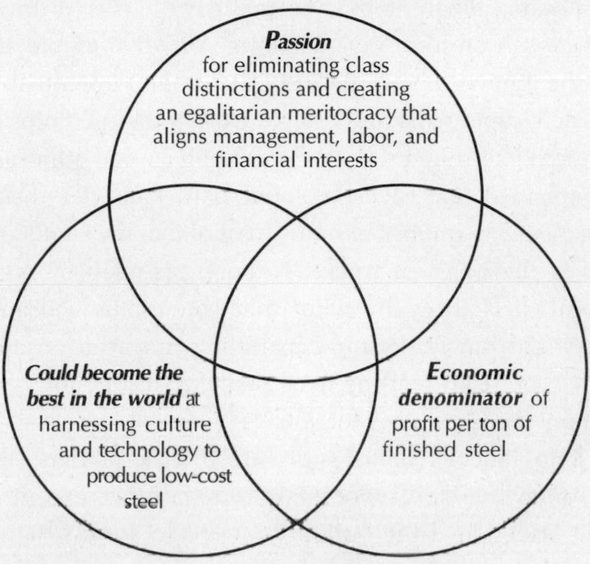

NUCOR'S THREE CIRCLES
1970–1995

lobby, which itself was not much larger than a closet. Instead of a corporate dining room, executives hosted visiting dignitaries at Phil's Diner, a strip mall sandwich shop across the street.[53]

Executives did not receive better benefits than frontline workers. In fact, executives had *fewer* perks. For example, all workers (but not executives) were eligible to receive $2,000 per year for each child for up to four years of post–high school education.[54] In one incident, a man came to Marvin Pohlman and said, "I have nine kids. Are you telling me that you'll pay for four years of school—college, trade school, whatever—for every single one of my kids?" Pohlman acknowledged that, yes, that's exactly what would happen. "The man just sat there and cried," said Pohlman. "I'll never forget it. It just captures in one moment so much of what we were trying to do."[55]

When Nucor had a highly profitable year, everyone in the company would have a very profitable year. Nucor workers became so well paid that one woman told her husband, "If you get fired from Nucor, I'll divorce you."[56] But when Nucor faced difficult times, everyone from top to bottom suffered. But people at the top suffered more. In the 1982 recession, for example, worker pay went down 25 percent, officer pay went down 60 percent, and the CEO's pay went down 75 percent.[57]

Nucor took extraordinary steps to keep at bay the class distinctions that eventually encroach on most organizations. All 7,000 employees' names appeared in the annual report, not just officers' and executives'.[58] Everyone except safety supervisors and visitors wore the same color hard hats. The color of hard hats might sound trivial, but it caused quite a stir. Some foremen complained that special-colored hard hats identified them as higher in the chain, an important status symbol that they could put on the back shelves of their cars or trucks. Nucor responded by organizing a series of forums to address the point that your status and authority in Nucor come from your leadership capabilities, not your position. If you don't like it—if you really feel you need that class distinction—well, then, Nucor is just not the right place for you.[59]

In contrast to Nucor's dental suite–sized headquarters, Bethlehem Steel built a twenty-one-story office complex to house its executive staff. At extra expense, it designed the building more like a cross than a rectangle—a design that accommodated the large number of vice presidents who needed corner offices. "The vice presidents . . . [had to have] windows in two directions, so it was out of that desire that we came up with the design," explained a Bethlehem executive.[60] In his book *Crisis in Bethlehem*, John Strohmeyer details a culture as far to the other end of the continuum from Nucor as you can imagine. He describes a fleet of corporate aircraft, used even for taking executives' children to college and flitting away to weekend hideaways. He describes a world-class eighteen-hole executive golf course, an executive country club renovated with Bethlehem corporate funds, and even how executive rank determined shower priority at the club.[61]

We came to the conclusion that Bethlehem executives saw the very purpose of their activities as the perpetuation of a class system that elevated them to elite status. Bethlehem did not decline in the 1970s and 1980s primarily because of imports or technology—Bethlehem declined first and foremost because it was a culture wherein people focused their efforts on negotiating the nuances of an intricate social hierarchy, not on customers, competitors, or changes in the external world.

From 1966 (at the start of its buildup) to 1999, Nucor posted thirty-four *consecutive* years of positive profitability, while over those same thirty-four years, Bethlehem lost money twelve times and its cumulative profitability added up to less than zero. By the 1990s, Nucor's profitability beat Bethlehem's every single year, and at the end of the century, Nucor—which had been less than a third the size of Bethlehem only a decade earlier—finally surpassed Bethlehem in total revenues.[62] Even more astounding, Nucor's average five-year profit per employee exceeded Bethlehem by almost ten times.[63] And for the investor, $1 invested in Nucor beat $1 invested in Bethlehem Steel by over 200 times.

To be fair, Bethlehem had one giant problem not faced by Nucor: adversarial labor relations and entrenched unions. Nucor had no union and enjoyed remarkably good relations with its workers. In fact, when union organizers visited one plant, workers felt so ferociously loyal to Nucor that *management* had to protect the union organizers from workers who began shouting and throwing sand at them.[64]

But the union argument begs a crucial question: *Why* did Nucor have such a better relationship with its workers in the first place? Because Ken Iverson and his team had a simple, crystalline Hedgehog Concept about aligning worker interests with management interests and—most importantly—because they were willing to go to almost extreme lengths to build the entire enterprise consistent with that concept. Call them a bit fanatical if you want, but to create great results *requires* a nearly fanatical dedication to the idea of consistency within the Hedgehog Concept.

START A "STOP DOING" LIST

Do you have a "to do" list?

Do you also have a "*stop* doing" list?

Most of us lead busy but undisciplined lives. We have ever-expanding "to do" lists, trying to build momentum by doing, doing, doing—and doing more. And it rarely works. Those who built the good-to-great companies, however, made as much use of "stop doing" lists as "to do" lists. They displayed a remarkable discipline to unplug all sorts of extraneous junk.

When Darwin Smith became CEO of Kimberly-Clark, he made great use of "stop doing" lists. He saw that playing the annual forecast game with Wall Street focused people too much on the short term, so he just stopped doing it. "On balance, I see no net advantage to our stockholders when we annually forecast future earnings," said Smith. "*We will not do it.*"[65] He saw "title creep" as a sign of class-consciousness and bureaucratic layering, so he simply unplugged titles. No one at the company would have a title, unless it was for a position where the outside world demanded a title. He saw increasing layers as the natural result of empire building.

So he simply unplugged a huge stack of layers with a simple elegant mechanism: If you couldn't justify to your peers the need for at least fifteen people reporting to you to fulfill your responsibilities, then you would have zero people reporting to you.[66] (Keep in mind that he did this in the 1970s, long before it became fashionable.) To reinforce the idea that Kimberly-Clark should begin thinking of itself as a consumer company, not a paper company, he unplugged Kimberly from all paper industry trade associations.[67]

The good-to-great companies institutionalized the discipline of "stop doing" through the use of a unique budget mechanism. Stop and think for a moment: What is the purpose of budgeting? Most answer that budgeting exists to decide how much to apportion to each activity, or to manage costs, or both. From a good-to-great perspective, both of these answers are wrong.

> In a good-to-great transformation, budgeting is a discipline to decide which arenas *should be fully funded and which should not be funded at all.* In other words, the budget process is not about figuring out how much each activity gets, but about determining which activities best support the Hedgehog Concept and should be fully strengthened and which should be eliminated entirely.

Kimberly-Clark didn't just reallocate resources from the paper business to the consumer business. It completely *eliminated* the paper business, sold the mills, and invested all the money into the emerging consumer business.

I had an interesting conversation with some executives from a company in the paper business. It's a good company, not yet a great one, and they had competed directly with Kimberly-Clark before Kimberly transformed itself into a consumer company. Out of curiosity, I asked them what they thought of Kimberly-Clark. "What Kimberly did is not fair," they said.

"Not fair?" I looked quizzical.

"Oh, sure, they've become a much more successful company. But, you know, if we'd sold our paper business and become a powerful consumer company, we could have been great, too. But we just have too much invested in it, and we couldn't have brought ourselves to do it."

If you look back on the good-to-great companies, they displayed remarkable courage to channel their resources into only one or a few arenas. Once they understood their three circles, they rarely hedged their bets. Recall Kroger's commitment to overturn its *entire* system to create superstores, while A&P clung to the "safety" of its older stores. Recall Abbott's commitment to put the bulk of its resources into becoming number one in diagnostics and hospital nutritionals, while Upjohn clung to its core pharmaceutical business (where it could never be the best in the world). Recall how Walgreens exited the profitable food-service business and focused all its might into one idea: the best, most convenient drugstores. Recall Gillette and Sensor, Nucor and the mini-mills, Kimberly-Clark and selling the mills to channel all its resources into the consumer business. They all had the guts to make huge investments, once they understood their Hedgehog Concept.

The most effective investment strategy is a highly undiversified portfolio when you are right. As facetious as that sounds, that's essentially the approach the good-to-great companies took. "Being right" means getting the Hedgehog Concept; "highly undiversified" means investing fully in those things that fit squarely within the three circles and getting rid of everything else.

Of course, the key here is the little caveat, "When you are right." *But how do you know when you're right?* In studying the companies, we learned that "being right" just isn't that hard if you have all the pieces in place. If you have Level 5 leaders who get the right people on the bus, if you confront the brutal facts of reality, if you create a climate where the truth is heard, if you have a Council and work within the three circles, if you frame all decisions in the context of a crystalline Hedgehog Concept, if you act from understanding, not bravado—if you do all these things, then you are likely to be right on the big decisions. The real question is, once you know the right thing, do you have the discipline to *do* the right thing and, equally important, to *stop doing* the wrong things?

CHAPTER SUMMARY

A CULTURE OF DISCIPLINE

KEY POINTS

- Sustained great results depend upon building a culture full of self-disciplined people who take disciplined action, fanatically consistent with the three circles.
- Bureaucratic cultures arise to compensate for incompetence and lack of discipline, which arise from having the wrong people on the bus in the first place. If you get the right people on the bus, and the wrong people off, you don't need stultifying bureaucracy.
- A culture of discipline involves a duality. On the one hand, it requires people who adhere to a consistent system; yet, on the other hand, it gives people freedom and responsibility within the framework of that system.
- A culture of discipline is not just about action. It is about getting disciplined *people* who engage in disciplined *thought* and who *then* take disciplined action.
- The good-to-great companies appear boring and pedestrian looking in from the outside, but upon closer inspection, they're full of people who display extreme diligence and a stunning intensity (they "rinse their cottage cheese").
- Do not confuse a culture of discipline with a tyrant who disciplines—they are very different concepts, one highly functional, the other highly dysfunctional. Savior CEOs who personally discipline through sheer force of personality usually fail to produce sustained results.
- The single most important form of discipline for sustained results is fanatical adherence to the Hedgehog Concept and the willingness to shun opportunities that fall outside the three circles.

UNEXPECTED FINDINGS

- The more an organization has the discipline to stay within its three circles, with almost religious consistency, the *more* it will have opportunities for growth.

- The fact that something is a "once-in-a-lifetime opportunity" is irrelevant, unless it fits within the three circles. A great company will have *many* once-in-a-lifetime opportunities.
- The purpose of budgeting in a good-to-great company is not to decide how much each activity gets, but to decide which arenas best fit with the Hedgehog Concept and should be *fully funded* and which should *not be funded at all.*
- "*Stop* doing" lists are more important than "to do" lists.

CHAPTER 7

TECHNOLOGY ACCELERATORS

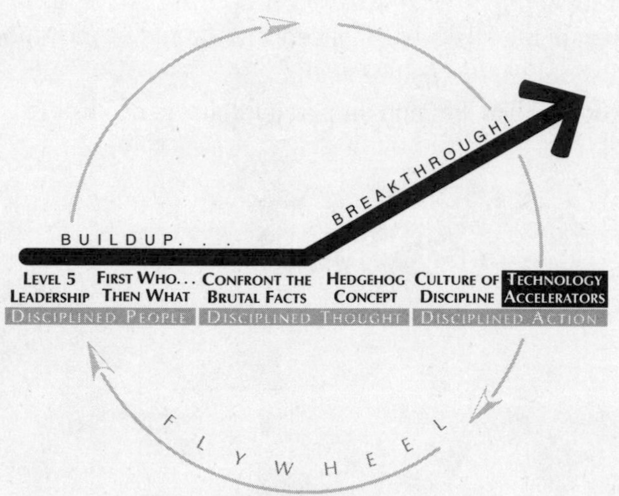

Most men would rather die, than think. Many do.

—BERTRAND RUSSELL[1]

On July 28, 1999, drugstore.com—one of the first Internet pharmacies—sold shares of its stock to the public. Within seconds of the opening bell, the stock multiplied nearly threefold to $65 per share. Four weeks later, the stock closed as high as $69, creating a market valuation of over $3.5 billion. Not bad for an enterprise that had sold products for less than nine months, had fewer than 500 employees, offered no hope of investor dividends for years (if not decades), and deliberately planned to lose hundreds of millions of dollars before turning a single dollar of profit.[2]

What rationale did people use to justify these rather extraordinary numbers? "New technology will change everything," the logic went. "The Internet is going to completely revolutionize all businesses," the gurus chanted. "It's the great Internet landgrab: Be there first, be there fast, build market share—no matter how expensive—and you win," yelled the entrepreneurs.

We entered a remarkable moment in history when the whole idea of trying to build a great company seemed quaint and outdated. "Built to

Flip" became the mantra of the day. Just tell people you were doing something, *anything*, connected to the Internet, and—presto!—you became rich by flipping shares to the public, even if you had no profits (or even a real company). Why take all the hard steps to go from buildup to breakthrough, creating a model that actually works, when you could yell, "New technology!" or "New economy!" and convince people to give you hundreds of millions of dollars?

Some entrepreneurs didn't even bother to suggest that they would build a real company at all, much less a great one. One even filed to go public in March of 2000 with an enterprise that consisted solely of an informational Web site and a business plan, nothing more. The entrepreneur admitted to the *Industry Standard* that it seemed strange to go public before starting a business, but that didn't stop him from trying to persuade investors to buy 1.1 million shares at $7 to $9 per share, despite having no revenues, no employees, no customers, no company.[3] With the new technology of the Internet, who needs all those archaic relics of the old economy? Or so the logic went.

At the high point of this frenzy, drugstore.com issued its challenge to Walgreens. At first, Walgreens' stock suffered from the invasion of the dotcoms, losing over 40 percent of its price in the months leading up to the drugstore.com public offering. Wrote *Forbes* in October 1999: "Investors seem to think that the Web race will be won by competitors who hit the ground running—companies like drugstore.com, which trades at 398 times revenue, rather than Walgreen, trading at 1.4 times revenue."[4] Analysts downgraded Walgreens' stock, and the pressure on Walgreens to react to the Internet threat increased as nearly $15 billion in market value evaporated.[5]

Walgreens' response in the midst of this frenzy?

"We're a crawl, walk, run company," Dan Jorndt told *Forbes* in describing his deliberate, methodical approach to the Internet. Instead of reacting like Chicken Little, Walgreens executives did something quite unusual for the times. They decided to pause and reflect. They decided to use their brains. They decided to think!

Slow at first (crawl), Walgreens began experimenting with a Web site while engaging in intense internal dialogue and debate about its implications, within the context of its own peculiar Hedgehog Concept. "How will the Internet connect to our convenience concept? How can we tie it to our economic denominator of cash flow per customer visit? How can we use the Web to enhance what we do better than any other company in the world and in a way that we're passionate about?" Throughout, Walgreens executives embraced the Stockdale Paradox: "We have complete faith that we can prevail in an Internet world as a great company; yet, we must also confront the brutal facts of reality about the Internet." One Walgreens executive told us a fun little story about this remarkable moment in history. An Internet leader made a statement about Walgreens along the lines of, "Oh, Walgreens. They're too old and stodgy for the Internet world. They'll be left behind." The Walgreens people, while irked by this arrogant comment from the Internet elite, never seriously considered a public response. Said one executive, "Let's quietly go about doing what we need to do, and it'll become clear soon enough that they just pulled the tail of the wrong dog."

Then a little faster (walk), Walgreens began to find ways to tie the Internet directly to its sophisticated inventory-and-distribution model and—ultimately—its convenience concept. Fill your prescription on-line, pop into your car and go to your local Walgreens drive-through (in whatever city you happen to be in at the moment), zoom past the window with hardly a moment's pause picking up your bottle of whatever. Or have it shipped to you, if that's more convenient. There was no manic lurching about, no hype, no bravado—just calm, deliberate pursuit of understanding, followed by calm, deliberate steps forward.

Then, finally (run!), Walgreens bet big, launching an Internet site as sophisticated and well designed as most pure dot-coms. Just before writing this chapter, in October 2000, we went on-line to use Walgreens.com. We found it as easy to use and the system of delivery as reliable and well thought out as Amazon.com (the reigning champion of e-commerce at the time). Precisely one year after the *Forbes* article, Walgreens had figured out how to harness the Internet to accelerate momentum, making it just that much more unstoppable. It announced (on its Web site) a significant increase in job openings, to support its sustained growth. From its low point in 1999 at the depths of the dot-com scare, Walgreens' stock price nearly doubled within a year.

And what of drugstore.com? Continuing to accumulate massive losses, it announced a layoff to conserve cash. At its high point, little more than a year earlier, drugstore.com traded at a price twenty-six times higher than at the time of this writing. It had lost nearly *all* of its initial value.[6] While Walgreens went from crawl to walk to run, drugstore.com went from run to walk to crawl.

Perhaps drugstore.com will figure out a sustainable model that works and become a great company. But it will not become great because of snazzy technology, hype, and an irrational stock market. It will only become a great company if it figures out how to apply technology to a coherent concept that reflects understanding of the three circles.

TECHNOLOGY AND THE HEDGEHOG CONCEPT

Now, you might be thinking: "But the Internet frenzy is just a speculative bubble that burst. So what? Everybody knew that the bubble was unsustainable, that it just couldn't last. What does that teach us about good to great?"

To be clear: The point of this chapter has little to do with the specifics of the Internet bubble, per se. Bubbles come and bubbles go. It happened with the railroads. It happened with electricity. It happened with radio. It happened with the personal computer. It happened with the Internet. And it will happen again with unforeseen new technologies.

Yet through all of this change, great companies have adapted and endured. Indeed, most of the truly great companies of the last hundred years—from Wal-Mart to Walgreens, from Procter & Gamble to Kimberly-Clark, from Merck to Abbott—trace their roots back through multiple generations of technology change, be it electricity, the television, or the Internet. They've adapted before and emerged great. The best ones will adapt again.

> Technology-induced change is nothing new. The real question is not, What is the role of technology? Rather, the real question is, How do good-to-great organizations *think differently* about technology?

We could have predicted that Walgreens would eventually figure out the Internet. The company had a history of making huge investments in technology long before other companies in its industry became tech savvy. In the early 1980s, it pioneered a massive network system called Intercom. The idea was simple: By linking all Walgreens stores electronically and sending customer data to a central source, it turned every Walgreens outlet in the country into a customer's local pharmacy. You live in Florida, but you're visiting Phoenix and need a prescription refill. No problem, the Phoenix store is linked to the central system, and it's just like going down to your hometown Walgreens store.

This might seem mundane by today's standards. But when Walgreens made the investment in Intercom in the late 1970s, no one else in the industry had anything like it. Eventually, Walgreens invested over $400 million in Intercom, including $100 million for its own satellite system.[7] Touring the Intercom headquarters—dubbed "Earth Station Walgreen"—"is like taking a trip through a NASA space center with its stunning array of sophisticated electronic gadgetry," wrote a trade journal.[8] Walgreens' technical staff became skilled at maintaining every piece of technology, rather than relying on outside specialists.[9] It didn't stop there. Walgreens pioneered the application of scanners, robotics, computerized inventory control, and advanced warehouse tracking systems. The Internet is just one more step in a continuous pattern.

Walgreens didn't adopt all of this advanced technology just for the sake of advanced technology or in fearful reaction to falling behind. No, it used technology as a tool to accelerate momentum after hitting breakthrough, and tied technology directly to its Hedgehog Concept of convenient drugstores increasing profit per customer visit. As an interesting aside, as technology became increasingly sophisticated in the late 1990s, Walgreens' CIO (chief information officer) was a registered pharmacist by training, not a technology guru.[10] Walgreens remained resolutely clear: Its Hedgehog Concept would drive its use of technology, not the other way around.

The Walgreens case reflects a general pattern. In every good-to-great case, we found technological sophistication. However, it was never technology per se, but the pioneering *application* of *carefully selected* technologies. Every good-to-great company became a pioneer in the application of technology, but the technologies themselves varied greatly. (See the table on page 150.)

Kroger, for example, was an early pioneer in the application of bar code scanners, which helped it accelerate past A&P by linking frontline purchases to backroom inventory management. This might not sound very exciting (inventory management is not something that tends to rivet readers), but think of it this way: Imagine walking back into the warehouse and instead of seeing boxes of cereal and crates of apples, you see stacks and stacks of dollar bills—hundreds of thousands and millions of freshly minted, crisp and crinkly dollar bills just sitting there on pallets, piled high to the ceiling. That's exactly how you should think of inventory. Every single case of canned carrots is not just a case of canned carrots, it's *cash.* And it's cash just sitting there useless, until you sell that case of canned carrots.

Now recall how Kroger systematically shed its dreary old and small grocery stores, replacing them with nice, big, shiny superstores. To accomplish this task ultimately required more than $9 billion of investment—cash that would somehow have to be pulled out of the low-margin grocery business. To put this in perspective, Kroger put more than *twice* its total annual profits into capital expenditures on average every year for *thirty* years.[11] Even more impressive, despite taking on $5.5 billion of junk bond debt to pay a onetime $40-per-share cash dividend plus an $8 junior debenture to fight off corporate raiders in 1988, Kroger continued its cash-intensive revamping throughout the 1980s and 1990s.[12] Kroger modernized and turned over all its stores, improved the customer's shopping experience, radically expanded the variety of products offered, and paid off billions of dollars of debt. Kroger's use of scanning technology to take hundreds of millions of crisp and crinkly dollar bills out of the warehouse and put them to better use became a key element in its ability to pull off its magic trick—pulling not one, not two, but *three* rabbits out of a hat.

Gillette also became a pioneer in the application of technology. But Gillette's technology accelerators lay largely in *manufacturing* technology. Think about the technology required to make billions—literally billions—of low-cost, high-tolerance razor blades. When you and I pick up a Gillette razor, we expect the blade to be perfect *and* we expect it to be inexpensive per shave. For example, to create the Sensor, Gillette invested over $200 million in design and development, most of it focused on manufacturing breakthroughs, and earned twenty-nine patents.[13] It pioneered the application of laser welding on a mass scale to shaving systems—a technology normally used for expensive and sophisticated products like heart pacemakers.[14] The whole key to Gillette's shaving systems lay in manufacturing technology so unique and proprietary that Gillette protected it the way Coca-Cola protects its secret formula, complete with armed guards and security clearances.[15]

TECHNOLOGY ACCELERATORS IN THE GOOD-TO-GREAT COMPANIES

Company	Technology Accelerators Linked to Hedgehog Concept during Transition Era
Abbott	Pioneered application of computer technology to increase economic denominator of profit per employee. *Not* a leader in pharmaceutical R&D—leaving that to Merck, Pfizer, and others that had a different Hedgehog Concept.
Circuit City	Pioneered application of sophisticated point-of-sale and inventory-tracking technologies—linked to the concept of being the "McDonald's" of big-ticket retailing, able to operate a geographically dispersed system with great consistency.
Fannie Mae	Pioneered application of sophisticated algorithms and computer analysis to more accurately assess mortgage risk, thereby increasing economic denominator of profit per risk level. "Smarter" system of risk analysis increases access to home mortgages for lower-income groups, linking to passion for democratizing home ownership.
Gillette	Pioneered application of sophisticated manufacturing technology for making billions of high-tolerance products at low cost with fantastic consistency. Protects manufacturing technology secrets with the same fanaticism that Coca-Cola protects its formula.
Kimberly-Clark	Pioneered application of manufacturing-process technology, especially in nonwoven materials, to support their passionate pursuit of product superiority. Sophisticated R&D labs; "babies crawl about with temperature and humidity sensors trailing from their tails."
Kroger	Pioneered application of computer and information technology to the continuous modernization of superstores. First to seriously experiment with scanners, which it linked to the entire cash-flow cycle, thereby providing funds for the massive store-revamping process.

Nucor	Pioneered application of the most advanced mini-mill steel manufacturing technology. "Shop the world over" for the most advanced technology. Willing to make huge bets (up to 50 percent of corporate net worth) on new technologies that others viewed as risky, such as continuous thin slab casting.
Philip Morris	Pioneered application of both packaging and manufacturing technology. Bet on technology to make flip-top boxes—the first packaging innovation in twenty years in the industry. First to use computer-based manufacturing. Huge investment in manufacturing center to experiment with, test, and refine advanced manufacturing and quality techniques.
Pitney Bowes	Pioneered application of advanced technology to the mailroom. At first, it took the form of mechanical postage meters. Later, Pitney invested heavily in electrical, software, communications, and Internet engineering for the most sophisticated back-office machines. Made huge R&D investment to reinvent basic postage meter technology in the 1980s.
Walgreens	Pioneered application of satellite communications and computer network technology, linked to its concept of convenient corner drugstores, tailored to the unique needs of specific demographics and locations. A "swallow your tonsils" big investment on a satellite system that links all stores together, like one giant web of a single corner pharmacy. "Like a trip through NASA space center." Led the rest of the industry by at least a decade.
Wells Fargo	Pioneered application of technologies that would increase economic denominator of profit per employee. Early leader in twenty-four-hour banking by phone, early adopter of ATMs, first to allow people to buy and sell mutual funds at an ATM, pioneer in Internet and electronic banking. Pioneered sophisticated mathematics to conduct better risk assessment in lending.

Technology as an Accelerator, Not a Creator, of Momentum

When Jim Johnson became CEO of Fannie Mae, following David Maxwell, he and his leadership team hired a consulting firm to conduct a technology audit. The lead consultant, Bill Kelvie, used a four-level ranking, with four being cutting edge and one being Stone Age. Fannie Mae ranked only a two. So, following the principle of "first who," Kelvie was hired to move the company ahead.[16] When Kelvie came to Fannie Mae in 1990, the company lagged about ten years behind Wall Street in the use of technology.

Over the next five years, Kelvie systematically took Fannie Mae from a 2 to a 3.8 on the four-point ranking.[17] He and his team created over 300 computer applications, including sophisticated analytical programs to control the $600 billion mortgage portfolio, on-line data warehouses covering 60 million properties and streamlined workflows, significantly reducing paper and clerical effort. "We moved technology out of the back office and harnessed it to transform every part of the business," said Kelvie. "We created an expert system that lowers the cost of becoming a home owner. Lenders using our technology reduced the loan-approval time from thirty days to thirty *minutes* and lowered the associated costs by over $1,000 per loan." To date, the system has saved home buyers nearly $4 billion.[18]

Notice that the Fannie Mae transition began in 1981, with the arrival of David Maxwell, yet the company lagged behind in the application of technology until the early 1990s. Yes, technology became of prime importance to Fannie Mae, but *after* it discovered its Hedgehog Concept and *after* it reached breakthrough. Technology was a key part of what Fannie Mae leaders called "the second wind" of the transformation and acted as an accelerating factor.[19] The same pattern holds for Kroger, Gillette, Walgreens, and all the good-to-great companies—the pioneering application of technology usually came late in the transition and never at the start.

> This brings us to the central point of the chapter. When used right, technology becomes an *accelerator* of momentum, not a creator of it. The good-to-great companies never began their transitions with pioneering technology, for the simple reason that you cannot make good

use of technology until you know which technologies are relevant. And which are those? Those—and *only* those—that link directly to the three intersecting circles of the Hedgehog Concept.

To make technology productive in a transformation from good to great means asking the following questions. Does the technology fit directly with your Hedgehog Concept? *If yes, then you need to become a pioneer in the application of that technology.* If no, then ask, do you need this technology at all? If yes, then all you need is parity. (You don't necessarily need the world's most advanced phone system to be a great company.) If no, then the technology is irrelevant, and you can ignore it.

We came to see the pioneering application of technology as just one more way in which the good-to-great companies remained disciplined within the frame of their Hedgehog Concept. Conceptually, their relationship to technology is no different from their relationship to any other category of decisions: disciplined people, who engage in disciplined thought, and who then take disciplined action. If a technology doesn't fit squarely within their three circles, they ignore all the hype and fear and just go about their business with a remarkable degree of equanimity. However, once they understand which technologies are relevant, they become fanatical and creative in the application of those technologies.

In the comparison companies, by contrast, we found only three cases of pioneering in the application of technology. Those three cases—Chrysler (computer-aided design), Harris (electronics applied to printing), and Rubbermaid (advanced manufacturing)—were all unsustained comparisons, which demonstrates that technology alone cannot create sustained great results. Chrysler, for instance, made superb use of advanced computer-aided and other design technologies but failed to link those technologies to a consistent Hedgehog Concept. As Chrysler strayed outside the three circles in the mid-1980s, from Gulfstream jets to Maserati sports cars, no advanced technology by itself could save the company from another massive downturn. Technology without a clear Hedgehog Concept, and without the discipline to stay within the three circles, cannot make a company great.

THE TECHNOLOGY TRAP

Two incidents stand out in my mind as I write this chapter. The first is *Time* magazine's selection in 1999 of Albert Einstein as "Person of the 20th Century." If you frame the person-of-the-century selection around the question, How different would the world be today if that person had not existed? the choice of Einstein is surprising, compared to leaders like Churchill, Hitler, Stalin, and Gandhi—people who truly changed the course of human history, for better or worse. Physicists point out that the scientific community would have reached an understanding of relativity with or without Einstein, perhaps five years later, certainly ten, but not fifty.[20] The Nazis never got the bomb, and the Allies would have won the Second World War without it (although it would have cost more Allied lives). Why did *Time* pick Einstein?

In explaining their selection, *Time* editors wrote: "It's hard to compare the influence of statesmen with that of scientists. Nevertheless, we can note that there are certain eras that were most defined by their politics, others by their culture, and others by their scientific advances. . . . So, how will the 20th century be remembered? Yes, for democracy. And, yes, for civil rights. But the 20th century will be most remembered for its earthshaking advances in science and technology . . . [which] . . . advanced the cause of freedom, in some ways more than any statesman did. In a century that will be remembered foremost for its science and technology . . . one person stands out as the paramount icon of our age . . . Albert Einstein."[21]

In essence, the *Time* editors didn't pick the person of the century so much as they picked the *theme* of the century—technology and science—and attached the most famous person to it. Interestingly, just a few days before the Einstein announcement, *Time* announced its person of the year for 1999. Who did it pick? None other than the poster child of e-commerce, Jeff Bezos of Amazon.com—reflecting yet again our cultural obsession with technology-driven change. Let me be clear. I neither agree nor disagree with *Time*'s choices. I simply find them interesting and illuminating, because they give us a window into our modern psyche. Clearly, a key item on our collective mind is technology, and its implications.

Which brings me to the second incident. Taking a short break from the rigors of writing this book, I traveled to Minnesota to teach sessions at the Masters Forum. The Masters Forum has held executive seminars for nearly fifteen years, and I was curious to know which themes appeared repeatedly over those years. "One of the consistent themes," said Jim Ericson and Patty Griffin Jensen, program directors, "is technology, change—and the connection between the two."

"Why do you suppose that is?" I asked.

"People don't know what they don't know," they said. "And they're always afraid that some new technology is going to sneak up on them from behind and knock them on the head. They don't understand technology, and many fear it. All they know for sure is that technology is an important force of change, and that they'd better pay attention to it."

Given our culture's obsession with technology, and given the pioneering application of technology in the good-to-great companies, you might expect that "technology" would absorb a significant portion of the discussion in our interviews with good-to-great executives.

> We were quite surprised to find that fully 80 percent of the good-to-great executives we interviewed didn't even mention technology as one of the top five factors in the transition. Furthermore, in the cases where they did mention technology, it had a median ranking of fourth, with only two executives of eighty-four interviewed ranking it number one.

If technology is so vitally important, why did the good-to-great executives talk so little about it? Certainly not because they ignored technology: They were technologically sophisticated and vastly superior to their comparisons. Furthermore, a number of the good-to-great companies received extensive media coverage and awards for their pioneering use of technology. Yet the executives hardly talked about technology. It's as if the media articles and the executives were discussing two totally different sets of companies!

Nucor, for example, became widely known as one of the most aggressive pioneers in the application of mini-mill steel manufacturing, with dozens of articles and two books that celebrated its bold investments in continuous thin slab casting and electric arc furnaces.[22] Nucor became a cornerstone case at business schools as an example of unseating the old order through the advanced application of new technologies.

But when we asked Ken Iverson, CEO of Nucor during its transition, to name the top five factors in the shift from good to great, where on the list do you think he put technology? First? No. Second? No. Third? Nope. Fourth? Not even. Fifth? Sorry, but no. "The primary factors," said Ken Iverson, "were the consistency of the company, and our ability to project its philosophies throughout the whole organization, enabled by our lack of layers and bureaucracy."[23]

Stop and think about that for a moment. Here we have a consummate case study of upending the old order with new technology, and the CEO who made it happen doesn't even list technology in the top five factors in the shift from good to great.

This same pattern continued throughout the Nucor interviews. Of the seven key executives and board members that we interviewed, only one picked technology as the number one factor in the shift, and most focused on other factors. A few executives did talk about Nucor's big bets on technology somewhere in the interview, but they emphasized other factors even more—getting people with a farmer work ethic on the bus, getting the right people in key management positions, the simple structure and lack of bureaucracy, the relentless performance culture that increases profit per ton of finished steel. Technology was part of the Nucor equation, but a secondary part. One Nucor executive summed up, "Twenty percent of our success is the new technology that we embrace . . . [but] eighty percent of our success is in the culture of our company."[24]

Indeed, you could have given the exact same technology at the exact same time to any number of companies with the exact same resources as Nucor—and even still, they would have failed to deliver Nucor's results. Like the Daytona 500, the primary variable in winning is not the car, but the driver and his team. Not that the car is unimportant, but it is secondary.

Mediocrity results first and foremost from management failure, not technological failure. Bethlehem Steel's difficulties had less to do with the mini-mill technology and more to do with its history of adversarial labor relations, which ultimately had its roots in unenlightened and ineffective management. Bethlehem had already begun its long slide before Nucor and the other mini-mills had taken significant market share.[25] In fact, by the time Nucor made its technological breakthrough with continuous thin slab casting in 1986, Bethlehem had already lost more than 80 percent of its value relative to the market. This is not to say that technology played no role in Bethlehem's demise; technology *did* play a role, and ultimately a significant one. But technology's role was as an *accelerator* of

Bethlehem's demise, *not* the cause of it. Again, it's the same principle at work—technology as an accelerator, not a cause—only in this comparison case it is operating in reverse.

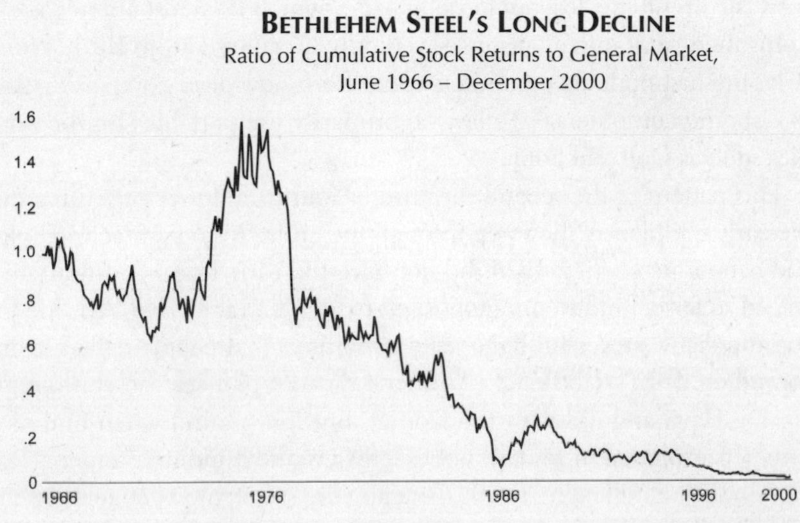

Indeed, when we examined the comparison companies, we did not find a single example of a comparison company's demise coming primarily from a technology torpedo that blew it out of the water. R. J. Reynolds lost its position as the number one tobacco company in the world not because of technology, but because RJR management thrashed about with undisciplined diversification and, later, went on a "let's make management rich at the expense of the company" buyout binge. A&P fell from the second-largest company in America to irrelevance not because it lagged behind Kroger in scanning technology, but because it lacked the discipline to confront the brutal facts of reality about the changing nature of grocery stores.

> The evidence from our study does not support the idea that technological change plays the principal role in the decline of once-great companies (or the perpetual mediocrity of others). Certainly, technology is important—you can't remain a laggard and hope to be great. But technology by itself is never a primary cause of either greatness or decline.

Throughout business history, early technology pioneers rarely prevail in the end. VisiCalc, for example, was the first major personal computer spreadsheet.[26] Where is VisiCalc today? Do you know anyone who uses it? And what of the company that pioneered it? Gone; it doesn't even exist. VisiCalc eventually lost out to Lotus 1-2-3, which itself lost out to Excel.[27] Lotus then went into a tailspin, saved only by selling out to IBM.[28] Similarly, the first portable computers came from now-dead companies, such as Osborne computers.[29] Today, we primarily use portables from companies such as Dell and Sony.

This pattern of the second (or third or fourth) follower prevailing over the early trailblazers shows up through the entire history of technological and economic change. IBM did not have the early lead in computers. It lagged so far behind Remington Rand (which had the UNIVAC, the first commercially successful large-scale computer) that people called its first computer "IBM's UNIVAC."[30] Boeing did not pioneer the commercial jet. De Havilland did with the Comet, but lost ground when one of its early jets exploded in midair, not exactly a brand-building moment. Boeing, slower to market, invested in making the safest, most reliable jets and dominated the airways for over three decades.[31] I could go on for pages. GE did not pioneer the AC electrical system; Westinghouse did.[32] Palm Computing did not pioneer the personal digital assistant; Apple did, with its high-profile Newton.[33] AOL did not pioneer the consumer Internet community; CompuServe and Prodigy did.[34]

We could make a long list of companies that were technology leaders but that failed to prevail in the end as great companies. It would be a fascinating list in itself, but all the examples would underscore a basic truth: Technology cannot turn a good enterprise into a great one, nor by itself prevent disaster.

History teaches this lesson repeatedly. Consider the United States debacle in Vietnam. The United States had the most technologically advanced fighting force the world has ever known. Super jet fighters. Helicopter gunships. Advanced weapons. Computers. Sophisticated communications. Miles of high-tech border sensors. Indeed, the reliance on technology created a false sense of invulnerability. The Americans lacked not technology, but a simple and coherent concept for the war, on which to attach that technology. It lurched back and forth across a variety of ineffective strategies, never getting the upper hand.

Meanwhile, the technologically inferior North Vietnamese forces adhered to a simple, coherent concept: a guerrilla war of attrition, aimed at methodically wearing down public support for the war at home. What little technology the North Vietnamese did employ, such as the AK 47 rifle (much more reliable and easier to maintain in the field than the complicated M-16), linked directly to that simple concept. And in the end, as you know, the United States—despite all its technological sophistication—did not succeed in Vietnam. If you ever find yourself thinking that technology alone holds the key to success, then think again of Vietnam.

Indeed, thoughtless reliance on technology is a *liability*, not an asset. Yes, when used right—when linked to a simple, clear, and coherent concept rooted in deep understanding—technology is an essential driver in accelerating forward momentum. But when used wrong—when grasped as an easy solution, without deep understanding of how it links to a clear and coherent concept—technology simply accelerates your own self-created demise.

TECHNOLOGY AND THE FEAR OF BEING LEFT BEHIND

The research team ferociously debated whether this topic merited its own chapter.

"There must be a technology chapter," said Scott Jones. "We're bombarded by the importance of technology these days at the business school. If we don't address it, we'll leave a huge hole in the book."

"But it seems to me," countered Brian Larsen, "that our technology finding is just a special case of disciplined action, and it belongs in the previous chapter. Disciplined action means staying within the three circles, and that's the essence of our technology finding."

"True, but it is a *very* special case," pointed out Scott Cederberg. "Every one of the companies became extreme pioneers in the application of technology long before the rest of the world became technology obsessed."

"But compared to other findings like Level 5, the Hedgehog Concept, and 'first who,' technology feels like a much smaller issue," retorted Amber Young. "I agree with Brian: Technology *is* important, but as a subset of discipline or perhaps the flywheel."

We argued throughout the summer. Then Chris Jones, in her typically quiet and thoughtful way, asked a key question: "*Why* did the good-to-great companies maintain such a balanced perspective on technology, when most companies become reactionary, lurching and running about like Chicken Little, as we're seeing with the Internet?"

Why indeed.

Chris's question led us to an essential difference between great companies and good companies, a difference that ultimately tipped the balance in favor of including this chapter.

If you had the opportunity to sit down and read all 2,000+ pages of transcripts from the good-to-great interviews, you'd be struck by the utter absence of talk about "competitive strategy." Yes, they did talk about strategy, and they did talk about performance, and they did talk about becoming the best, and they even talked about winning. But they never talked in reactionary terms and never defined their strategies principally in response to what others were doing. They talked in terms of what they were trying to create and how they were trying to improve relative to an absolute standard of excellence.

When we asked George Harvey to describe his motivation for bringing change to Pitney Bowes in the 1980s, he said: "I've always wanted to see Pitney Bowes as a great company. Let's start with that, all right? Let's just start there. That's a given that needs no justification or explanation. We're not there today. We won't be there tomorrow. There is always so much more to create for greatness in an ever-changing world."[35] Or as Wayne Sanders summed up about the ethos that came to typify the inner workings of Kimberly-Clark: "We're just never satisfied. We can be delighted, but never satisfied."[36]

Those who built the good-to-great companies weren't motivated by fear. They weren't driven by fear of what they didn't understand. They weren't driven by fear of looking like a chump. They weren't driven by fear of watching others hit it big while they didn't. They weren't driven by the fear of being hammered by the competition.

No, those who turn good into great are motivated by a deep *creative* urge and an *inner* compulsion for sheer unadulterated excellence *for its own sake.* Those who build and perpetuate mediocrity, in contrast, are motivated more by the fear of being left behind.

Never was there a better example of this difference than during the technology bubble of the late 1990s, which happened to take place right smack in the middle of the research on good to great. It served as an almost perfect stage to watch the difference between great and good play itself out, as the great ones responded like Walgreens—with calm equanimity and quiet deliberate steps forward—while the mediocre ones lurched about in fearful, frantic reaction.

Indeed, the big point of this chapter is not about technology per se. No technology, no matter how amazing—not computers, not telecommunications, not robotics, not the Internet—can by itself ignite a shift from good to great. No technology can make you Level 5. No technology can turn the wrong people into the right people. No technology can instill the discipline to confront brutal facts of reality, nor can it instill unwavering faith. No technology can supplant the need for deep understanding of the three circles and the translation of that understanding into a simple Hedgehog Concept. No technology can create a culture of discipline. No technology can instill the simple inner belief that leaving unrealized potential on the table—letting something remain good when it can become great—is a secular sin.

Those that stay true to these fundamentals and maintain their balance, even in times of great change and disruption, will accumulate the momentum that creates breakthrough momentum. Those that do not, those that fall into reactionary lurching about, will spiral downward or remain mediocre. This is the big-picture difference between great and good, the gestalt of the whole study captured in the metaphor of the flywheel versus the doom loop. And it is to that overarching contrast that we now turn.

CHAPTER SUMMARY

TECHNOLOGY ACCELERATORS

KEY POINTS

- Good-to-great organizations *think* differently about technology and technological change than mediocre ones.
- Good-to-great organizations avoid technology fads and bandwagons, yet they become pioneers in the application of *carefully selected* technologies.
- The key question about any technology is, Does the technology fit directly with your Hedgehog Concept? If yes, then you need to become a pioneer in the application of that technology. If no, then you can settle for parity or ignore it entirely.
- The good-to-great companies used technology as an *accelerator* of momentum, not a creator of it. *None* of the good-to-great companies began their transformations with pioneering technology, yet they *all* became pioneers in the application of technology once they grasped how it fit with their three circles and after they hit breakthrough.
- You could have taken the exact same leading-edge technologies pioneered at the good-to-great companies and handed them to their direct comparisons for free, and the comparisons still would have failed to produce anywhere near the same results.
- How a company reacts to technological change is a good indicator of its inner drive for greatness versus mediocrity. Great companies respond with thoughtfulness and creativity, driven by a compulsion to turn unrealized potential into results; mediocre companies react and lurch about, motivated by fear of being left behind.

UNEXPECTED FINDINGS

- The idea that technological change is the principal cause in the decline of once-great companies (or the perpetual mediocrity of others) is not supported by the evidence. Certainly, a company can't remain a laggard and hope to be great, but technology by itself is never a primary root cause of either greatness or decline.

- Across eighty-four interviews with good-to-great executives, fully 80 percent didn't even mention technology as one of the top five factors in the transformation. This is true even in companies famous for their pioneering application of technology, such as Nucor.
- "Crawl, walk, run" can be a very effective approach, even during times of rapid and radical technological change.

CHAPTER 8

THE FLYWHEEL AND THE DOOM LOOP

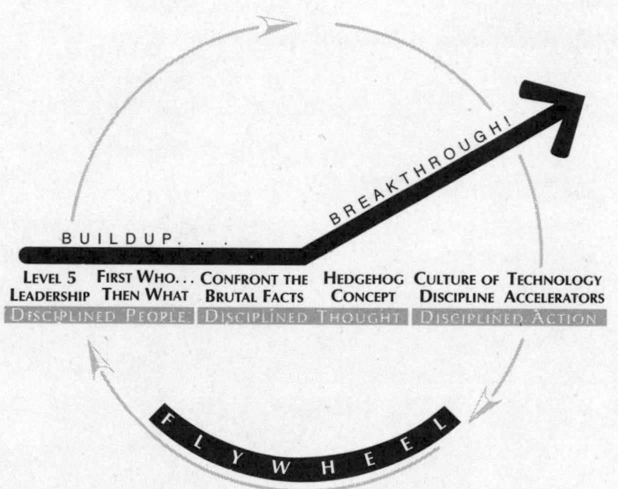

Revolution means turning the wheel.

—IGOR STRAVINSKY[1]

Picture a huge, heavy flywheel—a massive metal disk mounted horizontally on an axle, about 30 feet in diameter, 2 feet thick, and weighing about 5,000 pounds. Now imagine that your task is to get the flywheel rotating on the axle as fast and long as possible.

Pushing with great effort, you get the flywheel to inch forward, moving almost imperceptibly at first. You keep pushing and, after two or three hours of persistent effort, you get the flywheel to complete one entire turn.

You keep pushing, and the flywheel begins to move a bit faster, and with continued great effort, you move it around a second rotation. You keep pushing in a consistent direction. Three turns . . . four . . . five . . . six . . . the flywheel builds up speed . . . seven . . . eight . . . you keep pushing . . . nine . . . ten . . . it builds momentum . . . eleven . . . twelve . . . moving faster with each turn . . . twenty . . . thirty . . . fifty . . . a hundred.

Then, at some point—breakthrough! The momentum of the thing kicks in in your favor, hurling the flywheel forward, turn after turn . . . whoosh! . . . its own heavy weight working for you. You're pushing no harder than during the first rotation, but the flywheel goes faster and faster. Each turn of the flywheel builds upon work done earlier, compounding your investment of effort. A thousand times faster, then ten thousand, then a hundred thousand. The huge heavy disk flies forward, with almost unstoppable momentum.

Now suppose someone came along and asked, "What was the one big push that caused this thing to go so fast?"

You wouldn't be able to answer; it's just a nonsensical question. Was it the first push? The second? The fifth? The hundredth? No! It was *all* of them added together in an overall accumulation of effort applied in a consistent direction. Some pushes may have been bigger than others, but any single heave—no matter how large—reflects a small fraction of the entire cumulative effect upon the flywheel.

BUILDUP AND BREAKTHROUGH*

The flywheel image captures the overall feel of what it was like inside the companies as they went from good to great. No matter how dramatic the end result, the good-to-great transformations never happened in one fell swoop. There was no single defining action, no grand program, no one killer innovation, no solitary lucky break, no wrenching revolution. Good to great comes about by a cumulative process—step by step, action by action, decision by decision, turn by turn of the flywheel—that adds up to sustained and spectacular results.

Yet to read media accounts of the companies, you might draw an entirely different conclusion. Often, the media does not cover a company until the flywheel is already turning at a thousand rotations per minute. This entirely skews our perception of how such transformations happen, making it seem as if they jumped right to breakthrough as some sort of an overnight metamorphosis.

*Credit for the terms *buildup* and *breakthrough* should go to David S. Landes and his book, *The Wealth and Poverty of Nations: Why Some Are So Rich and Some So Poor* (New York: W. W. Norton & Company, 1998). On page 200, Landes writes: "The question is really twofold. First, why and how did any country break through the crust of habit and conventional knowledge to this new mode of production? Turning to the first, I would stress buildup—the accumulation of knowledge and know-how; and breakthrough—reaching and passing thresholds." When we read this paragraph, we noted its applicability to our study and decided to adopt these terms in describing the good-to-great companies.

For example, on August 27, 1984, *Forbes* magazine published an article on Circuit City. It was the first national-level profile *ever* published on the company. It wasn't that big of an article, just two pages, and it questioned whether Circuit City's recent growth could continue.[2] Still, there it was, the first public acknowledgment that Circuit City had broken through. The journalist had just identified a hot new company, almost like an overnight success story.

This particular overnight success story, however, had been more than a decade in the making. Alan Wurtzel had inherited CEO responsibility from his father in 1973, with the firm close to bankruptcy. First, he rebuilt his executive team and undertook an objective look at the brutal facts of reality, both internal and external. In 1974, still struggling with a crushing debt load, Wurtzel and his team began to experiment with a warehouse showroom style of retailing (large inventories of name brands, discount pricing, and immediate delivery) and built a prototype of this model in Richmond, Virginia, to sell appliances. In 1976, the company began to experiment with selling consumer electronics in the warehouse showroom format, and in 1977, it transformed the concept into the first-ever Circuit City store.

The concept met with success, and the company began systematically converting its stereo stores into Circuit City stores. In 1982—with nine years of accumulated turns on the flywheel—Wurtzel and his team committed fully to the concept of the Circuit City superstore. Over the next five years, as it shifted entirely to this concept, Circuit City generated the highest total return to shareholders of any company on the New York Stock Exchange.[3] From 1982 to 1999, Circuit City generated cumulative stock returns twenty-two times better than the market, handily beating Intel, Wal-Mart, GE, Hewlett-Packard, and Coca-Cola.

Not surprisingly, Circuit City then found itself a prime subject for media attention. Whereas we found no articles of any significance in the decade leading up the transition, we found ninety-seven articles' worth examining in the decade after the transition, twenty-two of them significant pieces. It's as if the company hadn't even existed prior to that, despite having traded on a major stock exchange since 1968, and despite the remarkable progress made by Wurtzel and his team in the decade leading up to the breakthrough point.

The Circuit City experience reflects a common pattern. In case after case, we found fewer articles in the decade leading up to the point of transition than in the decade after, by an average factor of nearly three times.[4]

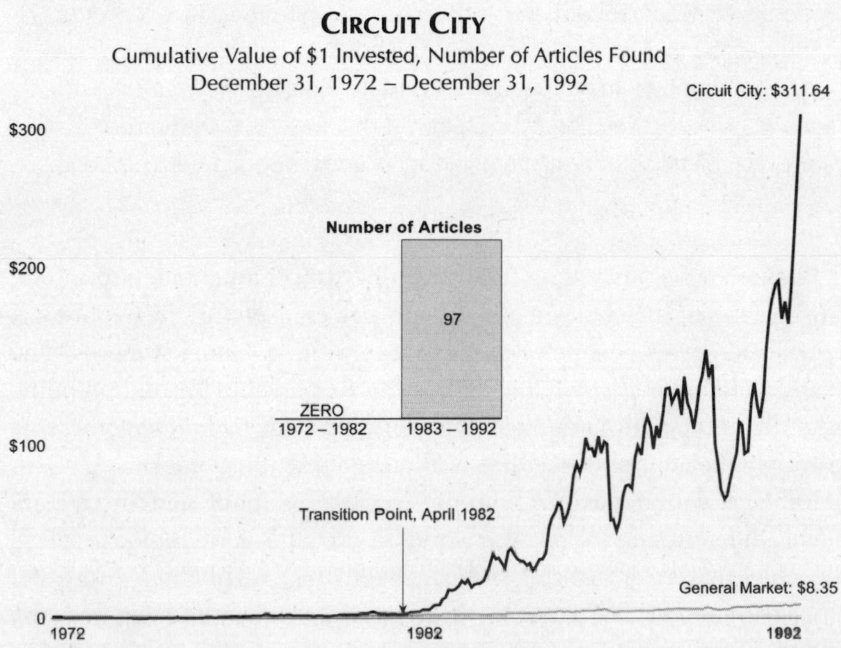

For example, Ken Iverson and Sam Siegel began turning the Nucor flywheel in 1965. For ten years, no one paid any attention, certainly not the financial press or the other steel companies. If you had asked executives at Bethlehem Steel or U.S. Steel about "The Nucor Threat" in 1970, they would have laughed, if they even recognized the company name at all (which is doubtful). By 1975, the year of its transition point on the stock chart, Nucor had already built its third mini-mill, long established its unique culture of productivity, and was well on its way to becoming the most profitable steel company in America.[5] Yet the first major article in *Business Week* did not appear until 1978, *thirteen years* after the start of the transition, and not in *Fortune* until *sixteen* years out. From 1965 through 1975, we found only eleven articles on Nucor, none of them significant. Then from 1976 through 1995, we collected ninety-six articles on Nucor, forty of them being major profiles or nationally prominent features.

Now, you might be thinking, "But we should expect that. Of course these companies would get more coverage after they become wildly successful. What's so important about that?"

Here's what's important. We've allowed the way transitions look from the *outside* to drive our perception of what they must feel like to those going through them on the *inside*. From the outside, they *look* like dramatic, almost revolutionary breakthroughs. But from the inside, they *feel* completely different, more like an organic development process.

Picture an egg just sitting there. No one pays it much attention until, one day, the egg cracks open and out jumps a chicken! All the major magazines and newspapers jump on the event, writing feature stories—"The Transformation of Egg to Chicken!" "The Remarkable Revolution of the Egg!" "Stunning Turnaround at Egg!"—as if the egg had undergone some overnight metamorphosis, radically altering itself into a chicken.

But what does it look like from the chicken's point of view? It's a completely different story. While the world ignored this dormant-looking egg, the chicken was evolving, growing, developing, incubating. From the chicken's point of view, cracking the egg is simply one more step in a long chain of steps leading up to that moment—a big step, to be sure, but hardly the radical, single-step transformation it looks like to those watching from outside the egg.

It's a silly analogy, granted. But I'm using it to highlight a very important finding from our research. We kept thinking that we'd find "the one big thing," the miracle moment that defined breakthrough. We even pushed for it in our interviews. But the good-to-great executives simply could not pinpoint a single key event or moment in time that exemplified the transition. Frequently, they chafed against the whole idea of allocating points and prioritizing factors. In every good-to-great company, at least one of the interviewees gave an unprompted admonishment, saying something along the lines of, "Look, you can't dissect this thing into a series of nice little boxes and factors, or identify the moment of 'Aha!' or the 'one big thing.' It was a whole bunch of interlocking pieces that built one upon another."

Even in the most dramatic case in our study—Kimberly-Clark selling the mills—the executives described an organic, cumulative process. "Darwin did not change the direction of the company overnight," said one Kimberly-Clark executive. "He evolved it over time."[6] "The transition wasn't like night and day," said another. "It was gradual, and I don't think it was entirely clear to everybody until a few years into it."[7] Of course, selling the mills was a gigantic push on the flywheel, but it was only one push. After selling the mills, the full transformation into the number one paper-based consumer products company required thousands of additional pushes on the flywheel, big and small, accumulated one on top of another. It took years to gain enough momentum for the press to openly herald Kimberly-Clark's shift from good to great. *Forbes* wrote, "When . . . Kimberly-Clark decided to go head to head against P&G . . . this magazine predicted disaster. What a dumb idea. As it turns out, it wasn't a dumb idea. It was a smart idea."[8] The amount of time between the two *Forbes* articles? *Twenty-one years.*

While working on the project, we made a habit of asking executives who visited our research laboratory what they would want to know from the research. One CEO asked, "What did they call what they were doing? Did they have a name for it? How did they talk about it at the time?" It's a great question, and we went back to look. The astounding answer: *They didn't call it anything.*

> The good-to-great companies had no name for their transformations. There was no launch event, no tag line, no programmatic feel whatsoever. Some executives said that they weren't even aware that a major transformation was under way until they were well into it. It was often more obvious to them after the fact than at the time.

Then it began to dawn on us: *There was no miracle moment*. (See the table on page 170.) Although it may have looked like a single-stroke breakthrough to those peering in from the outside, it was anything but that to people experiencing the transformation from within. Rather, it was a quiet, deliberate process of figuring out what needed to be done to create the best future results and then simply taking those steps, one after the other, turn by turn of the flywheel. After pushing on that flywheel in a consistent direction over an extended period of time, they'd inevitably hit a point of breakthrough.

"NO MIRACLE MOMENT" IN GOOD TO GREAT
(Representative Quotes from the Interviews)

Abbott	"It wasn't a blinding flash or sudden revelation from above."[9] "Our change was a major change, and yet in many respects simply a series of incremental changes—this is what made that change successful. We did this in a nice stepwise way and there were always a lot of common denominators between what we had already mastered and what we were embarking on."[10]
Circuit City	"The transition to focus on the superstore didn't happen overnight. We first considered the concept in 1974, but we didn't convert fully to Circuit City superstores until about ten years later, after we'd refined the concept and built enough momentum to bet our whole future on it."[11]
Fannie Mae	"There was no one magical event, no one turning point. It was a combination of things. More of an evolution, though the end results were dramatic."[12]
Gillette	"We didn't really make a big conscious decision or launch a big program to initiate a major change or transition. Individually and collectively we were coming to conclusions about what we could do to dramatically improve our performance."[13]
Kimberly-Clark	"I don't think it was done as bluntly as it sounds. These things don't happen overnight. They grow. The ideas grow and mushroom and come into being."[14]
Kroger	"It wasn't a flash from the blue. We had all been watching experimental superstores develop, and we were pretty well persuaded that the industry would go that way. The major thing that Lyle did was to say that we're going to change beginning *now*, on a very deliberate basis."[15]

Nucor	"We did not make a decision that this was what we stood for at any specific moment. It evolved through many agonizing arguments and fights. I am not sure that we knew exactly what we were fighting for until we looked back and said that we were fighting to establish who we were going to be."[16]
Philip Morris	"It's impossible to think of one big thing that would exemplify a shift from good to great because our success was evolutionary as opposed to revolutionary, building success upon success. I don't know that there was any single event."[17]
Pitney Bowes	"We didn't talk so much of change. We recognized early on not so much that we needed to change, but that we needed to evolve, which recognizes that we've got to do things differently. We realized that evolution is a whole different concept than change."[18]
Walgreens	"There was no seminal meeting or epiphany moment, no one big bright light that came on like a lightbulb. It was sort of an evolution thing."[19]
Wells Fargo	"It wasn't a single switch that was thrown at one time. Little by little, the themes became more apparent and stronger. When Carl became CEO, there wasn't any great wrenching. Dick led one stage of evolution and Carl the next, and it just proceeded smoothly, rather than an abrupt shift."[20]

When teaching this point, I sometimes use an example from outside my research that perfectly illustrates the idea: the UCLA Bruins basketball dynasty of the 1960s and early 1970s. Most basketball fans know that the Bruins won ten NCAA Championships in twelve years, at one point assembling a sixty-one-game winning streak, under the legendary coach John Wooden.[21]

But do you know how many years Wooden coached the Bruins before his first NCAA Championship? Fifteen. From 1948 to 1963, Wooden worked in relative obscurity before winning his first championship in 1964. Year by year, Coach Wooden built the underlying foundations, developing a recruiting system, implementing a consistent philosophy, and refining the full-court-press style of play. No one paid too much attention to the quiet, soft-spoken coach and his team until—wham!—they hit breakthrough and systematically crushed every serious competitor for more than a decade.

Like the Wooden dynasty, lasting transformations from good to great follow a general pattern of buildup followed by breakthrough. In some cases, the buildup-to-breakthrough stage takes a long time, in other cases, a shorter time. At Circuit City, the buildup stage lasted nine years, at Nucor ten years, whereas at Gillette it took only five years, at Fannie Mae only three years, and at Pitney Bowes about two years. But, no matter how short or long it took, every good-to-great transformation followed the same basic pattern—accumulating momentum, turn by turn of the flywheel—until buildup transformed into breakthrough.

NOT JUST A LUXURY OF CIRCUMSTANCE

It's important to understand that following the buildup-breakthrough flywheel model is not just a luxury of circumstance. People who say, "Hey, but we've got constraints that prevent us from taking this longer-term approach," should keep in mind that the good-to-great companies followed this model no matter how dire the short-term circumstances—deregulation in the case of Wells Fargo, looming bankruptcy in the cases of Nucor and Circuit City, potential takeover threats in the cases of Gillette and Kroger, or million-dollar-a-day losses in the case of Fannie Mae.

This also applies to managing the short-term pressures of Wall Street. "I just don't agree with those who say you can't build an enduring great company because Wall Street won't let you," said David Maxwell of Fannie Mae. "We communicated with analysts, to educate them on what we were doing and where we were going. At first, a lot of people didn't buy into that—you just have to accept that. But once we got through the dark days, we responded by doing better every single year. After a few years, because of our actual results, we became a hot stock and never looked back."[22] And a hot stock it was. During Maxwell's first two years, the stock lagged behind the market, but then it took off. From the end of 1984 to the year 2000, $1 invested in Fannie Mae multiplied sixty-four times, beating the general market—including the wildly inflated NASDAQ of the late 1990s—by nearly six times.

> The good-to-great companies were subject to the same short-term pressures from Wall Street as the comparison companies. Yet, unlike the comparison companies, they had the patience and discipline to follow the buildup-breakthrough flywheel model despite these pressures. And in the end, they attained extraordinary results by Wall Street's *own* measure of success.

The key, we learned, is to harness the flywheel to manage these short-term pressures. One particularly elegant method for doing so came from Abbott Laboratories, using a mechanism it called the Blue Plans. Each year, Abbott would tell Wall Street analysts that it expected to grow earnings a specified amount—say, 15 percent. At the same time, it would set an *internal* goal of a much higher growth rate—say, 25 percent, or even 30 percent. Meanwhile, it kept a rank-ordered list of proposed entrepreneurial projects that had not yet been funded—the Blue Plans. Toward the end of the year, Abbott would pick a number that exceeded analyst expectations but that fell short of its actual growth. It would then take the difference between the "make the analysts happy" growth and the actual growth and channel those funds into the Blue Plans. It was a brilliant mechanism for managing short-term pressures while systematically investing in the future.[23]

We found no evidence of anything like the Blue Plans at Abbott's comparison company. Instead, Upjohn executives would pump up the stock with a sales job ("Buy into our future"), reverently intoning the phrase "investing for the long-term," especially when the company failed to deliver current results.[24] Upjohn continually threw money after hare-brained projects like its Rogaine baldness cure, attempting to circumvent buildup and jump right to breakthrough with a big hit. Indeed, Upjohn reminded us of a gambler, putting a lot of chips on red at Las Vegas and saying, "See, we're investing for the future." Of course, when the future arrived, the promised results rarely appeared.

Not surprisingly, Abbott became a consistent performer and a favorite holding on Wall Street, while Upjohn became a consistent disappointment. From 1959 to Abbott's point of breakthrough in 1974, the two stocks roughly tracked each other. Then they dramatically diverged, with Upjohn falling more than six times behind Abbott before being acquired in 1995.

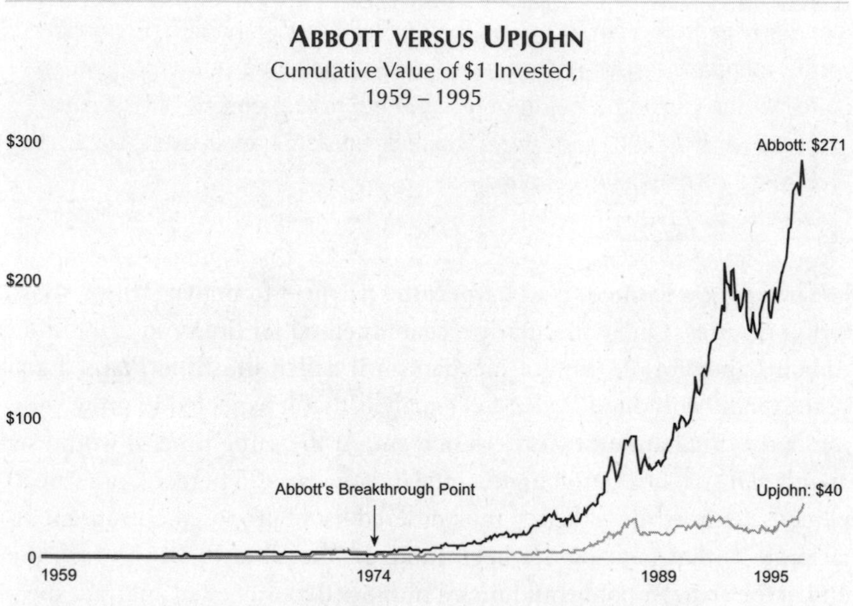

Like Fannie Mae and Abbott, all the good-to-great companies effectively managed Wall Street during their buildup-breakthrough years, and they saw no contradiction between the two. They simply focused on accumulating results, often practicing the time-honored discipline of underpromising and overdelivering. And as the results began to accumulate—as the flywheel built momentum—the investing community came along with great enthusiasm.

THE "FLYWHEEL EFFECT"

The good-to-great companies understood a simple truth: Tremendous power exists in the fact of continued improvement and the delivery of results. Point to tangible accomplishments—however incremental at first—and show how these steps fit into the context of an overall concept that will work. When you do this in such a way that people see and *feel* the buildup of momentum, they will line up with enthusiasm. We came to call this the flywheel effect, and it applies not only to outside investors but also to internal constituent groups.

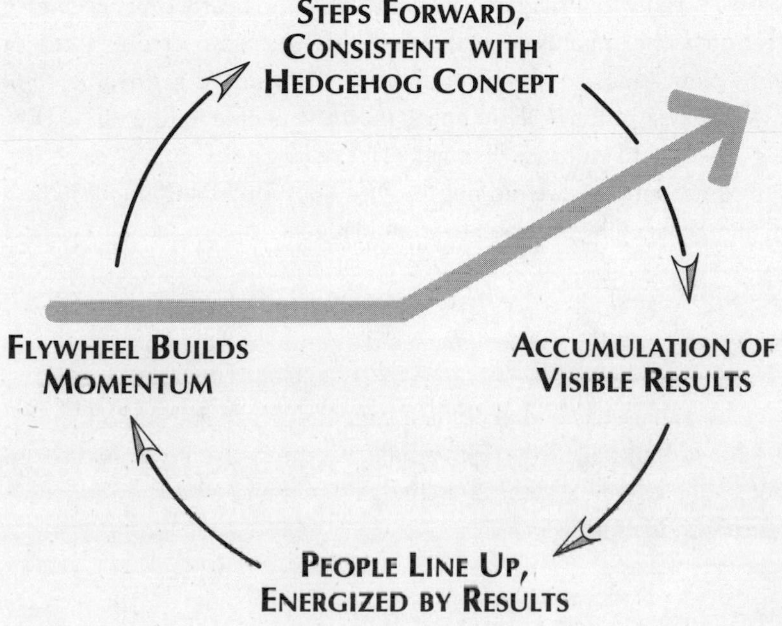

THE FLYWHEEL EFFECT

Let me share a story from the research. At a pivotal point in the study, members of the research team nearly revolted. Throwing their interview notes on the table, they asked, "Do we have to keep asking that stupid question?"

"What stupid question?" I asked.

"The one about commitment, alignment, and how they managed change."

"That's not a stupid question," I replied. "It's one of the most important."

"Well," said one team member, "a lot of the executives who made the transition—well, *they* think it's a stupid question. Some don't even understand the question!"

"Yes, we need to keep asking it," I said. "We need to be consistent across the interviews. And, besides, it's even more interesting that they don't understand the question. So, keep probing. We've got to understand how they overcame resistance to change and got people lined up."

I fully expected to find that getting everyone lined up—"creating alignment," to use the jargon—would be one of the top challenges faced by executives working to turn good into great. After all, nearly every executive who'd visited the laboratory had asked this question in one form or another. "How do we get the boat turned?" "How do we get people committed to the new vision?" "How do we motivate people to line up?" "How do we get people to embrace change?"

To my great surprise, we did not find the question of alignment to be a key challenge faced by the good-to-great leaders.

Clearly, the good-to-great companies did get incredible commitment and alignment—they artfully managed change—but they never really spent much time thinking about it. It was utterly transparent to them. We learned that under the right conditions, the problems of commitment, alignment, motivation, and change just melt away. They largely take care of themselves.

Consider Kroger. How do you get a company of over 50,000 people—cashiers, baggers, shelf stockers, produce washers, and so forth—to embrace a radical new strategy that will eventually change virtually every aspect of how the company builds and runs grocery stores? The answer is that *you don't.* Not in one big event or program, anyway.

Jim Herring, the Level 5 leader who initiated the transformation of Kroger, told us that he avoided any attempts at hoopla and motivation. Instead, he and his team began turning the flywheel, creating tangible evidence that their plans made sense. "We presented what we were doing in such a way that people saw our accomplishments," said Herring. "We tried to bring our plans to successful conclusion step by step, so that the mass of people would gain confidence from the successes, not just the words."[25] Herring understood that the way to get people lined up behind a bold new vision is to turn the flywheel consistent with that vision—from two turns to four, then four to eight, then eight to sixteen—and then to say, "See what we're doing, and how well it is working? Extrapolate from that, and that's where we're going."

The good-to-great companies tended not to publicly proclaim big goals at the outset. Rather, they began to spin the flywheel—understanding to action, step after step, turn after turn. After the flywheel built up momentum, they'd look up and say, "Hey, if we just keep pushing on this thing, there's no reason we can't accomplish X."

For example, Nucor began turning the flywheel in 1965, at first just trying to avoid bankruptcy, then later building its first steel mills because it could not find a reliable supplier. Nucor people discovered that they had a knack for making steel better and cheaper than anyone else, so they built two, and then three, additional mini-mills. They gained customers, then more customers, then more customers—whoosh!—the flywheel built momentum, turn by turn, month by month, year by year. Then, around 1975, it dawned on the Nucor people that if they just kept pushing on the flywheel, they could become the number one, most profitable steel company in America. Explained Marvin Pohlman: "I remember talking with Ken Iverson in 1975, and he said, 'Marv, I think we can become the number one steel company in the U.S.' 1975! And I said to him, 'Now, Ken, when are you going to be number one?' 'I don't know,' he said. 'But if we just keep doing what we're doing, there's no reason why we can't become number one.' "[26] It took over two decades, but Nucor kept pushing the flywheel, eventually generating greater profits than any other steel company on the Fortune 1000 list.[27]

When you let the flywheel do the talking, you don't need to fervently communicate your goals. People can just extrapolate from the momentum of the flywheel for themselves: "Hey, if we just keep doing this, look at where we can go!" As people decide among themselves to turn the fact of potential into the fact of results, the goal almost sets itself.

Stop and think about it for a minute. What do the right people want more than almost anything else? They want to be part of a winning team. They want to contribute to producing visible, tangible results. They want to feel the excitement of being involved in something *that just flat-out works.* When the right people see a simple plan born of confronting the brutal facts—a plan developed from understanding, not bravado—they are likely to say, "That'll work. Count me in." When they see the monolithic unity of the executive team behind the simple plan and the selfless, dedicated qualities of Level 5 leadership, they'll drop their cynicism. When people begin to feel the magic of momentum—when they begin to see tangible results, when they can *feel* the flywheel beginning to build speed—*that's* when the bulk of people line up to throw their shoulders against the wheel and push.

THE DOOM LOOP

We found a very different pattern at the comparison companies. Instead of a quiet, deliberate process of figuring out what needed to be done and then simply doing it, the comparison companies frequently launched new programs—often with great fanfare and hoopla aimed at "motivating the troops"—only to see the programs fail to produce sustained results. They sought the single defining action, the grand program, the one killer innovation, the miracle moment that would allow them to skip the arduous buildup stage and jump right to breakthrough. They would push the flywheel in one direction, then stop, change course, and throw it in a new direction—and then they would stop, change course, and throw it into yet another direction. After years of lurching back and forth, the comparison companies failed to build sustained momentum and fell instead into what we came to call the doom loop.

Consider the case of Warner-Lambert, the direct comparison company to Gillette.

In 1979, Warner-Lambert told *Business Week* that it aimed to be a leading consumer products company.[28]

One year later, in 1980, it did an abrupt about-face and turned its sights on health care, saying, "Our flat-out aim is to go after Merck, Lilly, SmithKline—everybody and his brother."[29]

In 1981, the company reversed course yet again and returned to diversification and consumer goods.[30]

Six years later, in 1987, Warner-Lambert did another U-turn, away from consumer goods, to try once again to be like Merck. (At the same time, the company spent three times as much on consumer-goods advertising as on R&D—a somewhat puzzling strategy, for a company trying to beat Merck.)[31]

In the early 1990s, reacting to Clinton-era health care reform, the company threw itself into reverse yet again and reembraced diversification and consumer brands.[32]

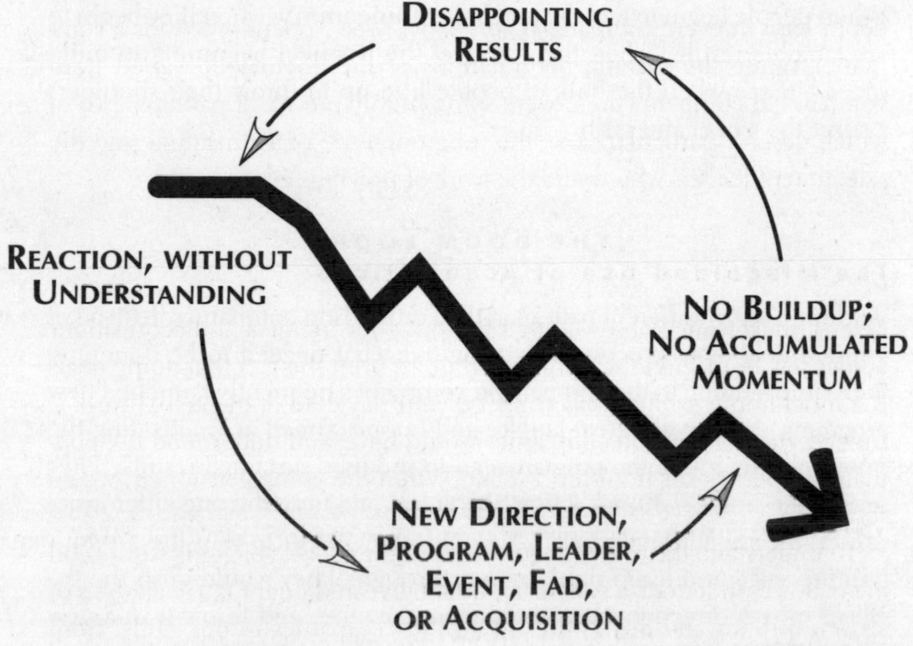

THE DOOM LOOP

Each new Warner-Lambert CEO brought his own new program and halted the momentum of his predecessor. Ward Hagen tried to create a breakthrough with an expensive acquisition in the hospital supply business in 1982. Three years later, his successor, Joe Williams, extracted Warner-Lambert from the hospital supply business and took a $550 million write-off.[33] He tried to focus the company on beating Merck, but *his* successor threw the company back to diversification and consumer goods. And so it went, back and forth, lurch and thrash, with each CEO trying to make a mark with his own program.

From 1979 through 1998, Warner-Lambert underwent three major restructurings—one per CEO—hacking away 20,000 people in search of quick breakthrough results. Time and again, the company would attain a burst of results, then slacken, never attaining the sustained momentum of a buildup-breakthrough flywheel. Stock returns flattened relative to the market and Warner-Lambert disappeared as an independent company, swallowed up by Pfizer.[34]

The Warner-Lambert case is extreme, but we found some version of the doom loop in every comparison company. (See Appendix 8.A for a summary.) While the specific permutations of the doom loop varied from company to company, there were some highly prevalent patterns, two of which deserve particular note: the misguided use of acquisitions and the selection of leaders who undid the work of previous generations.

The Misguided Use of Acquisitions

Peter Drucker once observed that the drive for mergers and acquisitions comes less from sound reasoning and more from the fact that doing deals is a much more exciting way to spend your day than doing actual work.[35] Indeed, the comparison companies would have well understood the popular bumper sticker from the 1980s, "When the going gets tough, we go shopping!"

To understand the role of acquisitions in the process of going from good to great, we undertook a systematic qualitative and quantitative analysis of all acquisitions and divestitures in all the companies in our study, from ten years before the transition date through 1998. While we noticed no particular pattern in the amount or scale of acquisitions, we *did* note a significant difference in the success rate of the acquisitions in the good-to-great companies versus the comparisons. (See Appendix 8.B.)

Why did the good-to-great companies have a substantially higher success rate with acquisitions, especially major acquisitions? The key to their success was that their big acquisitions generally took place *after* development of the Hedgehog Concept and *after* the flywheel had built significant momentum. They used acquisitions as an *accelerator* of flywheel momentum, not a creator of it.

In contrast, the comparison companies frequently tried to jump right to breakthrough via an acquisition or merger. It never worked. Often with their core business under siege, the comparison companies would dive into a big acquisition as a way to increase growth, diversify away their troubles, or make a CEO look good. Yet they never addressed the fundamental question: "What can we do better than any other company in the world, that fits our economic denominator and that we have passion for?" They never learned the simple truth that, while you can buy your way to growth, you absolutely cannot buy your way to greatness. Two big mediocrities joined together never make one great company.

Leaders Who Stop the Flywheel

The other frequently observed doom loop pattern is that of new leaders who stepped in, stopped an already spinning flywheel, and threw it in an entirely new direction. Consider Harris Corporation, which applied many of the good-to-great concepts in the early 1960s and began a classic buildup process that led to breakthrough results. George Dively and his successor, Richard Tullis, identified a Hedgehog Concept, based on the understanding that Harris could be the best in the world at applying technology to printing and communications. Although it did not adhere to this concept with perfect discipline (Tullis had a penchant for straying a bit outside the three circles), the company did make enough progress to produce significant results. It looked like a promising candidate for a good-to-great transformation, hitting breakthrough in 1975.

Then the flywheel came to a grinding halt.

In 1978, Joseph Boyd became chief executive. Boyd had previously been with Radiation, Inc., a corporation acquired by Harris years earlier. His first key decision as CEO was to move the company headquarters from Cleveland to Melbourne, Florida—Radiation's hometown, and the location of Boyd's house and forty-seven-foot powerboat, the *Lazy Rascal*.[36]

In 1983, Boyd threw a giant wrench into the flywheel by divesting the printing business. At the time, Harris was the number one producer of printing equipment in the world. The printing business was one of the most profitable parts of the company, generating nearly a third of total operating profits.[37] What did Boyd do with the proceeds from selling off this corporate gem? He threw the company headlong into the office automation business.

But could Harris become the best in the world in office automation? Not likely. "Horrendous" software-development problems delayed introduction of Harris' first workstation as the company stumbled onto the battlefield to confront IBM, DEC, and Wang.[38] Then, in an attempt to jump right to a new breakthrough, Harris spent *a third* of its entire corporate net worth to buy Lanier Business Products, a company in the low-end word processing business.[39] *Computerworld* magazine wrote: "Boyd targeted the automated office as a key. . . . Unfortunately, for Harris, the company had everything but an office product. The attempt to design and market a word processing system met with dismal failure . . . out of tune with the market, and had to be scrapped before introduction."[40]

The flywheel, which had been spinning with great momentum after Dively and Tullis, came detached from the axle, wobbled into the air, and then crashed to a grinding halt. From the end of 1973 to the end of 1978, Harris beat the market by more than five times. But from the end of 1978 to the end of 1983, Harris fell 39 percent behind the market, and by 1988 it had fallen over 70 percent behind. The doom loop replaced the flywheel.

THE FLYWHEEL AS A WRAPAROUND IDEA

When I look over the good-to-great transformations, the one word that keeps coming to mind is *consistency*. Another word offered to me by physics professor R. J. Peterson is *coherence*. "What is one plus one?" he asked, then paused for effect. "Four! In physics, we have been talking about the idea of coherence, the magnifying effect of one factor upon another. In reading about the flywheel, I couldn't help but think of the principle of coherence." However you phrase it, the basic idea is the same: Each piece of the system reinforces the other parts of the system to form an integrated whole that is much more powerful than the sum of the parts. It is only through consistency over time, through multiple generations, that you get maximum results.

In a sense, everything in this book is an exploration and description of the pieces of the buildup-to-breakthrough flywheel pattern. (See the table on page 183.) In standing back to survey the overall framework, we see that every factor works together to create this pattern, and each component produces a push on the flywheel.

HOW TO TELL IF YOU'RE ON THE FLYWHEEL OR IN THE DOOM LOOP

Signs That You're on the Flywheel (Good-to-Great Companies)	Signs That You're in the Doom Loop (Comparison Companies)
Follow a pattern of buildup leading to breakthrough.	Skip buildup and jump right to breakthrough.
Reach breakthrough by an accumulation of steps, one after the other, turn by turn of the flywheel; feels like an organic evolutionary process.	Implement big programs, radical change efforts, dramatic revolutions; chronic restructuring—always looking for a miracle moment or new savior.
Confront the brutal facts to see clearly what steps *must* be taken to build momentum.	Embrace fads and engage in management hoopla, rather than confront the brutal facts.
Attain *consistency* with a clear Hedgehog Concept, resolutely staying within the three circles.	Demonstrate chronic *inconsistency*—lurching back and forth and straying far outside the three circles.
Follow the pattern of disciplined people ("first who"), disciplined thought, disciplined action.	Jump right to action, without disciplined thought and without first getting the right people on the bus.
Harness appropriate technologies to your Hedgehog Concept, to accelerate momentum.	Run about like Chicken Little in reaction to technology change, fearful of being left behind.
Make major acquisitions *after* breakthrough (if at all) to *accelerate* momentum.	Make major acquisitions *before* breakthrough, in a doomed attempt to *create* momentum.
Spend little energy trying to motivate or align people; the momentum of the flywheel is infectious.	Spend a lot of energy trying to align and motivate people, rallying them around new visions.

Signs That You're on the Flywheel (Good-to-Great Companies)	Signs That You're in the Doom Loop (Comparison Companies)
Let results do most of the talking.	Sell the future, to compensate for lack of results.
Maintain consistency over time; each generation builds on the work of previous generations; the flywheel continues to build momentum.	Demonstrate inconsistency over time; each new leader brings a radical new path; the flywheel grinds to a halt, and the doom loop begins anew.

It all starts with Level 5 leaders, who naturally gravitate toward the flywheel model. They're less interested in flashy programs that make it look like they are *Leading!* with a capital *L*. They're more interested in the quiet, deliberate process of pushing on the flywheel to produce *Results!* with a capital *R*.

Getting the right people on the bus, the wrong people off the bus, and the right people in the right seats—these are all crucial steps in the early stages of buildup, very important pushes on the flywheel. Equally important is to remember the Stockdale Paradox: "We're not going to hit breakthrough by Christmas, but if we keep pushing in the right direction, we *will* eventually hit breakthrough." This process of confronting the brutal facts helps you see the obvious, albeit difficult, steps that must be taken to turn the flywheel. Faith in the endgame helps you live through the months or years of buildup.

Next, when you attain deep understanding about the three circles of your Hedgehog Concept and begin to push in a direction consistent with that understanding, you hit breakthrough momentum and accelerate with key accelerators, chief among them pioneering the application of technology tied directly back to your three circles. Ultimately, to reach breakthrough means having the discipline to make a series of good decisions consistent with your Hedgehog Concept—disciplined action, following from disciplined people who exercise disciplined thought. That's it. That's the essence of the breakthrough process.

In short, if you diligently and successfully apply each concept in the framework, and you continue to push in a consistent direction on the flywheel, accumulating momentum step by step and turn by turn, you will eventually reach breakthrough. It might not happen today, or tomorrow, or next week. It might not even happen next year. But it *will* happen.

And when it does, you will face an entirely new set of challenges: how to accelerate momentum in response to ever-rising expectations, and how to ensure that the flywheel continues to turn long into the future. In short, your challenge will no longer be how to go from good to great, but how to go from great to enduring great. And that is the subject of the last chapter.

CHAPTER SUMMARY

THE FLYWHEEL AND THE DOOM LOOP

KEY POINTS

- Good-to-great transformations often look like dramatic, revolutionary events to those observing from the outside, but they feel like organic, cumulative processes to people on the inside. The confusion of end outcomes (dramatic results) with process (organic and cumulative) skews our perception of what really works over the long haul.
- No matter how dramatic the end result, the good-to-great transformations never happened in one fell swoop. There was no single defining action, no grand program, no one killer innovation, no solitary lucky break, no miracle moment.
- Sustainable transformations follow a predictable pattern of buildup and breakthrough. Like pushing on a giant, heavy flywheel, it takes a lot of effort to get the thing moving at all, but with persistent pushing in a consistent direction over a long period of time, the flywheel builds momentum, eventually hitting a point of breakthrough.
- The comparison companies followed a different pattern, the doom loop. Rather than accumulating momentum—turn by turn of the flywheel—they tried to skip buildup and jump immediately to breakthrough. Then, with disappointing results, they'd lurch back and forth, failing to maintain a consistent direction.
- The comparison companies frequently tried to create a breakthrough with large, misguided acquisitions. The good-to-great companies, in contrast, principally used large acquisitions *after* breakthrough, to accelerate momentum in an already fast-spinning flywheel.

UNEXPECTED RESULTS

- Those inside the good-to-great companies were often unaware of the magnitude of their transformation at the time; only later, in retrospect, did it become clear. They had no name, tag line, launch event, or program to signify what they were doing at the time.

- The good-to-great leaders spent essentially no energy trying to "create alignment," "motivate the troops," or "manage change." Under the right conditions, the problems of commitment, alignment, motivation, and change largely take care of themselves. Alignment principally follows *from* results and momentum, not the other way around.
- The short-term pressures of Wall Street were not inconsistent with following this model. The flywheel effect is not in conflict with these pressures. Indeed, it is the key to managing them.

CHAPTER 9

FROM GOOD TO GREAT TO BUILT TO LAST

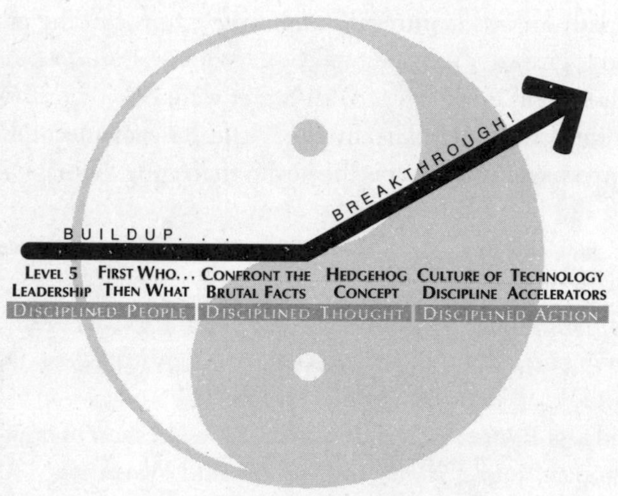

It is your Work in life that is the ultimate seduction.

—PABLO PICASSO[1]

When we began the *Good to Great* research project, we confronted a dilemma: How should we think about the ideas in *Built to Last* while doing the *Good to Great* research?

Briefly, *Built to Last,* based on a six-year research project conducted at Stanford Business School in the early 1990s, answered the question, What does it take to start and build an enduring great company from the ground up? My research mentor and coauthor Jerry I. Porras and I studied eighteen enduring great companies—institutions that stood the test of time, tracing their founding in some cases back to the 1800s, while becoming the iconic great companies of the late twentieth century. We examined companies like Procter & Gamble (founded in 1837), American Express (founded in 1850), Johnson & Johnson (founded in 1886), and GE (founded in 1892). One of the companies, Citicorp (now Citigroup), was founded in 1812, the same year Napoleon marched into Moscow! The "youngest" companies in the study were Wal-Mart and Sony, which trace their origins back to 1945. Similar to this book, we used direct comparison companies—3M versus Norton, Walt Disney versus Columbia Pictures, Marriott versus Howard Johnson, and so forth—for eighteen paired comparisons. In short, we sought to identify the essential distinctions between great companies and good companies as they endure over decades, even centuries.

When I had the first summer research team assembled for the good-to-great project, I asked, "What should be the role of *Built to Last* in doing this study?"

"I don't think it should play any role," said Brian Bagley. "I didn't join this team to do a derivative piece of work."

"Neither did I," added Alyson Sinclair. "I'm excited about a new project and a new question. It wouldn't be very fulfilling to just fill in the pieces of your other book."

"But wait a minute," I responded. "We spent six years on the previous study. It might be helpful to *build* on our previous work."

"I seem to recall that you got the idea for this study when a McKinsey partner said that *Built to Last* didn't answer the question of how to change a good company into a great one," noted Paul Weissman. "What if the answers *are different?*"

Back and forth, to and fro, the debate continued for a few weeks. Then Stefanie Judd weighed in with the argument that swayed me. "I love the ideas in *Built to Last* and that's what worries me," she said. "I'm afraid that if we start with *BTL* as the frame of reference, we'll just go around in circles, proving our own biases." It became clear that there would be substantially less risk in starting from scratch, setting out to discover what we would, whether it matched previous work or not.

Early in the research, then, we made a very important decision. We decided to conduct the research for *Good to Great* as if *Built to Last* didn't exist. This was the only way to clearly see the key factors in transforming a good company into a great one with minimal bias from previous work. Then we could return to ask, "How, if at all, do the two studies relate?"

Now, five years later, with this book complete, we can stand back to look at the two works in the context of each other. Surveying across the two studies, I offer the following four conclusions:

1. When I consider the enduring great companies from *Built to Last,* I now see substantial evidence that their early leaders followed the good-to-great framework. The only real difference is that they did so as entrepreneurs in small, early-stage enterprises trying to get off the ground, rather than as CEOs trying to transform established companies from good to great.
2. In an ironic twist, I now see *Good to Great* not as a sequel to *Built to Last,* but as a *prequel.* Apply the findings in this book to create sustained great results, as a start-up or an established organization, and then apply the findings in *Built to Last* to go from great results to an enduring great company.

Established Company *or* Start-up	+	*Good to Great* Concepts	→	Sustained Great Results	+	*Built to Last* Concepts	→	Enduring Great Company

3. To make the shift from a company with sustained great results to an enduring great company of iconic stature, apply the central concept from *Built to Last:* Discover your core values and purpose beyond just making money (core ideology) and combine this with the dynamic of preserve the core/stimulate progress.
4. A tremendous resonance exists between the two studies; the ideas from each enrich and inform the ideas in the other. In particular, *Good to Great* answers a fundamental question raised, but not answered, in *Built to Last:* What is the difference between a "good" BHAG (Big Hairy Audacious Goal) and a "bad" BHAG?

GOOD TO GREAT IN THE EARLY STAGES OF BUILT TO LAST

Looking back on the *Built to Last* study, it appears that the enduring great companies did in fact go through a process of buildup to breakthrough, following the good-to-great framework during their formative years.

Consider, for example, the buildup-breakthrough flywheel pattern in the evolution of Wal-Mart. Most people think that Sam Walton just exploded onto the scene with his visionary idea for rural discount retailing, hitting breakthrough almost as a start-up company. But nothing could be further from the truth.

Sam Walton began in 1945 with a single dime store. He didn't open his second store until seven years later. Walton built incrementally, step by step, turn by turn of the flywheel, until the Hedgehog Concept of large discount marts popped out as a natural evolutionary step in the mid-1960s. It took Walton a quarter of a century to grow from that single dime store to a chain of 38 Wal-Marts. Then, from 1970 to 2000, Wal-Mart hit breakthrough momentum and exploded to over 3,000 stores with over $150 billion (yes, billion) in revenues.[2] Just like the story of the chicken jumping out of the egg that we discussed in the flywheel chapter, Wal-Mart had been incubating for decades before the egg cracked open. As Sam Walton himself wrote:

> Somehow over the years people have gotten the impression that Wal-Mart was . . . just this great idea that turned into an overnight success. But . . . it was an outgrowth of everything we'd been doing since [1945]. . . . And like most overnight successes, it was about twenty years in the making.[3]

If there ever was a classic case of buildup leading to a Hedgehog Concept, followed by breakthrough momentum in the flywheel, Wal-Mart is it. The only difference is that Sam Walton followed the model as an entrepreneur building a great company from the ground up, rather than as a CEO transforming an established company from good to great. But it's the same basic idea.[4]

Hewlett-Packard provides another excellent example of the good-to-great ideas at work in the formative stages of a *Built to Last* company. For instance, Bill Hewlett and David Packard's entire founding concept for HP was not what, but *who*—starting with each other. They'd been best friends in graduate school and simply wanted to build a great company together that would attract other people with similar values and standards. The founding minutes of their first meeting on August 23, 1937, begin by stating that they would design, manufacture, and sell products in the electrical engineering fields, very broadly defined. But then those same founding minutes go on to say, "The question of *what* to manufacture was postponed. . . ."[5]

Hewlett and Packard stumbled around for months trying to come up with something, *anything,* that would get the company out of the garage. They considered yacht transmitters, air-conditioning control devices, medical devices, phonograph amplifiers, you name it. They built electronic

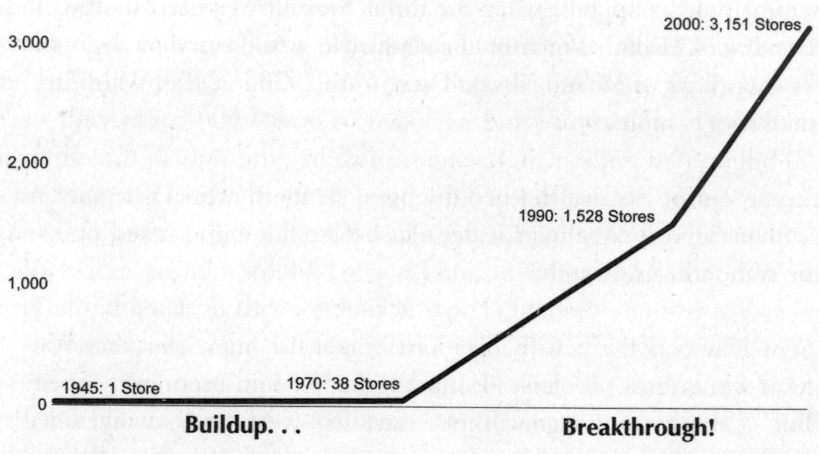

bowling alley sensors, a clock-drive for a telescope, and an electronic shock jiggle machine to help overweight people lose weight. It didn't really matter what the company made in the very early days, as long as it made a technical contribution and would enable Hewlett and Packard to build a company together and with other like-minded people.[6] It was the ultimate "first who . . . then what" start-up.

Later, as Hewlett and Packard scaled up, they stayed true to the guiding principle of "first who." After World War II, even as revenues shrank with the end of their wartime contracts, they hired a whole batch of fabulous people streaming out of government labs, with nothing specific in mind for them to do. Recall Packard's Law, which we cited in chapter 3: "No company can grow revenues consistently faster than its ability to get enough of the right people to implement that growth and still become a great company." Hewlett and Packard lived and breathed this concept and obtained a surplus of great people whenever the opportunity presented itself.

Hewlett and Packard were themselves consummate Level 5 leaders, first as entrepreneurs and later as company builders. Years after HP had established itself as one of the most important technology companies in the world, Hewlett maintained a remarkable personal humility. In 1972, HP vice president Barney Oliver wrote in a recommendation letter to the IEEE Awards Board for the Founders Award:

> While our success has been gratifying, it has not spoiled our founders. Only recently, at an executive council meeting, Hewlett remarked: "Look, we've grown because the industry grew. We were lucky enough to be sitting on the nose when the rocket took off. We don't deserve a damn bit of credit." After a moment's silence, while everyone digested this humbling comment, Packard said: "Well, Bill, at least we didn't louse it up completely."[7]

Shortly before his death, I had the opportunity to meet Dave Packard. Despite being one of Silicon Valley's first self-made billionaires, he lived in the same small house that he and his wife built for themselves in 1957, overlooking a simple orchard. The tiny kitchen, with its dated linoleum, and the simply furnished living room bespoke a man who needed no material symbols to proclaim "I'm a billionaire. I'm important. I'm successful." "His idea of a good time," said Bill Terry, who worked with Packard for thirty-six years, "was to get some of his friends together to string some barbed wire."[8] Packard bequeathed his $5.6 billion estate to a charitable foundation and, upon his death, his family created a eulogy pamphlet, with a photo of him sitting on a tractor in farming clothes. The caption made no reference to his stature as one of the great industrialists of the twentieth century.[9] It simply read: "David Packard, 1912–1996, Rancher, etc." Level 5, indeed.

CORE IDEOLOGY: THE EXTRA DIMENSION OF ENDURING GREATNESS

During our interview with Bill Hewlett, we asked him what he was most proud of in his long career. "As I look back on my life's work," he said, "I'm probably most proud of having helped create a company that by virtue of its values, practices, and success has had a tremendous impact on the way companies are managed around the world."[10] The "HP Way," as it became known, reflected a deeply held set of core values that distinguished the company more than any of its products. These values included technical contribution, respect for the individual, responsibility to the communities in which the company operates, and a deeply held belief that profit is *not* the fundamental goal of a company. These principles, while fairly standard today, were radical and progressive in the 1950s. David Packard said of businessmen from those days, "While they were reasonably polite in their disagreement, it was quite evident that they firmly believed that I was not one of *them,* and obviously not qualified to manage an important enterprise."[11]

Hewlett and Packard exemplify a key "extra dimension" that helped elevate their company to the elite status of an enduring great company, a vital dimension for making the transition from good to great to built to last. That extra dimension is a guiding philosophy or a "core ideology," which consists of core values and a core purpose (reason for being beyond just making money). These resemble the principles in the Declaration of Independence ("We hold these truths to be self-evident")—never perfectly followed, but always present as an inspiring standard and an answer to the question of *why* it is important that we exist.

> Enduring great companies don't exist merely to deliver returns to shareholders. Indeed, in a truly great company, profits and cash flow become like blood and water to a healthy body: They are absolutely essential for life, but they are not the very *point* of life.

We wrote in *Built to Last* about Merck's decision to develop and distribute a drug that cured river blindness. This painful disease afflicted over a million people with parasitic worms that swarm through the eyes to cause blindness. Because those who had the disease—tribal people in remote places like the Amazon—had no money, Merck initiated the creation of an independent distribution system to get the drug to remote villages and gave the drug away free to millions of people around the world.[12]

To be clear, Merck is not a charity organization, nor does it view itself as such. Indeed, it has consistently outperformed the market as a highly profitable company, growing to nearly $6 billion in profits and beating the market by over ten times from 1946 to 2000. Yet, despite its remarkable financial performance, Merck does not view its ultimate reason for being as making money. In 1950, George Merck 2d, son of the founder, set forth his company's philosophy:

> We try to remember that medicine is for the patient. . . . It is not for the profits. The profits follow, and if we have remembered that, they have never failed to appear. The better we have remembered it, the larger they have been.[13]

An important caveat to the concept of core values is that there are no specific "right" core values for becoming an enduring great company. No matter what core value you propose, we found an enduring great company that does not have that specific core value. A company need not have passion for its customers (Sony didn't), or respect for the individual (Disney didn't), or quality (Wal-Mart didn't), or social responsibility (Ford didn't) in order to become enduring and great. This was one of the most paradoxical findings from *Built to Last—core values are essential for enduring greatness, but it doesn't seem to matter what those core values are.* The point is not *what* core values you have, but *that* you have core values at all, that you know what they are, that you build them explicitly into the organization, and that you preserve them over time.

This notion of preserving your core ideology is a central feature of enduring great companies. The obvious question is, How do you preserve the core and yet adapt to a changing world? The answer: Embrace the key concept of preserve the core/stimulate progress.

> Enduring great companies preserve their core values and purpose while their business strategies and operating practices endlessly adapt to a changing world. This is the magical combination of "preserve the core and stimulate progress."

The story of Walt Disney exemplifies this duality. In 1923, an energetic twenty-one-year-old animator moved from Kansas City to Los Angeles and tried to get a job in the movie business. No film company would hire him, so he used his meager savings to rent a camera, set up a studio in his uncle's garage, and begin making animated cartoons. In 1934, Mr. Disney took the bold step, never before taken, to create successful full-length animated feature films, including *Snow White, Pinocchio, Fantasia,* and *Bambi.* In the 1950s, Disney moved into television with the *Mickey Mouse Club.* Also in the 1950s, Walt Disney paid a fateful visit to a number of amusement parks and came away disgusted, calling them "dirty, phony places, run by tough-looking people."[14] He decided that Disney could build something much better, perhaps even *the best in the world,* and the company launched a whole new business in theme parks, first with Disneyland and later with Walt Disney World and EPCOT Center.

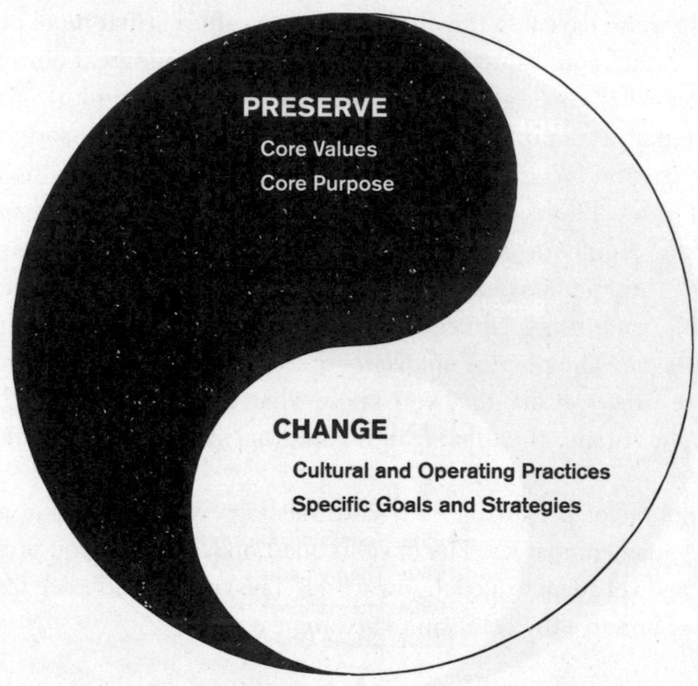

Over time, Disney theme parks have become a cornerstone experience for many families from all over the world.

Throughout all these dramatic changes—from cartoons to full-length feature animation, from the *Mickey Mouse Club* to Disney World—the company held firmly to a consistent set of core values that included passionate belief in creative imagination, fanatic attention to detail, abhorrence of cynicism, and preservation of the "Disney Magic." Mr. Disney also instilled a remarkable constancy of purpose that permeated every new Disney venture—namely, to bring happiness to millions, especially children. This purpose cut across national borders and has endured through time. When my wife and I visited Israel in 1995, we met the man who brought Disney products to the Middle East. "The whole idea," he told us with pride, "is to bring a smile to a child's face. That's really important here, where there aren't enough smiles on the children." Walt Disney provides a classic case of preserve the core and stimulate progress, holding a core ideology fixed while changing strategies and practices over time, and its adherence to this principle is the fundamental reason why it has endured as a great company.

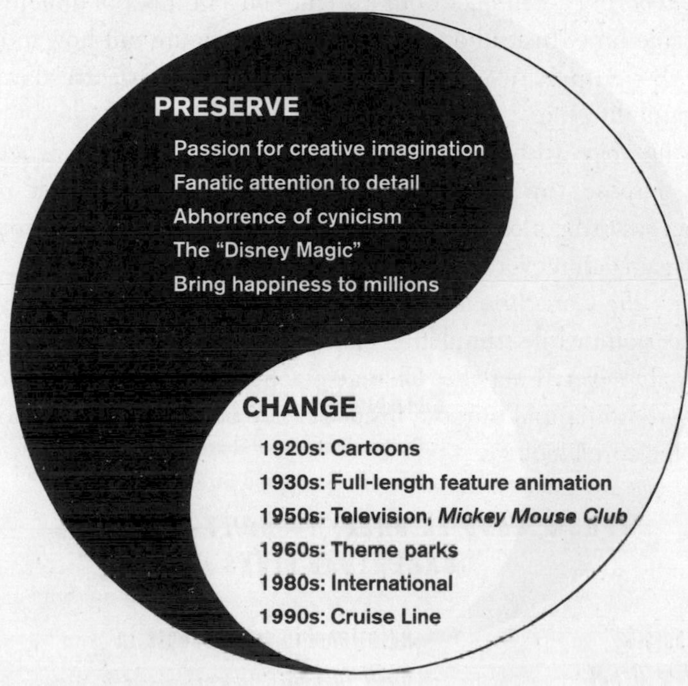

Preserve the Core/Stimulate Progress at Walt Disney Company, 1920s–1990s

GOOD BHAGS, BAD BHAGS, AND OTHER CONCEPTUAL LINKS

In the table on page 198, I've outlined a sketch of conceptual links between the two studies. As a general pattern, the *Good-to-Great* ideas appear to lay the groundwork for the ultimate success of the *Built to Last* ideas. I like to think of *Good to Great* as providing the core ideas for *getting* a flywheel turning from buildup through breakthrough, while *Built to Last* outlines the core ideas for *keeping* a flywheel accelerating long into the future and elevating a company to iconic stature. You will notice in examining the table that each of the *Good-to-Great* findings enables all four of the key ideas from *Built to Last*. To briefly review, those four key ideas are:

1. *Clock Building, Not Time Telling.* Build an organization that can endure and adapt through multiple generations of leaders and multiple product life cycles; the exact opposite of being built around a single great leader or a single great idea.

2. *Genius of AND.* Embrace both extremes on a number of dimensions at the same time. Instead of choosing A *OR* B, figure out how to have A *AND* B—purpose *AND* profit, continuity *AND* change, freedom *AND* responsibility, etc.
3. *Core Ideology.* Instill core values (essential and enduring tenets) and core purpose (fundamental reason for being beyond just making money) as principles to guide decisions and inspire people throughout the organization over a long period of time.
4. *Preserve the Core/Stimulate Progress.* Preserve the core ideology as an anchor point while stimulating change, improvement, innovation, and renewal in everything else. Change practices and strategies while holding core values and purpose fixed. Set and achieve BHAGs consistent with the core ideology.

FROM *GOOD TO GREAT* TO *BUILT TO LAST*: CONCEPTUAL LINKS

Concepts in *Good to Great*	Relationship to Concepts in *Built to Last**
Level 5 Leadership	***Clock Building, Not Time Telling:*** Level 5 leaders build a company that can tick along without them, rather than feeding their egos by becoming indispensable.
	Genius of AND: Personal humility *AND* professional will.
	Core Ideology: Level 5 leaders are ambitious for the company and what it stands for; they have a sense of purpose beyond their own success.
	Preserve the Core/Stimulate Progress: Level 5 leaders are relentless in stimulating progress toward tangible results and achievement, even if it means firing their brothers.

Concepts in *Good to Great*	Relationship to Concepts in *Built to Last**
First Who . . . Then What	***Clock Building, Not Time Telling:*** Practicing "first who" is clock building; practicing "first what" (setting strategy first) is time telling.
	Genius of AND: Get the right people on the bus *AND* the wrong people off the bus.
	Core Ideology: Practicing "first who" means selecting people more on their fit with the core values and purpose than on their skills and knowledge.
	Preserve the Core/Stimulate Progress: Practicing "first who" means a bias for promoting from within, which reinforces the core values.
Confront the Brutal Facts (Stockdale Paradox)	***Clock Building, Not Time Telling:*** Creating a climate where the truth is heard is clock building, especially if you create red flag mechanisms.
	Genius of AND: Confront the brutal facts of your current reality *AND* retain unwavering faith that you will prevail in the end—the *Stockdale Paradox.*
	Core Ideology: Confronting the brutal facts clarifies the values an organization truly holds as *core* versus those that it would like to hold as core.
	Preserve the Core/Stimulate Progress: Brutal facts clarify what *must* be done to stimulate progress.

Concepts in *Good to Great*	Relationship to Concepts in *Built to Last**
Hedgehog Concept (The Three Circles)	***Clock Building, Not Time Telling:*** The Council mechanism is consummate clock building.
	Genius of AND: Deep understanding *AND* incredible simplicity.
	Core Ideology: The "what you are passionate about" circle overlaps nicely with core values and purpose. Only those values about which you are so passionate that you would never, under any conditions, give them up qualify as truly *core.*
	Preserve the Core/Stimulate Progress: Good BHAGs flow from understanding; bad BHAGs flow from bravado. Great BHAGs sit right smack in the middle of the three circles.
Culture of Discipline	***Clock Building, Not Time Telling:*** Operating through sheer force of personality as a disciplinarian is time telling; building an enduring culture of discipline is clock building.
	Genius of AND: Freedom *AND* responsibility.
	Core Ideology: A culture of discipline ejects those who do not share the values and standards of an organization.
	Preserve the Core/Stimulate Progress: When you have a culture of discipline, you can give people more freedom to experiment and find their own best path to results.

Concepts in *Good to Great*	Relationship to Concepts in *Built to Last**
Technology Accelerators	***Clock Building, Not Time Telling:*** Technology accelerators are a key part of the clock.
	Genius of AND: Shun technology fads *AND* pioneer the application of technology.
	Core Ideology: In a great company, technology is subservient to core values, not the other way around.
	Preserve the Core/Stimulate Progress: The right technologies accelerate momentum in the flywheel, toward the achievement of BHAGs.
Flywheel, Not Doom Loop	***Clock Building, Not Time Telling:*** The flywheel effect creates the sustained building of momentum, and does not depend on the presence of a charismatic visionary to motivate people.
	Genius of AND: Evolutionary, incremental process *AND* revolutionary, dramatic results.
	Core Ideology: The doom loop makes it almost impossible to instill core values and purpose, as people chronically wonder, "Who are we? What do we stand for?"
	Preserve the Core/Stimulate Progress: The smooth consistency of the flywheel and the cumulative building of momentum to a point of breakthrough create the perfect conditions for instilling core values while stimulating change and progress.

* See *Built to Last: Successful Habits of Visionary Companies*, Collins and Porras, HarperBusiness, 1994.

I am not going to belabor all the links from the above table, but I would like to highlight one particularly powerful link: the connection between BHAGs and the three circles of the Hedgehog Concept. In *Built to Last,* we identified BHAGs as a key way to stimulate progress while preserving the core. A BHAG (pronounced *bee-hag,* short for "Big Hairy Audacious Goal") is a huge and daunting goal—like a big mountain to climb. It is clear, compelling, and people "get it" right away. A BHAG serves as a unifying focal point of effort, galvanizing people and creating team spirit as people strive toward a finish line. Like the 1960s NASA moon mission, a BHAG captures the imagination and grabs people in the gut.

However, as exciting as BHAGs are, we left a vital question unanswered. *What is the difference between a bad BHAG and a good BHAG?* Swimming from Australia to New Zealand would be a BHAG for me, but it would also kill me! We can now offer an answer to that question, drawing directly from the study of good-to-great companies.

> Bad BHAGs, it turns out, are set with *bravado;* good BHAGs are set with *understanding.* Indeed, when you combine quiet understanding of the three circles with the audacity of a BHAG, you get a powerful, almost magical mix.

A superb example of this comes from Boeing in the 1950s. Until the early 1950s, Boeing focused on building huge flying machines for the military—the B-17 Flying Fortress, the B-29 Superfortress, and the B-52 intercontinental jet bomber Stratofortress.[15] However, Boeing had virtually no presence in the commercial aircraft market, and the airlines showed no interest in buying aircraft from Boeing. ("You make great bombers up there in Seattle. Why don't you just stick with that," they said in response to Boeing's inquiries.) Today, we take for granted that most air travel takes place on Boeing jets, but in 1952, almost no one outside the military flew on Boeing.[16]

Wisely, through the 1940s, Boeing had stayed away from the commercial sphere, an arena in which McDonnell Douglas had vastly superior abilities in the smaller, propeller-driven planes that composed the commercial fleet.[17] In the early 1950s, however, Boeing saw an opportunity to leapfrog McDonnell Douglas by marrying its experience with large air-

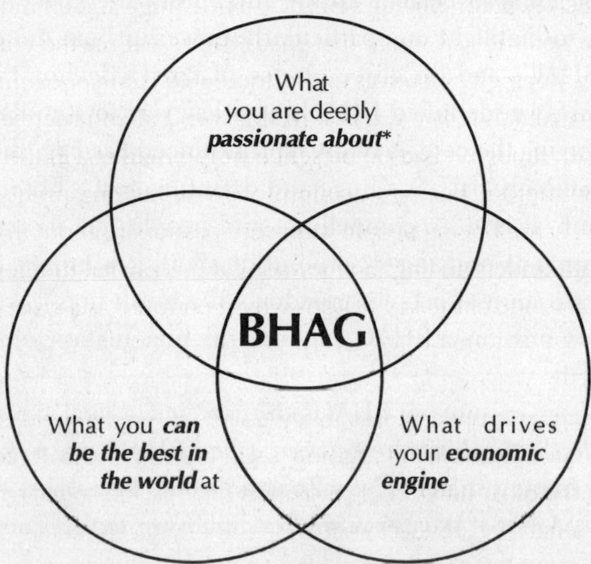

craft to its understanding of jet engines. Led by a Level 5 leader named Bill Allen, Boeing executives debated the wisdom of moving into the commercial sphere. They came to understand that, whereas Boeing could not have been the best commercial plane maker *a decade earlier*, the cumulative experience in jets and big planes they had gained from military contracts now made such a dream possible. They also came to see that the economics of commercial aircraft would be vastly superior to the military market and—of no small importance—they were just flat-out turned on by the whole idea of building a commercial jet.

So, in 1952, Bill Allen and his team made the decision to spend a quarter of the company's entire net worth to build a prototype jet that could be used for commercial aviation.[18] They built the 707 and launched Boeing on a bid to become the leading commercial aviation company in the world. Three decades later, after producing five of the most successful commercial jets in history (the 707, 727, 737, 747, and 757), Boeing stood as the absolute, unquestioned greatest company in the commercial airplane industry, worldwide.[19] Not until the late 1990s would Boeing's number one position be seriously challenged, and it would take a government consortium in the form of Airbus to do it.[20]

Here is the key point: Boeing's BHAG, while huge and daunting, was not any random goal. It was a goal that made sense within the context of the three circles. Boeing's executives understood with calm, equanimity that (1) the company *could become* the best in the world at commercial jet manufacturing even though it had no presence in the market, (2) the shift would significantly improve Boeing's economics by increasing profit per aircraft model, and (3) the Boeing people were very passionate about the idea. Boeing acted with understanding, not bravado, at this pivotal moment in its history, and that is one of the key reasons why it endured as a great company.

> The Boeing case underscores a key point: To remain great over time requires, on the one hand, staying squarely within the three circles while, on the other hand, being willing to change the specific *manifestation* of what's inside the three circles at any given moment. Boeing in 1952 never left the three circles or abandoned its core ideology, but it created an exciting new BHAG and adjusted its Hedgehog Concept to include commercial aircraft.

The three circle/BHAG framework provides one powerful example of how the ideas from the two studies link together, and I'd like to offer it here as a practical tool for creating this link within your own organization. Yet it alone will not make your company great and lasting. To create an enduring great company requires *all* the key concepts from both studies, tied together and applied consistently over time. *Furthermore, if you ever stop doing any one of the key ideas, your organization will inevitably slide backward toward mediocrity.* Remember, it is much easier to become great than to remain great. Ultimately, the consistent application of both studies, one building upon the other, gives the best chance for creating greatness that lasts.

WHY GREATNESS?

During a break at a seminar that I gave to a group of my ex-students from Stanford, one came up to me, brow furrowed. "Maybe I'm just not ambitious enough," he said. "But I don't really want to build a huge company. Is there something wrong with that?"

"Not at all," I replied. "Greatness doesn't depend on size." I then told him about Sina Simantob, who runs the building where I have my research laboratory. Sina has created a truly great institution. It's an old 1892 redbrick school building that has been renovated into the most extraordinary space, decorated and maintained with tremendous attention to detail, bordering on perfection. By one definition of results—attracting the most interesting people in Boulder, setting a standard that other local buildings measure themselves against, and generating the highest profit per foot of space—his small enterprise is truly a great institution in my hometown. Simantob has never defined greatness by size, and there is no reason for him to.

The student paused for a moment, then said: "Okay, I accept that I don't need to build a big company in order to have a great company. But even so, why should I try to build a great company? What if I just want to be successful?"

The question brought me up short. This was not a lazy person asking; he'd started his own business as a young man, put himself through law school, and after graduate school became a driven entrepreneur. He has remarkable energy, an intense and infectious enthusiasm. Of all the students I've known over the years, he is one that I have little doubt will be enormously successful. Yet he questions the whole idea of trying to build something great and lasting.

I can offer two answers.

First, I believe that it is no harder to build something great than to build something good. It might be statistically more *rare* to reach greatness, but it does not require more suffering than perpetuating mediocrity. Indeed, if some of the comparison companies in our study are any indication, it involves *less* suffering, and perhaps even less work. The beauty and power of the research findings is that they can radically simplify our lives while increasing our effectiveness. There is great solace in the simple fact of *clarity*—about what is vital, and what is not.

> Indeed, the point of this entire book is *not* that we should "add" these findings to what we are already doing and make ourselves even more overworked. No, the point is to realize that much of what we're doing is at best a waste of energy. If we organized the majority of our work time around applying these principles, and pretty much ignored or stopped doing everything else, our lives would be simpler and our results vastly improved.

Let me illustrate this point with a nonbusiness example, the last story of the book. The coaching staff of a high school cross-country running team recently got together for dinner after winning its second state championship in two years. The program had been transformed in the previous five years from good (top twenty in the state) to great (consistent contenders for the state championship, on both the boys' and girls' teams).

"I don't get it," said one of the coaches. "Why are we so successful? We don't work any harder than other teams. And what we do is just so simple. Why does it work?"

He was referring to the Hedgehog Concept of the program, captured in the simple statement: We run best at the end. We run best at the end of workouts. We run best at the end of races. And we run best at the end of the season, when it counts the most. Everything is geared to this simple idea, and the coaching staff knows how to create this effect better than any other team in the state. For example, they place a coach at the 2-mile mark (of a 3.1-mile race) to collect data as the runners go past. But unlike most teams, which collect *time* splits (minutes-per-mile running pace), this team collects *place* splits (what place the runners are in as they go by). Then the coaches calculate not how fast the runners go, but *how many competitors they pass at the end of the race*, from mile 2 to the finish. They then use this data to award "head bones" after each race. (Head bones are beads in the shape of shrunken skulls, which the kids make into necklaces and bracelets, symbolizing their vanquished competitors.) The kids learn how to pace themselves, and race with confidence: "We run best at the end," they think at the end of a hard race. "So, if I'm hurting bad, then my competitors must hurt a whole lot worse!"

Of equal importance is what they don't waste energy on. For example, when the head coach took over the program, she found herself burdened with expectations to do "fun programs" and "rah-rah stuff" to motivate the kids and keep them interested—parties, and special trips, and shopping adventures to Nike outlets, and inspirational speeches. She quickly put an end to nearly all that distracting (and time-consuming) activity. "Look," she said, "this program will be built on the idea that *running* is fun, racing is fun, improving is fun, and winning is fun. If you're not passionate about what we do here, then go find something else to do." The result: The number of kids in the program nearly tripled in five years, from thirty to eighty-two.

Before the boys' team won the first-ever state cross-country championship in the school's history, she didn't explicitly set the goal or try to "motivate" the kids toward it. Instead, she let the kids gain momentum, seeing for themselves—race by race, week by week—that they could beat anyone in the state. Then, one day out on a training run, one boy said to his teammates, "Hey, I think we could win state." "Yeah, I think so, too," said another. Everyone kept running, the goal quietly understood. The coaching staff never once mentioned the state championship idea until the kids saw for themselves that they could do it.

This created the strongest culture of discipline possible, as the seven varsity runners felt personally responsible for winning state—a commitment made not to the coaches, *but to each other*. One team member even called all of his teammates the night before the state race, just to make sure they were all getting ready for bed early. (No need for the coaches to be disciplinarians on this team.) Hammering through the last mile, passing competitors ("We run best at the end!"), each kid hurt, but knew it would hurt a lot more if he had to look his teammates in the eyes as the only one who failed to come through. No one failed, and the team beat every other team at the state meet by a large margin.

The head coach began rebuilding the whole program around the idea of "first who." One of the assistant coaches is a 300-pound ex-shot-putter (hardly the image of a lean distance runner), but he is without question the right who: He shares the values and has the traits needed to help build a great team. As the program built momentum, it attracted more kids and more great coaches. People want to be part of this spinning flywheel; they want to be part of a championship team; they want to be part of a first-class culture. When the cross-country team posts yet another championship banner in the gym, more kids sign up, the gene pool deepens, the team gets faster, which produces more championships, which attracts more kids, which creates even faster teams, and so forth and so on, in the infectious flywheel effect.

Are these coaches suffering more than other teams to create a great program? Are they working harder? No! In fact, all the assistant coaches have full-time professional jobs outside of coaching—engineers, computer technicians, teachers—and they work for essentially no pay, carving precious time out of their busy lives to be part of building a great program. They're just focusing on the right things, and not the wrong things. They're doing virtually everything we write about in this book, within their specific situation, and not wasting time on anything that doesn't fit. Simple, clean, straightforward, elegant—and a heck of a lot of fun.

The point of this story is that these ideas work. When you apply them in any situation, they make your life and your experience better, while improving results. And along the way, you just might make what you're building great. So, I ask again: If it's no harder (given these ideas), the results better, and the process so much more fun—well, *why wouldn't you go for greatness?*

To be clear, I am *not* suggesting that going from good to great is *easy*, or that every organization will successfully make the shift. By definition, it is not possible for everyone to be above average. But I *am* asserting that those who strive to turn good into great find the process no more painful or exhausting than those who settle for just letting things wallow along in mind-numbing mediocrity. Yes, turning good into great takes energy, but the building of momentum adds more energy back into the pool than it takes out. Conversely, perpetuating mediocrity is an inherently depressing process and drains much more energy out of the pool than it puts back in.

But there is a second answer to the question of why greatness, one that is at the very heart of what motivated us to undertake this huge project in the first place: the search for meaning, or more precisely, the search for meaningful work.

I asked the head coach of the cross-country program why she felt compelled to make it great. She paused before answering. "That's a really good question." Long pause. "It's really hard to answer." More pause. "I guess . . . it's because I really care about what we're doing. I believe in running and the impact it can make on these kids' lives. I want them to have a great experience, and to have the experience of being part of something absolutely first class."

Now for the interesting twist: The coach has an MBA from an elite business school and is a Phi Beta Kappa graduate in economics, having won the prize for the best undergraduate honors thesis at one of the most selective universities in the world. She found, however, that most of what her classmates went on to do—investment banking on Wall Street, starting Internet companies, management consulting, working for IBM, or whatever—held no meaning for her. She just didn't care enough about those endeavors to *want* to make them great. For her, those jobs held no meaningful purpose. And so she made the decision to search for meaningful work—work about which she would have such passion that the question, Why try for greatness? would seem almost tautological. If you're doing something you care that much about, and you believe in its purpose deeply enough, then it is impossible to imagine *not* trying to make it great. It's just a given.

I've tried to imagine the Level 5 leaders of the companies we've studied answering the question "Why greatness?" Of course, most would say: "We're not great—we could be so much better." But pushed to answer, "Why try for greatness?" I believe they would respond much like the cross-country coach. They're doing something they really care about, about which they have great passion. Like Bill Hewlett, they might care first and foremost about creating a company that by virtue of its values and success has a tremendous impact on the way companies are managed around the world. Or like Ken Iverson, they might feel a crusader's purpose to obliterate the oppressive class hierarchies that cause degradation of both labor and management. Or like Darwin Smith at Kimberly-Clark, they might derive a tremendous sense of purpose from the inner quest for excellence itself, being driven from within to make anything they touch the best it can be. Or perhaps like Lyle Everingham at Kroger or Cork Walgreen at Walgreens, they might have grown up in the business and just really love it. You don't need to have some grand existential reason for why you love what you're doing or to care deeply about your work (although you might). All that matters is that you do love it and that you do care.

So, the question of Why greatness? is almost a nonsense question. If you're engaged in work that you love and care about, for whatever reason, then the question needs no answer. The question is not why, but *how*.

Indeed, the real question is not, "Why greatness?" but "What work makes you feel compelled to try to create greatness?" If you have to ask the question, "Why should we try to make it great? Isn't success enough?" then you're probably engaged in the wrong line of work.

Perhaps your quest to be part of building something great will not fall in your business life. But find it somewhere. If not in corporate life, then perhaps in making your church great. If not there, then perhaps a nonprofit, or a community organization, or a class you teach. Get involved in something that you care so much about that you want to make it the greatest it can possibly be, not because of what you will get, but just because it can be done.

When you do this, you will start to grow, inevitably, toward becoming a Level 5 leader. Early in the book, we wondered about how to become

Level 5, and we suggested that you start by practicing the rest of the findings. But under what conditions will you have the drive and discipline to fully practice the other findings? Perhaps it is when you care deeply enough about the work in which you are engaged, and when your responsibilities line up with your own personal three circles.

When all these pieces come together, not only does your work move toward greatness, but so does your life. For, in the end, it is impossible to have a great life unless it is a meaningful life. And it is very difficult to have a meaningful life without meaningful work. Perhaps, then, you might gain that rare tranquillity that comes from knowing that you've had a hand in creating something of intrinsic excellence that makes a contribution. Indeed, you might even gain that deepest of all satisfactions: knowing that your short time here on this earth has been well spent, and that it mattered.

EPILOGUE

FREQUENTLY ASKED QUESTIONS

Q: Did you originally identify more than eleven good-to-great possibilities and, if so, what good-to-great examples did not make it into the study?

The eleven good-to-great companies were the *only* examples from our initial universe of Fortune 500 companies that met all the criteria for entrance into the study; they do not represent a sample. (See Appendix 1.A for the selection process we used.) The fact that we studied the *total* set of companies that met our criteria should increase our confidence in the findings. We do not need to worry that a second set of companies in the Fortune 500 went from good to great—not by our criteria, anyway—by other methods.

Q: Why did only eleven companies make the cut?

There are three principal reasons. First, we used a *very* tough standard (three times the market over fifteen years) as our metric of great results. Second, the fifteen-year sustainability requirement is difficult to meet. Many companies show a sharp rise for five or ten years with a hit product or charismatic leader, but few companies manage to achieve fifteen years. Third, we were looking for a very specific pattern: sustained great results *preceded by* a sustained period of average results (or worse). Great companies are easy to find, but *good-to-great* companies are much more rare. When you add all these factors together, it is not surprising that we identified only eleven examples.

I would like to stress, however, that the "only eleven" finding should not be discouraging. We had to set a cutoff and we chose a very tough one. If we had set a slightly lower hurdle—say, 2.5 times the market or ten years of sustainability—then many more companies would have qualified. After completing the research, I am convinced that many organizations can make the journey from good to great if they apply the lessons in this book. The problem is not the statistical odds; the problem is that people are squandering their time and resources on the wrong things.

Q: What about statistical significance, given that only eleven companies made the final cut as good-to-great examples and the total study size is twenty-eight companies (with comparisons)?

We engaged two leading professors to help us resolve this question, one statistician and one applied mathematician. The statistician, Jeffrey T. Luftig at the

University of Colorado, looked at our dilemma and concluded that we do *not* have a statistics problem, pointing out that the concept of "statistical significance" applies only when sampling of data is involved. "Look, you didn't *sample* companies," he said. "You did a very purposeful *selection* and found the eleven companies from the Fortune 500 that met your criteria. When you put these eleven against the seventeen comparison companies, the probabilities that the concepts in your framework appear by random chance are essentially zero." When we asked University of Colorado applied mathematics professor William P. Briggs to examine our research method, he framed the question thus: What is the probability of finding by chance a group of eleven companies, all of whose members display the primary traits you discovered while the direct comparisons do not possess those traits? He concluded that the probability is less than 1 in 17 million. There is virtually no chance that we simply found eleven random events that just happened to show the good-to-great pattern we were looking for. We can conclude with confidence that the traits we found are strongly associated with transformations from good to great.

Q: Why did you limit your research to publicly traded corporations?

Publicly traded corporations have two advantages for research: a widely agreed upon definition of results (so we can rigorously select a study set) and a plethora of easily accessible data. Privately held corporations have limited information available, which would be particularly problematic with comparison companies. The beauty of publicly traded companies is that we don't need their cooperation to obtain data. Whether they like it or not, vast amounts of information about them are a matter of public record.

Q: Why did you limit your research to U.S. corporations?

We concluded that rigor in selection outweighed the benefits of an international study set. The absence of apples-to-apples stock return data from non-U.S. exchanges would undermine the consistency of our selection process. The comparative research process eliminates contextual "noise" (similar companies, industries, sizes, ages, and so forth) and gives us much greater confidence in the fundamental nature of our findings than having a geographically diverse study set. Nonetheless, I suspect that our findings will prove useful across geographies. A number of the companies in our study are global enterprises and the same concepts applied wherever they did business. Also, I believe that much of what we found—Level 5 leadership and the flywheel, for instance—will be harder to swallow for *Americans* than for people from other cultures.

Q: Why don't any high-technology companies appear in the study set?

Most technology companies were eliminated from consideration because they are not old enough to show the good-to-great pattern. We required at least thirty years of history to consider a company for the study (fifteen years of good results followed by fifteen years of great results). Of the technology companies that *did* have more than thirty years of history, none showed the specific good-to-great pattern we were looking for. Intel, for example, never had a fifteen-year period of only good performance; Intel has always been great. If this study were to be repeated in ten or twenty years, I would fully expect that high-technology companies would make the list.

Q: How does *Good to Great* apply to companies that are *already* great?

I suggest that they use both *Good to Great* and *Built to Last* to help them better understand *why* they are great, so that they can keep doing the right things. As Robert Burgelman, one of my favorite professors from Stanford Business School, taught me years ago, "The single biggest danger in business and life, other than outright failure, is to be successful without being resolutely clear about *why* you are successful in the first place."

Q: How do you explain recent difficulties at some of the good-to-great companies?

Every company—no matter how great—faces difficult times. There are no enduring great companies that have a perfect, unblemished record. They *all* have ups and downs. The critical factor is not the absence of difficulty but the ability to bounce back and emerge stronger.

Furthermore, if any company ceases to practice all of the findings, it will eventually slide backward. It is not any one variable in isolation that makes a company great; it is the combination of all of the pieces working together in an integrated package *consistently and over time.* Two current cases illustrate this point.

One current case for concern is Gillette, which produced eighteen years of exceptional performance—rising to over 9 times the market from 1980 to 1998—but stumbled in 1999. We believe the principal source of this difficulty lies in Gillette's need for greater discipline in sticking to businesses that fit squarely inside the three circles of its Hedgehog Concept. Of even greater concern is the clamoring from industry analysts that Gillette needs a charismatic CEO from outside the company to come in and shake things up. If Gillette brings in a Level 4 leader, then the probability that Gillette will prove to be an *enduring* great company will diminish considerably.

Another troubling case is Nucor, which hit its peak in 1994 at fourteen times the market, then fell off considerably as it experienced management turmoil in the wake of Ken Iverson's retirement. Iverson's chosen successor

Will Gillette Go from Good to Great to Built to Last?

Ratio of Cumulative Stock Returns to General Market, 1927 – 2000

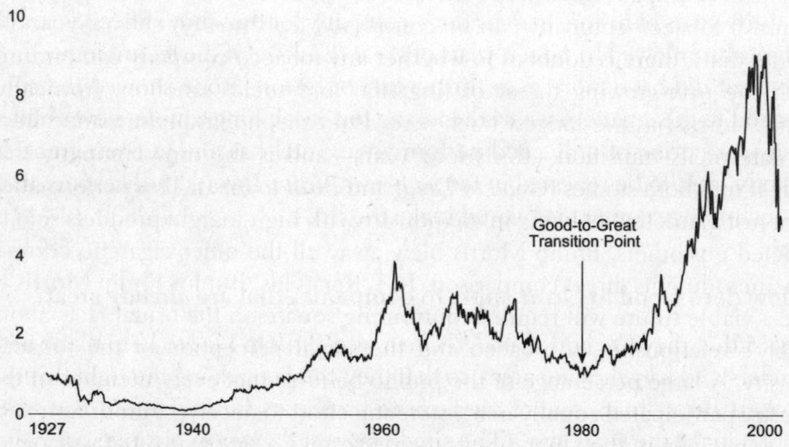

lasted only a short time in the job, before being ousted in an ugly executive-suite battle. One of the architects of this boardroom coup indicated in the *Charlotte News and Observer* (June 11, 1999, page D1) that Iverson had fallen from Level 5 leadership in his old age and had begun to display more egocentric Level 4 traits. "In his heyday, Ken was a giant of a man," he said, "but he wanted to take this company to the grave with him." Iverson tells a different story, arguing that the real problem is current management's desire to diversify Nucor away from its Hedgehog Concept. "Iverson just shakes his head," wrote the *News and Observer*, "saying it was to get away from diversification that Nucor became a narrowly focused steel products company in the first place." Whatever the case—loss of Level 5 leadership or straying from the Hedgehog Concept, or both—the future of Nucor as a great company remains uncertain at the time of this writing.

That being said, it is worth noting that most of the good-to-great companies are still going strong at the time of this writing. Seven of the eleven companies have thus far generated over twenty years of extraordinary performance from their transition dates, with the median of the entire group being *twenty-four years* of exceptional results—a remarkable record by any measure.

Q: How do you reconcile Philip Morris as a "great" company with the fact that it sells tobacco?

Perhaps no company anywhere generates as much antipathy as Philip Morris. Even if a tobacco company can be considered truly great (and many would dispute that), there is doubt as to whether any tobacco company can endure, given the ever-growing threat of litigation and social sanction. Ironically, Philip Morris has the longest track record of exceptional performance from the date of its transition—thirty-four years—and is the only company that made it into both studies (*Good to Great* and *Built to Last*). This performance is not just a function of being in an industry with high-margin products sold to addicted customers. Philip Morris blew away all the other cigarette companies, including its direct comparison, R. J. Reynolds. But for Philip Morris to have a viable future will require confronting square-on the brutal facts about society's relationship to tobacco and the social perception of the tobacco industry. A large percentage of the public believes that every member of the industry participated equally in a systematic effort to deceive. Fair or not, people—especially in the United States—can forgive a lot of sins, but will never forget or forgive feeling lied to.

Whatever one's personal feelings about the tobacco industry (and there was a wide range of feelings on the research team and some very heated debates), having Philip Morris in both *Good to Great* and *Built to Last* has proved very instructive. It has taught me that it is not the *content* of a company's values that correlates with performance, but the *strength of conviction* with which it holds those values, whatever they might be. This is one of those findings that I find difficult to swallow, but that are completely supported by the data. (For further discussion of this topic, see chapter 3 of *Built to Last*, pages 65–71.)

Q: Can a company have a Hedgehog Concept *and* have a highly diverse business portfolio?

Our study strongly suggests that highly diversified firms and conglomerates will rarely produce sustained great results. One obvious exception to this is GE, but we can explain this case by suggesting that GE has a very unusual and subtle Hedgehog Concept that unifies its agglomeration of enterprises. What can GE do better than any company in the world? Develop first-rate general managers. In our view, that is the essence of GE's Hedgehog Concept. And what would be GE's economic denominator? Profit per top-quartile management talent. Think about it this way: You have two business opportunities, both that might generate $X million in profits. But suppose one of those businesses would drain three times the amount of top-quartile management talent to achieve those profits as the other business. The one that drains less management talent would fit with the Hedgehog Concept and the other would not. Finally, what does GE pride itself on more than anything else? Having the best set of general managers in the world. This is their *true* passion—more than lightbulbs, jet engines, or television programming. GE's Hedgehog Concept, properly conceived, enables the company to operate in a diverse set of businesses yet remain squarely focused on the intersection of the three circles.

Q: What is the role of the board of directors in a transformation from good to great?

First, boards play a key role in picking Level 5 leaders. The recent spate of boards enamored with charismatic CEOs, especially "rock star" celebrity types, is one of the most damaging trends for the long-term health of companies. Boards should familiarize themselves with the characteristics of Level 5 leadership and install such leaders into positions of responsibility. Second, boards at corporations should distinguish between share *value* and share *price*. Boards have no responsibility to a large chunk of the people who own company shares at any given moment, namely the share*flippers;* they should refocus their energies on creating great companies that build value for the share*holders*. Managing the stock for anything less than a five-to-ten-year horizon confuses price and value and is irresponsible to shareholders. For a superb look at the board's role in taking a company from good to great, I recommend the book *Resisting Hostile Takeovers* by Rita Ricardo-Campbell (Praeger Publishers, 1997). Ms. Ricardo-Campbell was a Gillette board member during the Colman Mockler era and provides a detailed account of how a responsible board wrestled with the difficult and complex question of price versus value.

Q: Can hot young technology companies in a go-go world have Level 5 leaders?

My answer is two words: *John Morgridge.* Mr. Morgridge was the transition CEO who turned a small, struggling company in the Bay Area into one of the great technology companies of the last decade. With the flywheel turning, this unassuming and relatively unknown man stepped into the background and turned the company over to the next generation of leadership. I doubt you've ever heard of John Morgridge, but I suspect you've heard of the company. It goes by the name Cisco Systems.

Q: How can you practice the discipline of "first who" when there is a shortage of outstanding people?

First, at the top levels of your organization, you absolutely *must* have the discipline not to hire until you find the right people. The *single* most harmful step you can take in a journey from good to great is to put the wrong people in key positions. Second, widen your definition of "right people" to focus more on the character attributes of the person and less on specialized knowledge.

People can learn skills and acquire knowledge, but they cannot learn the essential character traits that make them right for your organization. Third—and this is key—take advantage of difficult economic times to hire great people, even if you don't have a specific job in mind. A year before I wrote these words, nearly everyone bemoaned the difficulty of attracting top talent away from hot technology and Internet companies. Now the bubble has burst, and tens of thousands of talented people have been cast into the streets. Level 5 leaders will view this as the single best opportunity to come along in two decades—not a market or technology opportunity, but a *people* opportunity. They will take advantage of this moment and hire as many of the very best people they can afford and *then* figure out what they are going to do with them.

Q: How can you practice the discipline of the "right people on the bus and the wrong people off the bus" in situations where it is very hard to get the wrong people off the bus—such as academic institutions and government agencies?

The same basic idea applies, but it takes more time to accomplish. A prominent medical school, for example, went through a transformation from good to great in the 1960s and 1970s. The director of academic medicine changed the entire faculty, but it took him two decades. He could not fire tenured professors, but he could hire the right people for every opening, gradually creating an environment where the wrong people felt increasingly uncomfortable and eventually retired or decided to go elsewhere. Also, you can use the Council mechanism to your advantage. (See chapter 5.) Fill Council seats entirely with the right people, and just ignore the others. Yes, you might still have to carry the wrong people along, but you can essentially restrict them to backseats on the bus by not including them on the Council.

Q: I'm an entrepreneur running a small company, how do these ideas apply to me?

Directly. See chapter 9, where I discuss the application of the good-to-great ideas in the context of small and early-stage companies.

Q: I'm not a CEO. What can I do with these findings?

Plenty. The best answer I can give is to reread the story at the end of chapter 9 about the high school cross-country coach.

Q: Where and how should I begin?

First, familiarize yourself with all the findings. Remember, no single finding *by itself* makes a great organization; you need to have them all working together as an integrated set. Then work sequentially through the framework, starting with "first who" and moving through all the major components. Meanwhile, work continuously on your own development toward Level 5 leadership. I have laid out this book in a sequence consistent with what we observed in the companies; the very structure of the book is a road map. I wish you the best of luck on your journey from good to great.

APPENDIX 1.A:

SELECTION PROCESS FOR GOOD-TO-GREAT COMPANIES

Research-team member Peter Van Genderen was instrumental in the creation of the selection criteria and in the "death march of financial analysis" required to use the criteria to find the good-to-great companies.

Criteria for Selection as a Good-to-Great Company

1. The company shows a pattern of "good" performance punctuated by a transition point, after which it shifts to "great" performance. We define "great" performance as a cumulative total stock return of at least 3 times the general market for the period from the point of transition through fifteen years (T + 15). We define "good" performance as a cumulative total stock return no better than 1.25 times the general stock market for the fifteen years prior to the point of transition. Additionally, the ratio of the cumulative stock return for the fifteen years after the point of transition divided by the ratio of the cumulative stock return for the fifteen years prior to the point of transition must exceed 3.
2. The good-to-great performance pattern must be a *company* shift, *not an industry event.* In other words, the company must demonstrate the pattern not only relative to the market, but also relative to its industry.
3. At the transition point, the company must have been an established, ongoing company, not a start-up. This was defined as having operations for at least twenty-five years prior to the transition point. Additionally, it had to have been publicly traded with stock return data available at least ten years prior to the transition point.
4. The transition point had to occur before 1985 so that we would have enough data to assess the sustainability of the transition. Good-to-great transitions that occurred after 1985 might have been good-to-great shifts; however, by the time we completed our research, we would be unable to calculate their fifteen-year ratio of cumulative returns to the general market.
5. Whatever the year of transition, the company still had to be a significant, ongoing, stand-alone company at the time of selection into the next stage of the research study. To satisfy this criterion, the company had to appear in the 1995 Fortune 500 rankings, published in 1996.

6. Finally, at the time of selection, the company should still show an upward trend. For any company where T + 15 falls before 1996, the slope of cumulative stock returns relative to the market from the initial point of transition to 1996 should equal or exceed the slope of 3/15 required to satisfy criterion 1 for the T + 15 phase.

Good-to-Great Selection Process

We used a sifting process with increasingly tighter screens to find our companies. The sifting process had four layers of analysis:

Screening Process for Selecting Good-to-Great Companies

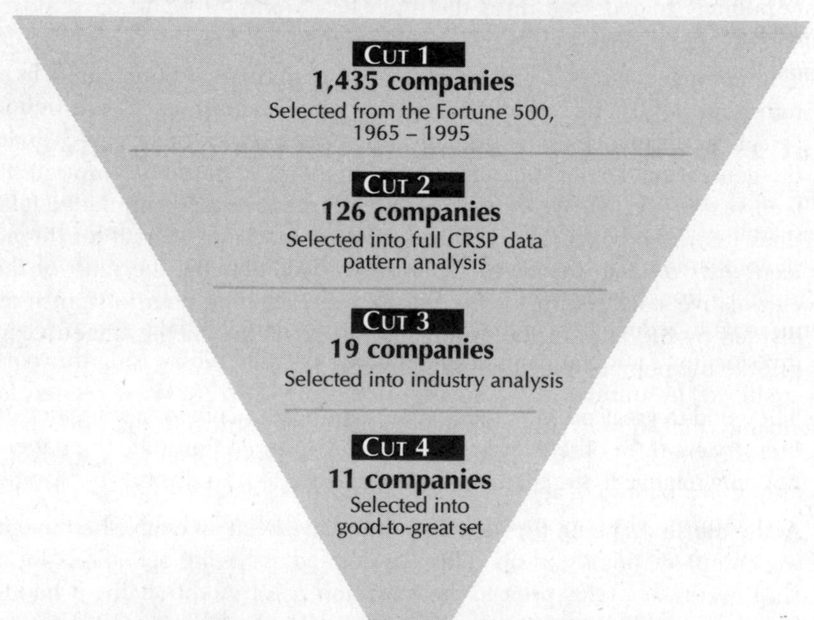

Cut 1: From the Universe of Companies to 1,435 Companies

We elected to begin our search with a list of companies that appeared on the *Fortune* rankings of America's largest public companies, going as far back as 1965, when the list came into existence. Our initial list consisted of all companies that appeared on the 1965, 1975, 1985, and 1995 listings. There were 1,435 such companies. Most people know these rankings as the "Fortune 500," although the total number of companies listed may be as many as 1,000 because *Fortune* occasionally changes the size and format of its lists. As a base set to begin our analysis, the *Fortune* largest-companies ranking has two key advantages. First, it lists only companies of substantial size (companies earn their way onto the list by annual revenues). Therefore, nearly every company in the *Fortune* ranking met our criterion of being an established ongoing company at the time of transition. Second, all companies in the *Fortune* rankings are publicly traded, which allowed us to use financial stock return data as the basis for more rigorous screening and analysis. Privately held companies, which do not have to meet the same accounting and disclosure standards, offer no opportunity for an apples-to-apples, direct comparison analysis of performance. Restricting our set to the *Fortune* rankings has one obvious disadvantage: It limits our analysis to U.S.-based companies. We concluded, however, that greater rigor in the selection process—made possible by using only publicly traded U.S. firms that hold to a common reporting standard (apples-to-apples stock return data)—outweighed the benefits of an international data set.

Cut 2: From 1,435 Companies to 126 Companies

Our next step was to use data from the University of Chicago Center for Research in Security Prices (CRSP) to make our final selection of good-to-great companies. We needed, however, a method to pare down the number of companies to a manageable size. We used the published *Fortune* rates-of-return data to reduce the candidate list. *Fortune* calculates the ten-year return to investors for each company in the rankings back to 1965. Using this data, we reduced the number of companies from 1,435 to 126. We screened for companies that showed substantially above-average returns in the time spans of 1985–1995, 1975–1995, and 1965–1995. We also looked for companies that showed a pattern of above-average returns preceded by average or below-average returns. More specifically, the 126 companies selected passed any *one* of the following tests:

Test 1: The compound annual total return to investors over the period 1985–1995 exceeded the compound annual average return to investors for the *Fortune* Industrial and Service listings over the same period by 30 percent (i.e., total returns exceeded average returns by 1.3 times), *and* the company showed evidence of average or below-average performance in the prior two decades (1965–1985).

Test 2: The compound annual total return to investors over the period 1975–1995 exceeded the compound annual average return to investors for the *Fortune* Industrial and Service listings over the same period by 30 percent (i.e., total returns exceeded average returns by 1.3 times), *and* the company showed evidence of average or below-average performance in the prior decade (1965–1975).

Test 3: The compound annual total return to investors over the period 1965–1995 exceeded the compound annual average return to investors for the *Fortune* Industrial and Service listings over the same period by 30 percent (i.e., total returns exceeded average returns by 1.3 times). The *Fortune* listings do not contain ten-year returns before 1965, so we decided to include all top performers over the three-decade period in the initial set.

Test 4: Companies founded after 1970 and whose total return to investors over the period 1985–1995 or 1975–1995 exceeded the average return to investors for the *Fortune* Industrial and Service listings over the same period by 30 percent (i.e., total returns exceeded average returns by 1.3 times) but that did not meet the above criteria due to a lack of data in the *Fortune* list in prior decades. This allowed us to closely consider any companies that performed well in later decades but did not show up earlier on the *Fortune* listings. The 1970 cutoff also allowed us to identify and eliminate from consideration any companies with histories too short to be a legitimate transition company.

Cut 3: From 126 Companies to 19 Companies

Drawing upon the research database at the University of Chicago Center for Research in Securities Pricing (CRSP), we analyzed the cumulative stock returns of each candidate company relative to the general market, looking for the good-to-great stock return pattern. Any company that met any *one* of the Cut 3 elimination criteria was eliminated at this stage.

CUT 3 ELIMINATION CRITERIA

Any company that met any *one* of the following elimination criteria was eliminated at this stage.

Terminology used in Cut 3 elimination criteria:

T year: Year we identified as the point at which performance began an upward trend—the "transition year," based on when the actual stock returns showed a visible upward shift.

X period: Era of *observable* "good" performance relative to the market immediately prior to the T year.

Y period: Era of substantially above market performance immediately following the T year.

Cut 3 Elimination Criterion #1: The company displays a continual upward trend relative to the market over the entire time covered by CRSP data—there is no X period.

Cut 3 Elimination Criterion #2: The company shows a flat to gradual rise relative to the market. There is no obvious shift to breakthrough performance.

Cut 3 Elimination Criterion #3: The company demonstrates a transition, but an X period of less than ten years. In other words, the pretransition average performance data was not long enough to demonstrate a fundamental transition. In some cases, the company likely had more years of X period performance prior to the transition year, but the stock became traded on the NASDAQ, NYSE, or AMEX during the X period; therefore, our data did not go back far enough to verify an X period.

Cut 3 Elimination Criterion #4: The company demonstrates a transition from terrible performance to average performance relative to the market. In other words, we eliminated classic turnaround situations where the company pulled out of a downward trend and into a trajectory parallel with the general market.

Cut 3 Elimination Criterion #5: The company demonstrates a transition, but after 1985. Good-to-great transitions that occurred after 1985 might also have been legitimate good-to-great candidates. By the time we completed our research, however, we would not be able to verify that their fifteen-year ratio of cumulative returns to the general market met the three-to-one criterion.

Cut 3 Elimination Criterion #6: The company shows a transition to increased performance, but the rise in performance is not sustained. After the initial rise, it goes flat or declines relative to the market until the time of consideration for selection into the study.

Cut 3 Elimination Criterion #7: The company demonstrates a volatile pattern of returns—large upward and downward swings—with no clear X period, Y period, or T year.

Cut 3 Elimination Criterion #8: A complete set of CRSP data is not available before 1975, making it impossible to identify a verifiable X period of ten years.

Cut 3 Elimination Criterion #9: There is a transition pattern, but the company demonstrated a period of such spectacular performance prior to the X period that there is substantial evidence that the company is a *great* company that had fallen temporarily on difficult times, rather than a good or mediocre company that became great. The classic example is Walt Disney.

Cut 3 Elimination Criterion #10: The company is acquired, has merged, or is otherwise eliminated from consideration as a stand-alone company by the time of the final Cut 3 analysis.

Cut 3 Elimination Criterion #11: The company shows a mild transition but falls short of three times the market.

CUT 3 ANALYSIS RESULTS

	Companies Admitted in Cut 2	Outcome in Cut 3
1	AFLAC, Inc.	Eliminated, criterion 3
2	AMP, Inc.	Eliminated, criterion 6
3	Abbott Labs	Accepted into Cut 4 analysis
4	Albertson's, Inc.	Eliminated, criterion 1
5	Alco Standard, Corp.	Eliminated, criterion 3
6	Allegheny Teledyne, Inc.	Eliminated, criterion 6
7	ALLTEL Corp.	Eliminated, criterion 2
8	American Express Co.	Eliminated, criteria 6, 7
9	American Stores Co.	Eliminated, criterion 6
10	Anheuser-Busch Companies, Inc.	Eliminated, criterion 2
11	Applied Materials, Inc.	Eliminated, criterion 5
12	Archer Daniels Midland Co.	Eliminated, criterion 6
13	Automatic Data Processing	Eliminated, criterion 1
14	BANC ONE Corp.	Eliminated, criterion 6
15	Bank of New York, Inc.	Eliminated, criterion 2
16	Barnett Banks	Eliminated, criteria 3, 6
17	Berkshire Hathaway, Inc.	Eliminated, criterion 1
18	Boeing Co.	Eliminated, criterion 1
19	Browning-Ferris Industries	Eliminated, criterion 3
20	Campbell Soup Co.	Eliminated, criterion 2
21	Cardinal Health	Eliminated, criterion 8
22	Chrysler	Eliminated, criterion 6
23	Circuit City Stores, Inc.	Accepted into Cut 4 analysis
24	Coca-Cola Co.	Accepted into Cut 4 analysis
25	Colgate-Palmolive Co.	Eliminated, criterion 11
26	Comerica, Inc.	Eliminated, criterion 3
27	Computer Associates	Eliminated, criterion 8
28	Computer Sciences Corp.	Eliminated, criteria 6, 7
29	ConAgra, Inc.	Eliminated, criterion 3
30	Conseco	Eliminated, criterion 8
31	CPC International (later Bestfoods)	Accepted into Cut 4 analysis
32	CSX	Eliminated, criterion 8
33	Dean Foods Co.	Eliminated, criterion 7
34	Dillard's	Eliminated, criterion 6
35	Dover Corp.	Eliminated, criteria 3, 6
36	DuPont	Eliminated, criterion 11
37	Engelhard Corp.	Eliminated, criterion 2
38	FMC Corp.	Eliminated, criterion 7
39	Federal National Mortgage Assn.	Accepted into Cut 4 analysis
40	First Interstate Bancorp	Eliminated, criterion 2

Companies Admitted in Cut 2	Outcome in Cut 3
41 First Union Corp.	Eliminated, criteria 3, 6
42 Fleet Financial Group, Inc.	Eliminated, criterion 6
43 Fleetwood Enterprises, Inc.	Eliminated, criterion 7
44 Foster Wheeler Corp.	Eliminated, criterion 6
45 GPU, Inc.	Eliminated, criterion 2
46 The Gap, Inc.	Eliminated, criterion 8
47 GEICO	Eliminated, criterion 10
48 General Dynamics Corp.	Eliminated, criterion 7
49 General Electric Co.	Eliminated, criteria 5, 11
50 General Mills, Inc.	Accepted into Cut 4 analysis
51 General Re Corp.	Eliminated, criterion 2
52 Giant Foods, Inc.	Eliminated, criterion 6
53 Gillette Co.	Accepted into Cut 4 analysis
54 Golden West Financial Corp.	Eliminated, criterion 3
55 Hasbro, Inc.	Eliminated, criterion 6
56 Heinz, H. J. Co.	Accepted into Cut 4 analysis
57 Hershey Foods Corp.	Accepted into Cut 4 analysis
58 Hewlett-Packard Co.	Eliminated, criterion 7
59 Humana, Inc.	Eliminated, criteria 3, 6
60 Illinois Tool Works, Inc.	Eliminated, criterion 2
61 Intel Corp.	Eliminated, criterion 1
62 Johnson & Johnson	Eliminated, criteria 6, 7
63 Johnson Controls, Inc.	Eliminated, criterion 6
64 Kellogg Co.	Accepted into Cut 4 analysis
65 Kelly Services, Inc.	Eliminated, criteria 3, 6
66 KeyCorp	Eliminated, criterion 3
67 Kimberly-Clark Corp.	Accepted into Cut 4 analysis
68 Kroger Co.	Accepted into Cut 4 analysis
69 Eli Lilly and Co.	Eliminated, criterion 2
70 Loews Corp.	Eliminated, criteria 3, 6
71 Loral Corp.	Eliminated, criterion 7
72 Lowe's Companies, Inc.	Eliminated, criterion 2
73 MCI Communications Corp.	Eliminated, criterion 7
74 Mapco, Inc.	Eliminated, criteria 3, 6
75 Masco Corp.	Eliminated, criteria 3, 6
76 Mattel	Eliminated, criteria 3, 6
77 McDonald's Corp.	Eliminated, criterion 7
78 Melville	Eliminated, criterion 10
79 Merck & Co., Inc.	Eliminated, criterion 1
80 Mobil Corp.	Eliminated, criterion 2
81 Monsanto Co.	Eliminated, criteria 4, 5
82 Motorola, Inc.	Eliminated, criterion 1
83 Newell Co.	Eliminated, criteria 3, 6

Companies Admitted in Cut 2	Outcome in Cut 3
84 Nike, Inc.	Eliminated, criteria 1, 7
85 Norwest Corp.	Eliminated, criterion 5
86 Nucor Corp.	Accepted into Cut 4 analysis
87 Olsten Corp.	Eliminated, criteria 1, 7
88 Owens-Corning	Eliminated, criterion 2
89 PACCAR, Inc.	Eliminated, criterion 2
90 PacifiCare Health Systems	Eliminated, criterion 8
91 Pepsico, Inc.	Accepted into Cut 4 analysis
92 Pfizer, Inc.	Eliminated, criterion 1
93 Phelps Dodge Corp.	Eliminated, criterion 2
94 Philip Morris Companies, Inc.	Accepted into Cut 4 analysis
95 Pitney Bowes, Inc.	Accepted into Cut 4 analysis
96 Procter & Gamble Co.	Eliminated, criteria 2, 5
97 Progressive Corp.	Eliminated, criteria 1, 3
98 Raytheon Co.	Eliminated, criterion 6
99 Reebok	Eliminated, criterion 8
100 Republic New York	Eliminated, criteria 3, 6
101 Rockwell International Corp.	Eliminated, criteria 3, 6
102 SCI Systems, Inc.	Eliminated, criterion 7
103 SAFECO Corp.	Eliminated, criterion 2
104 Sara Lee Corp.	Accepted into Cut 4 analysis
105 Schering-Plough Corp.	Eliminated, criterion 7
106 ServiceMaster Co.	Eliminated, criterion 7
107 Shaw Industries, Inc.	Eliminated, criteria 3, 6
108 Sonoco Products Co.	Eliminated, criteria 3, 6
109 Southwest Airlines Co.	Eliminated, criterion 1
110 State Street Boston Corp.	Eliminated, criterion 3
111 SunTrust Banks	Eliminated, criterion 8
112 SYSCO Corp.	Eliminated, criteria 3, 6
113 Tandy Corp.	Eliminated, criterion 6
114 Tele-Communications, Inc.	Eliminated, criteria 3, 6
115 Turner Broadcasting	Eliminated, criterion 8
116 Tyco International, Ltd.	Eliminated, criteria 2, 6
117 Tyson Foods, Inc.	Eliminated, criteria 1, 3
118 Union Carbide Corp.	Eliminated, criterion 6
119 U.S. Bancorp	Eliminated, criterion 2
120 VF Corp.	Eliminated, criterion 6
121 Wal-Mart Stores, Inc.	Eliminated, criterion 1
122 Walgreens Co.	Accepted into Cut 4 analysis
123 Walt Disney	Eliminated, criterion 9
124 Warner-Lambert Co.	Eliminated, criterion 6, 7
125 Wells Fargo & Co.	Accepted into Cut 4 analysis
126 Winn-Dixie Stores, Inc.	Eliminated, criterion 7

Cut 4: From Nineteen Companies to Eleven Good-to-Great Companies

We wanted to find *companies* that made a transition, not industries that made a transition; merely being in the right industry at the right time would not qualify a company for the study. To separate industry transitions from company transitions, we decided to repeat the CRSP analysis for the remaining nineteen companies, only this time against a composite industry index rather than the general stock market. Companies that showed a transition relative to their industry would be selected for the final study set.

For each of the remaining nineteen companies, we looked back in time via the S&P industry composites and created an industry set of companies *at the time of transition* (within five years). We then acquired CRSP stock return data on all of the companies in the industry composite. If the company had multiple industry lines of business, we used two separate industry tests. We then created an industry cumulative returns index against which we plotted the cumulative returns for the transition company. This allowed us to identify and eliminate from the study any companies that did not show the transition pattern relative to their industry.

Through industry analysis, we eliminated eight companies. Sara Lee, Heinz, Hershey, Kellogg, CPC, and General Mills demonstrated a dramatic upward shift relative to the general stock market in about 1980, but none of these companies demonstrated a shift relative to the food industry. Coca-Cola and Pepsico demonstrated a dramatic upward shift relative to the general stock market in about 1960 and again in 1980, but neither demonstrated a shift relative to the beverage industry. We therefore ended up with eleven companies that made it through Cuts 1 through 4 and into the research study. (Note: At the time of initial selection into the study, three of the companies did not yet have a full fifteen years of cumulative stock data—Circuit City, Fannie Mae, and Wells Fargo. We continued to monitor the data until they hit T + 15 years, to ensure that they would meet the "three times the market over fifteen years" standard of performance. All three did, and remained in the study.)

APPENDIX 1.B

DIRECT COMPARISON SELECTIONS

Direct Comparison Selection Process

The purpose of the direct comparison analysis is to create as close to a "historical controlled experiment" as possible. The idea is simple: By finding companies that were approximately the same ages and had similar opportunities, lines of business, and success profiles as each of the good-to-great companies at the time of transition, we were able to conduct direct comparative analysis in our research, looking for the *distinguishing* variables that account for the transition from good to great. Our objective was to find companies that *could* have done what the good-to-great companies did, but failed to do so, and then ask: "What was different?" We performed a systematic and methodical collection and scoring of all obvious comparison candidates for each good-to-great company, using the following six criteria.

Business Fit: At the time of transition, the comparison candidate had similar products and services as the good-to-great company.

Size Fit: At the time of transition, the comparison candidate was the same basic size as the good-to-great company. We applied a consistent scoring matrix based upon the ratio of the comparison candidate revenues divided by the good-to-great company revenues at the time of transition.

Age Fit: The comparison candidate was founded in the same era as the good-to-great company. We applied a consistent scoring matrix based upon a calculated age ratio of the comparison candidate to the good-to-great company.

Stock Chart Fit: The cumulative stock returns to market chart of the comparison candidate roughly tracks the pattern of the good-to-great company until the point of transition, at which point the trajectories of the two companies separate, with the good-to-great company outperforming the comparison candidate from that point on.

Conservative Test: At the time of transition, the comparison candidate was *more* successful than the good-to-great company—larger and more profitable, with a stronger market position and better reputation. This is a critical test, stacking the deck against our good-to-great companies.

Face Validity: This takes into account two factors: (1) The comparison candidate is in a similar line of business at the time of selection into the study, and (2) the comparison candidate is less successful than the good-to-great company at the time of selection into the study.

Thus, face validity and conservative test work together: Conservative test ensures that the comparison company was *stronger* than the good-to-great company *at the year of the good-to-great company's transition*, and *weaker* than the good-to-great company *at the time of selection* into the study.

We scored each comparison candidate on each of the above six criteria on a scale of 1 to 4:

4 = The comparison candidate fits the criteria extremely well—there are no issues or qualifiers.

3 = The comparison candidate fits the criteria reasonably well—there are minor issues or qualifiers that keep it from getting a 4.

2 = The comparison candidate fits the criteria poorly—there are major issues and concerns.

1 = The comparison candidate fails the criteria.

The following table shows the comparison candidates for each good-to-great company with their average score across the six criteria. The comparison candidate selected as the direct comparison appears at the top of each list.

Abbott	
Upjohn	4.00
Richardson-Merrill	3.25
G. D. Searle & Co	3.00
Sterling Drugs	2.83
Schering-Plough	2.70
Bristol-Meyers	2.67
Norwich	2.67
Parke-Davis	2.40
SmithKline Beecham	2.33
Pfizer	2.33
Warner-Lambert	2.17

Circuit City

Silo	3.40
Tandy	3.25
Best Buy	1.83

Fannie Mae

Great Western Financial Corp.	2.83
Sallie Mae	2.67
Freddie Mac	2.50
H. F. Ahmanson & Co.	2.33
Household International	2.33
Continental Bancorp	2.20
First Charter	1.60

Gillette

Warner-Lambert	2.67
Avon	2.50
Procter & Gamble	2.33
Unilever	2.33
International Flavors & Fragrances	2.33
Revlon	2.33
The Clorox Company	2.33
Colgate-Palmolive	2.25
Cheeseborough-Ponds	2.00
Bic	1.50
Alberto-Culver	1.50
American Safety Razor	1.50
Purex Corporation	1.00
Fabergé	1.00

Kimberly-Clark

Company	
Scott Paper Company*	3.50
The Mead Corporation	3.50
Crown Zellerbach	3.25
St. Regis Paper Company	3.13
International Paper	2.92
Union Camp Corporation	2.67
Georgia-Pacific	2.50
The Westvaco Corporation	2.50

*Scott Paper was selected due to being a more direct competitor as the transition unfolded.

Kroger

Company	
A&P	3.17
Safeway	2.58
Winn-Dixie	2.50
American Stores	2.42
Giant Foods, Inc.	2.33
Jewel	2.25
Albertson's	2.08
Food Fair	1.50
Grand Union	1.00

Nucor

Bethlehem Steel Corporation	3.00
Inland Steel Industries, Inc.*	3.00
USX	2.92
National Steel Corporation	2.60
Florida Steel	2.50
Northwestern Steel and Wire Co.	2.40
The Interlake Corporation	2.00
Allegheny Teledyne	1.83
Republic Steel Corporation	1.75
Lykes Corporation	1.60
Wheeling	1.50

*Inland scores higher only in the category of age fit. Bethlehem scores higher in conservative fit and face validity; therefore, we selected Bethlehem in the tie-breaker.

Philip Morris

R. J. Reynolds Tobacco	3.50
American Tobacco	3.40
Liggett Group, Inc.	3.25
Lorillard Industries	3.20

Pitney Bowes

Addressograph-Multigraph	3.42
Burroughs (now Unisys)	2.83
Smith-Corona	2.58
Xerox	2.33
NCR	2.25
IBM	2.00
Control Data	1.33

Walgreens

Eckerd	3.42
Revco D.S., Inc.	2.67
Rite Aid Corporation	2.17

Wells Fargo

Bank of America	3.33
First Chicago	3.17
NationsBank	3.17
Mellon	3.00
Continental Illinois	3.00
Bank of Boston	2.83
First Interstate	2.25
Norwest	2.17
First Pennsylvania	2.00
Interfirst	1.75

APPENDIX 1.C

UNSUSTAINED COMPARISONS

Unsustained Comparison	Number of Years of Rise*	Ratio of Cumulative Stock Returns to Market during the Years of Rise	Ratio of Cumulative Stock Returns to Market during the Next Ten Years†
Burroughs	10.08	13.76	0.21
Chrysler	5.67	10.54	0.69
Harris	6.42	6.63	0.16
Hasbro	6.33	35.00	0.63
Rubbermaid	10.83	6.97	0.31‡
Teledyne	9.42	17.95	0.22
Median	7.92	12.15	0.26
Unsustained Average	8.125	15.14	0.37
Good-to-Great Average over the analogous period		4.91§	2.02‖

* This is the number of years from the moment of upward transition to the peak of the rise, when the unsustained comparison begins to decline again relative to the market.

† Whenever the ratio of returns to the market is less than 1.0, this indicates a *decline* in value relative to the market. For example, if the ratio is 0.20, then for every dollar you invest in the company, you fall 80 percent below what you would have earned had you invested that same dollar in the general market over the same time period.

‡ The data for Rubbermaid goes 7.17 years after the peak, at which point the company is acquired.

§ Calculated as: For each good-to-great company, calculate the ratio of cumulative returns to the market from *its* moment of upward transition to 8.125 years (8.125 is the average rise cycle of the unsustained companies), and then calculate the average across the eleven good-to-great companies at T + 8.125.

(Place $1 in market and in company on transition date and take out on T + 8.125.)
|| For each good-to-great company, calculate the ratio of cumulative returns to the market from T + 8.125 to T + 18.125, and average across the eleven good-to-great companies at T + 18.125. (Place $1 in market and in company on T + 8.125, and take it out on T + 18.125.) If a company data ends before T + 18.125, use the last available data cell in the average. For Wells Fargo, we use the last cell prior to the Norwest merger in 1998 (10/30/88).

The following chart shows a classic unsustained comparison pattern:

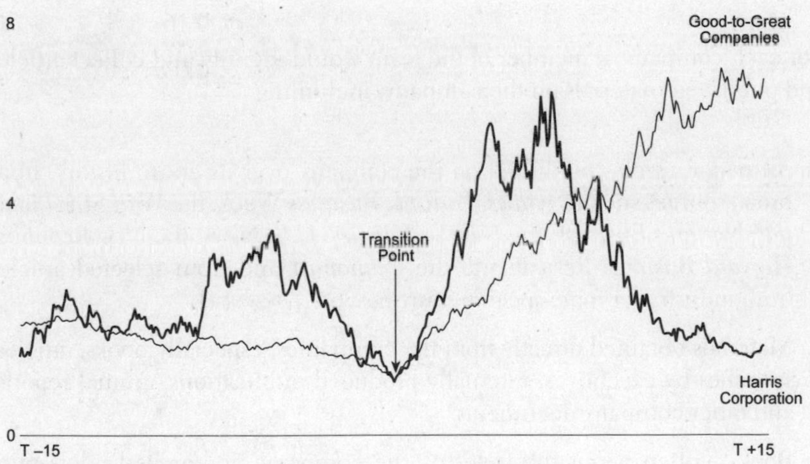

APPENDIX 1.D

OVERVIEW OF RESEARCH STEPS

Once the twenty-eight companies had been selected (eleven good-to-great, eleven direct comparison, six unsustained comparison), the following steps and analyses were taken by the research team.

COMPANY CODING DOCUMENTS

For each company, a member of the team would identify and collect articles and published materials on the company, including:

1. All major articles published on the company over its entire history, from broad sources such as *Forbes, Fortune, Business* Week, the *Wall Street Journal, Nation's Business*, the *New York Times, U.S. News*, the *New Republic, Harvard Business Review*, and the *Economist* and from selected articles from industry- or topic-specific sources.
2. Materials obtained directly from the companies, especially books, articles, speeches by executives, internally produced publications, annual reports, and other company documents.
3. Books written about the industry, the company, and/or its leaders published either by the company or by outside observers.
4. Business school case studies and industry analyses.
5. Business and industry reference materials, such as the *Biographical Dictionary of American Business Leaders*, the *International Directory of Company Histories, Hoover's Handbook of Companies, Development of American Industries*, and similar sources.
6. Annual reports, proxy statements, analyst reports, and any other materials available on the company, especially during the transition era.

Then for each company, the researcher would systematically code all of the information into a "coding document," organized according to the following categories, proceeding chronologically from the founding of the company to the present day:

Coding Category 1—Organizing Arrangements: "Hard" items such as organization structure, policies and procedures, systems, rewards and incentives, ownership structure.

Coding Category 2—Social Factors: "Soft" items such as the company's cultural practices, people policies and practices, norms, rituals, mythology and stories, group dynamics, management style, and related items.

Coding Category 3—Business Strategy, Strategic Process: Primary elements of the company's strategy. Process of setting strategy. Includes significant mergers and acquisitions.

Coding Category 4—Markets, Competitors, and Environment: Significant aspects of the company's competitive and external environment—primary competitors, significant competitor activities, major market shifts, dramatic national or international events, government regulations, industry structural issues, dramatic technology changes, and related items. Includes data about the company's relationship to Wall Street.

Coding Category 5—Leadership: Leadership of the firm—key executives, CEOs, presidents, board members. Interesting data on leadership succession, leadership style, and so on.

Coding Category 6—Products and Services: Significant products and services in the company's history.

Coding Category 7—Physical Setting and Location: Significant aspects of the way the company handled physical space—plant and office layout, new facilities, etc. Includes any significant decisions regarding the geographic location of key parts of the company.

Coding Category 8—Use of Technology: How the company used technology: information technology, state-of-the-art processes and equipment, advanced job configurations, and related items.

Coding Category 9—Vision: Core Values, Purpose, and BHAGs: Were these variables present? If yes, how did they come into being? Did the organization have them at certain points in its history and not others? What role did they play? If it had strong values and purpose, did they remain intact or become diluted?

Coding Category 10A (for Direct Comparisons Only)—Change/Transition Activities during Transition Era of Corresponding Good-to-Great Company: Major attempts to change the company, to stimulate a transition, during the ten years prior and ten years after the transition date in the corresponding good-to-great company.

Coding Category 10B (for Unsustained Comparisons Only)—Attempted Transition Era: For the ten years leading up to and then during the "attempted transition era," major change/transition initiatives and supporting activities undertaken by the company.

Coding Category 11 (for Unsustained Comparisons Only)—Posttransition Decline: For the ten years following the attempted transition era, major factors that seem to have contributed to the company not sustaining its transition.

FINANCIAL SPREADSHEET ANALYSIS

We conducted extensive financial analysis for each company, examining all financial variables for 980 combined years of data (35 years on average per company for 28 companies). This comprised gathering raw income and balance sheet data and examining the following variables in both the pre- and posttransition decades:

Total sales in nominal and real (inflation-adjusted) dollars
Sales growth
Profit growth
Profit margin
Return on sales
Sales per employee in nominal and real dollars
Profit per employee in nominal and real dollars
PP&E (property, plant, and equipment)
Dividend payout ratio
Selling, general, and administrative expenses as a percent of sales
Research and development as a percent of sales
Collection period in days
Inventory turnover ratio
Return on equity
Ratio of debt to equity
Ratio of long-term debt to equity
Interest expense as a percent of sales
High stock price to earnings per share
Low stock price to earnings per share
Average stock price to earnings per share

EXECUTIVE INTERVIEWS

We conducted interviews of senior management and members of the board, focusing on people who were in office during the transition era. We transcribed all interviews and synthesized the data into content analysis findings.

COMPANY AND NUMBER OF INTERVIEWS CONDUCTED

Company	Interviews
Abbott	8
Circuit City	8
Fannie Mae	10
Gillette	6
Kimberly-Clark	7
Kroger	6
Nucor	7
Philip Morris	6
Pitney Bowes	9
Walgreens	8
Wells Fargo	9
Total	84

Interview Questions

Could you briefly give an overview of your relationship to the company—years involved and primary responsibilities held?

What do you see as the top five factors that contributed to or caused the upward shift in performance during the years [ten years before transition] to [ten years after transition]?

Now let's return to each of those five factors, and I'd like you to allocate a total of 100 points to those factors, according to their overall importance to the transition (total across all five factors equals 100 points).

Could you please elaborate on the [top two or three] factors? Can you give me specific examples that illustrate the factor?

Did the company make a conscious decision to initiate a major change or transition during this time frame?

[If a conscious decision:] To the best of your recollection, when did the company begin to make the key decisions that led to the transition (what year, approximately)?

[If a conscious decision:] What sparked the decision to undertake a major transition?

What was the process by which the company made key decisions and developed key strategies during the transition era—not what decisions the company made, but how did it go about making them?

What was the role, if any, of outside consultants and advisors in making the key decisions?

On a scale of 1 to 10, what confidence did you have in the decisions at the time they were made, before you knew their outcome? (Ten means you had great confidence that they were very good decisions with high probability of success. One means you had little confidence in the decisions; they seemed risky—a roll of the dice.)

[If had confidence of 6 or greater:] What gave you such confidence in the decisions?

How did the company get commitment and alignment with its decisions?

Can you cite a specific example of how this took place?

What did you try during the transition that didn't work?

How did the company manage the short-term pressures of Wall Street while making long-term changes and investments for the future?

Many companies undertake change programs and initiatives, yet their efforts do not produce lasting results. One of the remarkable aspects of [good-to-great company's] transition is that it has endured—it was not just a short-term upswing. We find this extraordinary. What makes [good-to-great company] different? What were the primary factors in the endurance of the transition far beyond the first few years?

We will be comparing [good-to-great company] to [comparison company], which was in your industry at the time of your transition but—unlike [good-to-great company]—did not show a significant and lasting shift in performance. What was different about [good-to-great company] that enabled it to make this transition? Other companies could have done what you did, but didn't; what did you have that they didn't?

Can you think of one particularly powerful example or vignette from your experience or observation that, to you, exemplifies the essence of the shift from good to great at [good-to-great company]?

Who else would you strongly recommend that we interview?

- *Inside management during and after the transition.*
- *External board members or other key outside people.*

Are there any questions we didn't ask, but should have?

SPECIAL ANALYSIS UNITS

We undertook a series of special analysis units. These units were designed to shed light on the question of good to great by systematic comparison and (where possible) quantification of key variables between the good-to-great companies and the comparison companies.

Acquisitions and Divestitures

This analysis unit sought to understand the role of acquisitions and divestments in the transition from good to great.

Objectives:

1. What is the quantitative difference in acquisitions and divestments, if any, between the pretransition and posttransition eras for the good-to-great companies?
2. How do the good-to-great companies differ in acquisitions and divestments from the direct comparisons?
3. How do the good-to-great companies differ in acquisitions and divestments from the unsustained comparisons?

To do this analysis, we created a database for each company, year by year:

1. List of acquisitions made during the year and their financial attributes.
2. Total number of acquisitions made during the year.

3. Total combined size of all acquisitions made during the year.
4. List of divestments made during the year and their financial attributes.
5. Total number of divestments made during the year.
6. Total combined size of all divestments made during the year.

Using this data, we did eight major analyses:

1. Good-to-great companies: pre- and posttransition.
2. Good-to-great companies versus comparison companies: pre- and posttransition.
3. Unsustained transition companies: pre- and posttransition decades.
4. Summary pre- and postdecade analysis: good-to-great companies versus direct comparisons versus unsustained comparisons.
5. Good-to-great companies: transition date to present.
6. Good-to-great companies versus comparison companies: transition date to 1998.
7. Unsustained comparisons: transition date to 1998. Do the same analysis as for the good-to-great companies from transition date to 1998.
8. Summary, transition date to 1998: good-to-great companies versus direct comparisons versus unsustained comparisons.

In addition, this analysis looked at the qualitative aspects of acquisitions and divestitures, examining questions such as:

1. Overall strategy of acquisitions.
2. Overall strategy of integrating acquisitions.
3. The ultimate success of each major acquisition.
4. Ultimate success of the overall acquisition strategy.

Industry Performance Analysis

In this analysis, we looked at the performance of the companies versus the performance of the industries. The purpose of the analysis was to determine whether the companies were in highly attractive industries at the time of the transition. We created spreadsheets that quantified each industry versus the company, to determine the relationship between the two.

We compared each good-to-great company's industry relative to all other industries that appeared in the *Standard & Poor's Analyst's Handbook* for a period from the transition year to 1995. We used the following procedure:

1. For each good-to-great company, determine all industries that are listed in the *S&P Analyst's Handbook* from the year of transition to 1995.
2. For each of these industries, use the total returns from the transition year of the corresponding company to 1995 to determine the percentage change in total returns for a period from the transition year to 1995.
3. Rank the industries according to their percentage returns over this period.

Executive Churn Analysis

This analysis unit looked at the extent to which the executive teams changed in the companies during crucial points in their history.

Using *Moody's Company Information Reports*, we calculated churn in the good-to-great companies versus comparison companies:

- Average percent of departures over pretransition decade.
- Average percent of departures over posttransition decade.
- Average percent of additions over pretransition decade.
- Average percent of additions over posttransition decade.
- Average total churn percentage over pretransition decade.
- Average total churn percentage over posttransition decade.
- Same analyses repeated out to 1998.

Objectives:

1. What is the quantitative difference in executive churn and/or continuity, if any, between the pretransition and posttransition eras for the good-to-great companies?
2. How do the good-to-great companies differ in executive churn and/or continuity from the direct comparisons?
3. How do the good-to-great companies differ in executive churn and/or continuity from the unsustained comparisons?

CEO Analysis:

We examined a total of fifty-six CEOs. For each set of CEOs during the transition era in all three sets of companies (good-to-great, direct comparison, and unsustained comparison), we did a qualitative examination of:

1. Management style.
2. Executive persona.
3. Personal life.
4. What they saw as their top five priorities as CEO.

Also, for each good-to-great company, direct comparison, and unsustained comparison, we examined the CEO background and tenure. Beginning with CEOs in place ten years prior to the transition year through 1997, we determined:

1. Whether the CEO was brought in from the outside *directly* into the role of CEO (i.e., hired as CEO).
2. Number of years of employment with the company prior to becoming CEO.
3. Age at the time of becoming CEO.
4. Start year and end year of tenure in CEO role.
5. Number of years CEO position was held.
6. Responsibility held immediately prior to becoming CEO.
7. Factors in selection of that person as CEO (why picked as CEO).
8. Education (especially study areas—e.g., law, business—and degrees held).
9. Work experience and other experiences (e.g., military) prior to joining the company.

Executive Compensation

This unit examined executive compensation across the companies in our study. For the twenty-eight companies in the study, from ten years before the transition point to 1998, we collected data and performed a wide variety of analyses.

1. Total of all officers' and directors' salary + bonus as a percent of net worth at transition year.
2. CEO's total cash compensation as a percent of net worth at transition year.
3. CEO's salary + bonus as a percent of net worth at transition year.
4. Difference between CEO's salary + bonus and average of top four executives' salary + bonus as a percent of net worth at transition year and at transition year + 10 years.

5. Average of all officers' and directors' salary + bonus as a percent of net worth at transition year.
6. Total of all officers' and directors' salary + bonus at transition year.
7. Total of all officers' and directors' salary + bonus as a percent of sales at transition year.
8. Total of all officers' and directors' salary + bonus as a percent of assets at transition year.
9. Top four executives' total cash compensation as a percent of net worth at transition year.
10. Top four executives' salary + bonus as a percent of net worth at transition year.
11. Average of all officers' and directors' salary + bonus at transition year.
12. CEO's salary + bonus as a percent of net income.
13. Difference between CEO's and average of top four executives' salary + bonus.
14. Difference between CEO's and average of top four executives' salary + bonus as a percent of sales.
15. Difference between CEO's and average of top four executives' salary + bonus as a percent of net income.
16. Average of all officers' and directors' salary + bonus as a percent of sales at transition year.
17. Average of all officers' and directors' salary + bonus as a percent of net income at transition year.
18. Total of all officers' and directors' salary + bonus as a percent of net income at transition year.
19. CEO's total cash compensation as a percent of net income at transition year.
20. Value of stocks granted per year to CEO as a percent of net worth at transition year.
21. Value of stocks granted per year to top four executives as a percent of sales at transition year.
22. Value of stocks granted per year to top four executives as a percent of assets at transition year.
23. Value of stocks granted per year to top four executives as a percent of net worth at transition year.

24. CEO salary + bonus as a percent of sales at transition + 10 years.
25. Top four executives' salary + bonus as a percent of sales at transition year + 10 years.

Objectives:

1. What is the quantitative difference in executive compensation, if any, between the pretransition and posttransition eras for the good-to-great companies?
2. How do the good-to-great companies differ in executive compensation from the direct comparisons?
3. How do the good-to-great companies differ in executive compensation from the unsustained comparisons?

Role of Layoffs

In this unit, we sought to examine the good-to-great companies, the direct comparisons, and the unsustained comparisons for evidence of layoffs as a significant conscious tactic in an attempt to improve company performance. We examined:

1. Total employment head count year by year, from ten years prior to transition through 1998.
2. Evidence of layoffs as a significant tactic in an attempt to improve company performance during the ten years prior and ten years after the date of transition.
3. If layoffs did occur, then calculate the number of people laid off, nominally and as a percent of the total workforce.

Corporate Ownership Analysis

The point of this analysis was to determine if there were any significant differences in the corporate ownership of the good-to-great and direct comparisons. We looked at:

1. The presence of large-block shareholders and groups.
2. The extent of board ownership.
3. The extent of executive ownership.

Media Hype Analysis

This unit looked at the degree of "media hype" surrounding the good-to-great companies, direct comparisons, and unsustained comparisons. For the period ten years before to ten years after the transition date for each of the companies, we looked at:

1. Total number of articles in the pre- and posttransition decades and for the two decades combined.
2. Total number of "feature" articles on the company in the pre- and posttransition decades and for the two decades combined.
3. Total number of the above articles that explicitly talk about a "transition," "rebound," "turnaround," "transformation," under way at the company in the pre- and posttransition decades and for the two decades combined.
4. Total number of "highly positive" articles, total number of "neutral" articles (from slightly negative to slightly positive), and total number of "highly negative" articles in the pre- and posttransition decades and for the two decades combined.

Technology Analysis

This unit examined the role of technology, drawing largely upon executive interviews and written source materials:

1. Pioneering applications of technology.
2. Timing of technology.
3. Criteria for selection and use of specific technologies.
4. Role of technology in decline of comparison companies.

COMPARATIVE ANALYSES FRAMEWORKS

Finally, in addition to the above, we performed a number of comparative analyses frameworks as we moved through the project. These were less detailed analyses than those above, although they all did derive directly from the research evidence. They included:

The use of bold corporate moves
Evolutionary versus revolutionary corporate process
Executive class versus egalitarianism
Causes of decline in once-great comparison companies
Three-circle analysis and fit with core values and purpose

Length of buildup period before breakthrough
Timing of Hedgehog Concept with breakthrough date
Core business versus Hedgehog Concept analysis
Succession analysis and success rates of successors
Role of leadership in the decline of once-great comparison companies

APPENDIX 2.A

INSIDE VERSUS OUTSIDE CEO ANALYSIS

The following tables show the total number of inside versus outside CEOs within each company. For each good-to-great company, we examined all the CEOs from ten years prior to the transition date to 1998. For the direct comparison company, we did the same analysis, using the corresponding good-to-great company's transition date. For each unsustained comparison company, we examined the period from ten years prior to its attempted transition date to 1998. We counted any CEO who had been with the company for one year or less as an outsider.

Good-to-Great Companies	Number of CEOs	Number of Outsiders	Percent of Outsiders
Abbott	6	0	0%
Circuit City	3	0	0%
Fannie Mae	4	2	50%
Gillette	3	0	0%
Kimberly-Clark	4	0	0%
Kroger	4	0	0%
Nucor	2	0	0%
Philip Morris	6	0	0%
Pitney Bowes	4	0	0%
Walgreens	3	0	0%
Wells Fargo	3	0	0%
Total	42	2	4.76%

Direct Comparison Companies	Number of CEOs	Number of Outsiders	Percent of Outsiders
Upjohn	6	2	33%
Silo	6	4	67%
Great Western	3	0	0%
Warner-Lambert	5	1	20%
Scott Paper	5	1	20%
A&P	7	2	29%
Bethlehem Steel	6	0	0%
R. J. Reynolds	9	3	33%
Addressograph	10	7	70%
Eckerd	3	0	0%
Bank of America	5	0	0%
Total	65	20	30.77%

Unsustained Comparison Companies	Number of CEOs	Number of Outsiders	Percent of Outsiders
Burroughs	6	2	33%
Chrysler	4	3	75%
Harris	5	0	0%
Hasbro	3	0	0%
Rubbermaid	4	1	25%
Teledyne	3	0	0%
Total	25	6	24%
Total Comparison Set	90	26	28.89%

SUMMARY ANALYSIS

	Total Number of CEOs	Total Number of Outsiders	Percent of Outsiders	Ratio of Comparison to Good-to-Great
Good-to-Great Companies	42	2	4.76%	
Direct Comparison Companies	65	20	30.77%	6.46
Unsustained Comparison Companies	25	6	24.00%	5.04
Total Comparison Set	90	26	28.89%	6.07

	Number of Companies	Number of Companies That Hired an Outside CEO	Percent of Companies That Hired Outside CEO	Ratio of Comparison to Good-to-Great
Good-to-Great Companies	11	1	9.09%	
Direct Comparison Companies	11	7	63.64%	7.00
Unsustained Comparison Companies	6	3	50.00%	5.50
Total Comparison Set	17	10	58.82%	6.47

APPENDIX 5.A:

INDUSTRY ANALYSIS RANKINGS

We compared each good-to-great company's industry relative to all other industries that appeared in the *Standard & Poor's Analyst's Handbook* for a period from the transition year to 1995. We used the following procedure:

1. For each good-to-great company, determine all industries that are listed in the *S&P Analyst's Handbook* from the year of transition to 1995.
2. For each of these industries, use the total returns from the transition year of the corresponding company to 1995, to determine the percentage change in total returns for a period from the transition year to 1995.
3. Rank the industries according to their percentage returns over this period.

The following table shows that a company does not need to be in a great-performing industry to produce a transition to great results.

INDUSTRY PERFORMANCE FROM TRANSITION YEAR TO 1995, CORRESPONDING TO EACH COMPANY

Company	Years of Calculation	Number of Industries Ranked	Industry That Best Reflects Company	Rank of That Industry	Percentile of Industry
Abbott	1974–1995	70	Medical products	28	40%
Circuit City	1982–1995	80	Retail specialty	17	21%
Fannie Mae	1984–1995	90	S&L*	69	77%
Gillette	1980–1995	76	Cosmetics	19	25%
Kimberly-Clark	1972–1995	64	Household products	18	28%
Kroger	1973–1995	66	Retail food chain	12	19%
Nucor	1975–1995	71	Steel	70	99%

Company	Years of Calculation	Number of Industries Ranked	Industry That Best Reflects Company	Rank of That Industry	Percentile of Industry
Philip Morris	1972–1995†	57	Tobacco	2	4%
Pitney Bowes	1974–1995	70	Computer systems	68	97%
Walgreens	1975–1995	71	Retail drugstore	13	18%
Wells Fargo	1983–1995	84	Major regional banks	64	76%

*The savings and loan industry was deemed the best proxy for Fannie Mae.
†Philip Morris dates from 1972 because S&P data is not available before that date.

APPENDIX 8.A:

DOOM LOOP BEHAVIOR IN THE COMPARISON COMPANIES

DIRECT COMPARISONS

A&P

A&P vacillated, shifting from one strategy to another, always looking for a single stroke to quickly solve its problems. Held pep rallies, launched programs, grabbed fads, fired CEOs, hired CEOs, and fired them yet again. Article headlines for A&P during the years of decline read, "Heralding the Trumpet of Change," "Awakening the Giant," "Renewing A&P," and "Great Expectations." The expectations were never realized.[1]

Addressograph

Went into a Chicken Little "The Sky Is Falling" panic about the decline of its core business. Tried a quixotic "total corporate rejuvenation," throwing itself into the office automation field against IBM, Xerox, and Kodak. When this failed, the next CEO engineered a "strategic flip-flop" away from office automation. Then, "like a brain surgeon vanishing from the operating room in the middle of an operation," that CEO resigned after less than a year. The next CEO does another "180-degree turn" and buys his way into offset printing. It fails; the company takes a write-off. Four CEOs in six years, leading up to 1984. Later, not one, but two bankruptcies.[2]

Bank of America

Went into a reactionary revolution mode in response to deregulation. Fell behind in ATMs and technology, then threw itself into an expensive catch-wup program. Fell behind in California, then launched a crash program to catch-up. Tried to "pull off its own version of Mao's Cultural Revolution" by hiring corporate change consultants who led "corporate encounter groups" and tried to institute a "rah-rah approach to management." Lurched after Charles Schwab; culture clash erupted, and later sold it back. Lurched after Security Pacific, trying to emulate Wells Fargo's Crocker merger; acquisition failed, creating a multibillion-dollar write-off.[3]

Bethlehem Steel

Vacillated back and forth: diversification, then focus on steel, then back to diversification, then back to steel. Fell behind in technology and modernization, then launched a crash program to catch up. Management reacted to the unions, then unions reacted to management, then management reacted to unions, then unions reacted to management, and so on. Meanwhile, foreign competitors and Nucor snuck in from below to devour market share.[4]

Eckerd

Fell into doom loop by making unrelated acquisitions, in search of growth, but without any guiding Hedgehog Concept. Bought a candy company, a chain of department stores, a security service, and a food-service supplier. In the biggest disaster, it bought American Home Video; lost $31 million, then sold it off to Tandy at $72 million below book value. Eckerd never fully recovered, got bought in a leveraged buyout, and later sold out to J. C. Penney.[5]

Great Western Financial

Inconsistency of program. Would zig one way (trying to look more like a bank), then zag another way (trying to become a diversified firm). Into insurance, then later out of insurance. Into leasing and manufactured housing, then back to focus on finance and banking. "Don't worry about what you call us—a bank, an S&L or a Zebra." Held together by the personal vision of the CEO, but when he retired, Great Western stumbled under its unwieldy, incoherent model, fell into reactionary restructuring, and sold out to Washington Mutual.[6]

R. J. Reynolds

As RJR began to slip and found itself under siege from antitobacco forces, it reacted by throwing itself into ill-considered acquisitions, such as Sea-Land. It bought Sea-Land and poured over $2 billion into trying to make it work (all the while, its tobacco factories were falling apart from underinvestment), then sold it at a loss five years later. With each new CEO, it got a new strategy. Later, after losing its number one spot to Philip Morris, RJR threw itself into a leveraged buyout, designed primarily to enrich management rather than build the company.[7]

Scott Paper

Fell into reactionary diversification as its core business came under attack from Procter & Gamble and Kimberly-Clark. With each new CEO, Scott got a new road, a new direction, a new vision. With fanfare, Scott undertook radical change efforts in the late 1980s, but never answered the question, What can we be the best in the world at? Fell into restructuring mode. Hired Al Dunlap, known as Chainsaw Al, who cut 41 percent of the workforce in one fell swoop and then sold the company.[8]

Silo

Vacuum left after death of Sidney Cooper. Next generation pursued growth for growth's sake. Whereas Circuit City would go into a region, build a distribution center, and fill every surrounding town with a store, Silo irrationally jumped from city to city, one store here, another store there, creating a totally unsystematic hodgepodge agglomeration of stores, with no regional economies of scale. Did not stick with a consistent concept or layout. Silo acquired by Cyclops, then Cyclops acquired by Dixons. Management fired by new owners.[9]

Upjohn

Fell into a pattern of selling the future ("The future never looked brighter") and hyping the potential of new products. But results failed to match the hype. Upjohn stock became volatile and speculative—up and down, up and down again—as it sold the sizzle, but never delivered the steak. Later, like a gambler at Las Vegas, it threw its chips on "savior products," such as Rogaine baldness cure. Persistent product problems, with Halcion and others, exacerbated the swings. Eventually succumbed to restructuring disease and merged with Pharmacia.[10]

Warner-Lambert

Lurched back and forth, from consumer products to pharmaceuticals and health care, then back again, then both at the same time, then back to one, then back to the other. Each new CEO had a new vision, and new restructuring, stopping the momentum of his predecessor and starting the flywheel back in another direction. Tried to ignite breakthrough with bold acquisitions, but failed and took hundreds of millions in write-offs. In the end, after years of inconsistent programs, it lurched into the arms of Pfizer, ending its turbulent existence as an independent company.[11]

UNSUSTAINED COMPARISONS

Burroughs

During its rise, Burroughs' CEO, "a brilliant but abusive man," led a sweeping total reengineering. Cost cutting led to morale problems, which led to losing good people. Picked a weak successor. He failed and was replaced by a "brilliant, brash, overly aggressive" CEO who set a new direction, blaming the prior generation. Another massive reorganization, 400 executives leave in one purge. Posters adorned the walls, touting new programs. The company restructured again. Got yet another CEO who tried yet another restructuring, another new direction. More decline, and then another CEO.[12]

Chrysler

Five years of stellar performance, then decline back into crisis. "Like so many patients with a heart condition, we'd survived emergency surgery several years before only to revert to our old unhealthy lifestyle," wrote an insider. Diverted attention into Italian sports cars, corporate jet business, and defense. Revived in second turnaround in 1990s, but eventually sold out to Daimler.[13]

Harris

Rose with a CEO who had a Hedgehog Concept in his head, and who produced an initial flywheel effect. But he did not instill this concept into his executive team. Later, when he retired, executives replaced the Hedgehog Concept with a growth mantra. Harris lurched off into office automation, which proved to be a disaster, and then into a series of unrelated acquisitions. Fell into the "sell the sizzle, but never deliver the steak" syndrome. The flywheel came to a grinding halt.[14]

Hasbro

Hasbro is the one comparison company that nearly got it all right. It built spectacular results by consistently pursuing the Hedgehog Concept of revitalizing classic toy brands, like G.I. Joe. Unfortunately, the architect of the initial transformation died unexpectedly at a young age.His successor appeared to be more a Level 3 (competent manager) than a Level 5 leader. The flywheel slowed. The CEO reacted with restructuring and eventually hired an outsider to rebuild momentum.[15]

Rubbermaid

If there ever was a company that skipped the buildup stage, it's Rubbermaid. Its transition CEO launched "a complete restructuring of the company, a very dramatic and traumatic undertaking." Growth became the mantra, growth even at the expense of long-term momentum in the flywheel. When the CEO retired, it became clear that he was the primary force in the flywheel, not a strong team guided by a systematic Hedgehog Concept. The flywheel slowed; the company succumbed to restructuring disease and selling the future without delivering results. Rubbermaid fell from *Fortune*'s number one most admired to being acquired by Newell, in just five years.[16]

Teledyne

Teledyne rose and fell with the genius of one man, Henry Singleton, known as the Sphinx. The company's Hedgehog Concept was, in essence: Follow Henry's brain. Singleton engineered over a hundred acquisitions, in fields from electronics to exotic metals. The problems arose when Henry retired and took his brain with him. Teledyne fell into a downward spiral, eventually merging with Allegheny.[17]

APPENDIX 8.B

SUMMARY OF ACQUISITION ANALYSIS

GOOD-TO-GREAT COMPANIES VERSUS COMPARISON COMPANIES*

Company	Total Number of Acquisitions during Era Studied	Total Number of Divestitures during Era Studied	Overall Success Rate of Acquisitions Strategy
Abbott	21	5	+2
Upjohn	25	7	NA
Circuit City	1	0	+3
Silo	4	0	–1
Fannie Mae	0	0	+3
Great Western	21	3	–1
Gillette	39	20	+3
Warner-Lambert	32	14	–1
Kimberly-Clark	22	18	+2
Scott Paper	18	24	–2
Kroger	11	9	+2
A&P	14	4	–3
Nucor	2	3	+3
Bethlehem Steel	10	23	–3
Philip Morris	55	19	+1
R. J. Reynolds	36	29	–3
Pitney Bowes	17	8	+1
Addressograph	19	9	–3
Walgreens	11	8	+3
Eckerd	22	9	–1

Company	Total Number of Acquisitions during Era Studied	Total Number of Divestitures during Era Studied	Overall Success Rate of Acquisitions Strategy
Wells Fargo	17	6	+3
Bank of America	22	13	+1
Burroughs	22	7	–2
Chrysler	14	15	–1
Harris	42	7	–1
Hasbro	14	0	+1
Rubbermaid	20	5	+3
Teledyne	85	3	–2

*To construct this table, we determined the total number of acquisitions conducted by each company from the pretransition decade to 1998. We then assessed each acquisition on a scale of –3 to +3, basing our rankings on both financial and qualitative analysis, and created an average score based on these scores. In the case of Upjohn, we could not obtain enough research data to conduct a thorough analysis and thus did not assign a score to the company.

NOTES

CHAPTER 1

1. Beryl Markham, *West with the Night* (San Francisco: North Point Press, 1983), 25.
2. Stock return calculations in this book were determined using data from the University of Chicago Center for Research in Security Prices (CRSP).

   Key definitions:

   - *Monthly Total Return:* The total return to shareholders in a given month, including dividends reinvested, for an individual security.
   - *Cumulative Stock Return:* The compounded value of $Y invested in an individual security between times t1 and t2, using the formula: $Y × (1 + Monthly Total Return @ m1) × (1 + Monthly Total Return @ m2) × . . . (1 + Monthly Total Return @ t2); where m1 = end of the first month following t1, m2 = end of the second month following t1, and so forth.
   - *General Stock Market* (also called the *General Market* or just the *Market*): NYSE/AMEX/NASDAQ value-weighted return, which consists of the combined market value of all companies traded on these exchanges (including dividends reinvested) weighted by the capitalization of the company divided by the capitalization of the market.
   - *Cumulative Return Ratio to the Market:* At the end of any given time, this ratio is calculated as the cumulative return of $Y invested in the company divided by the cumulative return of $Y invested in the general stock market, where the $Y is invested in both the company and the market on the same date.
   - *Transition Date* (for good-to-great companies): The precise transition date for a good-to-great company is the date when the company's performance—in terms of cumulative stock returns relative to the general stock market—turns upward after a period of market to below-market performance, and never again falls below this point.

3. Using University of Chicago Center for Research in Security Prices data, cumulative returns were calculated from December 31, 1984, to December 31, 1999, for GE and the general market, all dividends reinvested, adjusted for stock splits.
4. The chart on page 2 was created using the following methodology:

1. For each good-to-great company, invest $1 at the transition date minus 15 years. Also invest $1 in the general market. Calculate the cumulative stock return of $1 invested at the transition date minus 15 years through the transition date plus 15 years for the good-to-great company and the general market. In the case of CRSP data not being available (usually because the company was not yet publicly traded, merged, or was acquired), use market returns in lieu of company returns.
2. For each good-to-great company, calculate the ratio of cumulative stock returns to the general market from t – 15 to t + 15 to create a "ratio of cumulative returns" curve.
3. Shift this "ratio of cumulative returns curve" for each good-to-great company such that at the transition date, the ratio of cumulative stock returns to the market equals precisely 1. This shifts the transition dates for all the good-to-great companies to a common reference point—time t. Do this by dividing the ratio of cumulative stock returns to the market at *each* month (calculated in step 2) from t – 15 to t + 15 by the ratio of the cumulative stock return number calculated at *precisely* the transition date.
4. Use these shifted returns to calculate the average ratio of cumulative stock returns to the market across all eleven good-to-great companies at each month t – 15 to t + 15. In other words, calculate the average of the calculation in step 3 at t – 15 across all eleven companies, then t – 15 plus 1 month for all eleven companies, plus 2 months, and so forth, for all 360 months. This creates the combined, cumulative returns relative to the market curve for the good-to-great companies.
5. For each direct comparison company, repeat steps 1–3 above, using the same dates for the direct comparison company as for its counterpart good-to-great company.
6. For the direct comparison companies as a set, repeat step 4 above.
7. This chart shows the good-to-great companies versus the direct comparison companies, cumulative returns ratio to the market, t – 15 to t + 15, with t as a common reference point where the ratio to the market is set to 1.0.

The chart on page 4 was created using the following methodology:

1. For each good-to-great company, invest $1 on December 31, 1964 (the date of the first transition in our study).
2. For each good-to-great company, calculate cumulative stock returns at the market rate of return through the transition-date month, then switch over to using returns from the good-to-great company. For any missing CRSP data (usually because the company was not yet publicly traded, merged, or was acquired), use the market rate of return in lieu of company returns.

3. For each month from December 31, 1964, through December 31, 1999, add the cumulative returns across all eleven companies and divide by 11. This gives the cumulative return of $1 invested in the entire set.
4. For the general market, invest $1 on December 31, 1964, and carry through December 31, 1999.
5. For each direct comparison company repeat steps 1–3, holding the company at the market rate until the date of transition for the corresponding good-to-great company. Notes: RJR held at market rate from May 31, 1989, to December 31, 1999, as the company emerged from its LBO in different pieces (RJR and Nabisco).
6. This chart shows the market versus the comparison companies versus the good-to-great companies, the value of $1 invested from December 31, 1964, to year 2000.

CHAPTER 2

1. David McCullough, *Truman* (New York: Simon & Schuster, 1992), 564.
2. Robert Spector, based on research and a manuscript by William W. Wicks, *Shared Values: A History of Kimberly-Clark* (Connecticut: Greenwich Publishing Group, 1997), 101.
3. "Darwin Smith May Have Done Too Good a Job," *Business Week*, August 1, 1988, 57; "Rae Takes On the Paper Industry's Tough Lone Wolf," *Globe and Mail*, July 20, 1991; "Former CEO of K-C Dies," *Dallas Morning News*, December 27, 1995, 1D.
4. Research Interview #5-E, page 26.
5. Research Interview #5-E, page 26.
6. "Darwin Smith May Have Done Too Good a Job," *Business Week*, August 1, 1988, 57.
7. "Darwin Smith May Have Done Too Good a Job," *Business Week*, August 1, 1988, 57; "Kimberly-Clark Bets, Wins on Innovation," *Wall Street Journal*, November 22, 1991, A5; "Darwin E. Smith, 69, Executive Who Remade a Paper Company," *New York Times*, December 28, 1995, B9; Robert Spector, based on research and a manuscript by William W. Wicks, *Shared Values: A History of Kimberly-Clark* (Connecticut: Greenwich Publishing Group, 1997), 101.
8. Robert Spector, based on research and a manuscript by William W. Wicks, *Shared Values: A History of Kimberly-Clark* (Connecticut: Greenwich Publishing Group, 1997), 112.
9. *International Directory of Company Histories*, vol. 3 (Chicago: St. James Press, 1991), 40; "Kimberly-Clark—Aiming for the Consumer," *Financial World*, April 1, 1970, 15.
10. Robert Spector, based on research and a manuscript by William W. Wicks, *Shared Values: A History of Kimberly-Clark* (Connecticut: Green-

wich Publishing Group, 1997), 106, 112; "Darwin E. Smith, 69, Executive Who Remade a Paper Company," *New York Times*, December 28, 1995, B9; "Former CEO of K-C Dies," *Dallas Morning News*, December 27, 1995, 1D; Research Interview #5-E, page 6; "Paper Tiger: How Kimberly-Clark Wraps Its Bottom Line in Disposable Huggies," *Wall Street Journal*, July 23, 1987, 1.

11. "The Battle of the Bottoms," *Forbes*, March 24, 1997, 98.
12. "The Battle of the Bottoms," *Forbes*, March 24, 1997, 98.
13. Robert Spector, based on research and a manuscript by William W. Wicks, *Shared Values: A History of Kimberly-Clark* (Connecticut: Greenwich Publishing Group, 1997), 10.
14. Shelby Foote, *The Civil War: A Narrative: Red River to Appomattox* (New York: Random House, 1975), 1040; James M. McPherson, *Battle Cry of Freedom: The Civil War Era* (New York: Ballantine Books, 1989), 854.
15. Gordon McKibben, *Cutting Edge: Gillette's Journey to Global Leadership* (Boston: Harvard Business School Press, 1998), 14.
16. Company "Chronology," Gillette corporate typescript, 1995; Gordon McKibben, *Cutting Edge: Gillette's Journey to Global Leadership* (Boston: Harvard Business School Press, 1998), 198, 199; Rita Ricardo-Campbell, *Resisting Hostile Takeovers: The Case of Gillette* (Connecticut: Praeger Publishers, 1997), 153.
17. Gordon McKibben, *Cutting Edge: Gillette's Journey to Global Leadership* (Boston: Harvard Business School Press, 1998), 159.
18. Rita Ricardo-Campbell, *Resisting Hostile Takeovers: The Case of Gillette* (Connecticut: Praeger Publishers, 1997).
19. Author conversation with Gillette CEO, summer 2000. "We invested almost $1.5 billion in Sensor and Mach3. We believed that these projects would have been scrapped had the takeover happened."
20. Gordon McKibben, *Cutting Edge: Gillette's Journey to Global Leadership* (Boston: Harvard Business School Press, 1998), 158. Calculations run using CRSP data.
21. Gordon McKibben, *Cutting Edge: Gillette's Journey to Global Leadership* (Boston: Harvard Business School Press, 1998), 254.
22. "Maxwell Relinquishes Rights to $5.5 Million Final Retirement Payment," *PR Newswire*, January 21, 1992; "$5.5 Million Declined by Ex-Official," *Washington Post*, January 22, 1992, F1.
23. "Iacocca's Last Stand," *Fortune*, April 20, 1992, 63.
24. "Sincere Tyranny," *Forbes*, January 28, 1985, 54.
25. "Managing: Leaders of Corporate Change," *Fortune*, December 14, 1992, 104.
26. "Chairman Quits Post," *New York Times*, November 17, 1992, D5; "Rubbermaid's Sad Succession Tale," *New York Times*, July 5, 1987, C1.
27. "Is Rubbermaid Reacting Too Late?" *New York Times*, December 22, 1996, A1.

28. Research Interview #7-D, page 17.
29. Chris Jones and Duane Duffy, "Media Hype Analysis" (unpublished), *Good to Great* research project, summers 1998, 1999.
30. "Did CEO Dunlap Save Scott Paper—or Just Pretty It Up? The Shredder," *Business Week*, January 15, 1996.
31. "Did CEO Dunlap Save Scott Paper—or Just Pretty It Up? The Shredder," *Business Week*, January 15, 1996; "Chain Saw Al to the Rescue?" *Forbes*, August 26, 1996; "After the Fall," *Across the Board*, April 1996, 28–33; "Only the Paranoid Survive," *Worth Online*, October 1996; Albert J. Dunlap with Bob Andelman, *Mean Business: How I Save Bad Companies and Make Good Companies Great* (New York: Fireside, 1997), 20.
32. Albert J. Dunlap with Bob Andelman, *Mean Business: How I Save Bad Companies and Make Good Companies Great* (New York: Fireside, 1997), 132.
33. The cases where a charismatic CEO eventually became a liability for the company were Great Western, Warner-Lambert, Scott Paper, Bethlehem Steel, R. J. Reynolds, Addressograph-Multigraph, Eckerd, Bank of America, Burroughs, Chrysler, Rubbermaid, and Teledyne.
34. "President Iacocca," *Wall Street Journal*, July 28, 1982, 1; "Iacocca Hands Over the Keys to Chrysler," *Investor's Business Daily*, January 4, 1993, 1.
35. "Iacocca Hands Over the Keys to Chrysler," *Investor's Business Daily*, January 4, 1993, 1.
36. "How Chrysler Filled Detroit's Biggest Shoes," *Wall Street Journal*, September 7, 1994, B1.
37. "Why Certain Stocks," *Wall Street Journal*, April 13, 1995, A1; "Chrysler's New Plan: Sell Cars," *Fortune*, June 26, 1995, 19.
38. "Will Success Spoil Chrysler?" *Fortune*, January 10, 1994; "Company of the Year: Chrysler Has the Hot Cars. More Important, It Has a Smart, Disciplined Management Team," *Forbes*, January 13, 1997, 82; "Daimler-Benz Will Acquire Chrysler in $36 Billion Deal That Will Reshape Industry," *New York Times*, May 7, 1998, A6.
39. Research Interview #1-A, page 3; Research Interview #1-G, page 35; "A Drugmaker's Return to Health," *Business Week*, April 26, 1976, 38; Herman Kogan, *The Long White Line: The Story of Abbott Laboratories* (New York: Random House, 1963), 249.
40. The Upjohn Company, *International Directory of Company Histories*, 707; "The Medicine Men of Kalamazoo," *Fortune*, July 1959, 106.
41. Leigh Wilbanks, "CEO Analysis Unit" (unpublished), *Good to Great* research project, summer 1998.
42. University of Chicago Center for Research in Securities Prices data, all dividends reinvested and adjusted for stock splits.
43. Research Interview #10-D, pages 9–10.
44. Herman Kogan and Rick Kogan, *Pharmacist to the Nation* (Deerfield, Ill.: Walgreens Company, 1989), 236; Research Interview #10-F, page 3.

45. Research Interview #2-G, page 10.
46. University of Chicago Center for Research in Securities Prices data, all dividends reinvested and adjusted for stock splits.
47. Research Interview #2-G, page 16.
48. Research Interview #7-H, page 12.
49. Research Interview #8-A, pages 4–5, 9, 10.
50. Joseph F. Cullman 3d, *I'm a Lucky Guy* (Joseph F. Cullman 3d, 1998), 1.
51. "Searching for Profits at Bethlehem," *New York Times*, December 25, 1983, C1.
52. "Steel Man Ken Iverson," *Inc.*, April 1, 1986, 40.
53. Jeffrey L. Rodengen, *The Legend of the Nucor Corporation* (Fort Lauderdale, Fla.: Write Stuff Enterprises, 1997), 71.
54. Joseph F. Cullman 3d, *I'm a Lucky Guy* (Joseph F. Cullman 3d, 1998).
55. Gordon McKibben, *Cutting Edge: Gillette's Journey to Global Leadership* (Boston: Harvard Business School Press, 1998), 78–79.

CHAPTER 3

1. Tom Wolfe, *The Electric Kool-Aid Acid Test* (New York: Bantam, 1999), 83.
2. Warren Buffett, *The Essays of Warren Buffett: Lessons for Corporate America*, selected, arranged, and introduced by Lawrence A. Cunningham (Lawrence A. Cunningham, Benjamin N. Cardozo School of Law, Yeshiva University, 1998), 97.
3. Research Interview #11-B, page 5.
4. Duane Duffy, "Industry Analysis Unit" (unpublished), *Good to Great* research project, summer 1998, CRSP financial data analysis.
5. Research Interview #11-H, page 5; "A Banker Even Keynes Might Love," *Forbes*, July 2, 1984, 40.
6. Research Interview #11-F, pages 1–2, 5.
7. Research Interview #11-H, pages 15, 20.
8. Gary Hector, *Breaking the Bank: The Decline of BankAmerica* (Little, Brown & Company, 1988), 145.
9. "Big Quarterly Deficit Stuns BankAmerica," *Wall Street Journal*, July 18, 1985, A1.
10. Gary Hector, *Breaking the Bank: The Decline of BankAmerica* (Little, Brown & Company, 1988), 73, 143; "Big Quarterly Deficit Stuns BankAmerica," *Wall Street Journal*, July 18, 1985, A1; "Autocrat Tom Clausen," *Wall Street Journal*, October 17, 1986, 1; further confirmed in conversation between Jim Collins and two former Bank of America executives, July–August 2000.
11. "Combat Banking," *Wall Street Journal*, October 2, 1989, A1.

12. Research Interview #3-I, page 7.
13. Research Interview #3-I, pages 3–14.
14. Research Interview #3-I, page 7.
15. Research Interview #3-I, pages 3, 15.
16. Research Interview #3-A, page 13.
17. Research Interview #3-D, page 6.
18. "Eckerd Ad Message: Tailored to Fit," *Chainstore Age Executive,* May 1988, 242; "Heard on the Street," *Wall Street Journal,* January 21, 1964, B25; "Jack Eckerd Resigns as Chief Executive," *Wall Street Journal,* July 24, 1974, 17; "J. C. Penney Gets Eckerd Shares," *Wall Street Journal,* December 18, 1996, B10; "J. C. Penney Has Seen the Future," *Kiplinger's Personal Finance Magazine,* February 1, 1997, 28.
19. Research Interview #10-E, page 16.
20. "Tuning In," *Forbes,* April 13, 1981, 96; "Video Follies," *Forbes,* November 5, 1984, 43; Research Interview #10-F, page 10.
21. "The Forbes Four Hundred," *Forbes,* October 17, 1994, 200.
22. *International Directory of Company Histories,* vol. 10 (Chicago: St. James Press, 1995), 520.
23. *International Directory of Company Histories,* vol. 10 (Chicago: St. James Press, 1995); "Making Big Waves with Small Fish," *Business Week,* December 30, 1967, 36.
24. "The Sphinx Speaks," *Forbes,* February 20, 1978, 33.
25. "The Singular Henry Singleton," *Forbes,* July 9, 1979, 45.
26. Scott Jones, "Executive Compensation Analysis Unit" (unpublished), *Good to Great* research project, summer 1999.
27. Jim Collins, "Summary Changes in Compensation Analysis, Summary Notes #5" (unpublished), *Good to Great* research project, summer 1999.
28. "Nucor Gets Loan," *Wall Street Journal,* March 3, 1972, 11; "Nucor's Big-Buck Incentives," *Business Week,* September 21, 1981, 42.
29. "A New Philosophy," *Winston-Salem Journal,* March 21, 1993; "Changing the Rules of the Game," *Planning Review,* September/October 1993, 9.
30. "How Nucor Crawfordsville Works," *Iron Age New Steel,* December 1995, 36–52.
31. "A New Philosophy," *Winston-Salem Journal,* March 21, 1993.
32. "Nucor Gets Loan," *Wall Street Journal,* March 3, 1972, B11.
33. Research Interview #9-F, page 29.
34. Joseph F. Cullman 3d, *I'm a Lucky Guy* (Joseph F. Cullman 3d, 1998), 82.
35. "Bold Banker: Wells Fargo Takeover of Crocker Is Yielding Profit but Some Pain," *Wall Street Journal,* August 5, 1986, A1.
36. "Bold Banker: Wells Fargo Takeover of Crocker Is Yielding Profit but Some Pain," *Wall Street Journal,* August 5, 1986, A1.
37. Research Interview #11-G, page 10; Research Interview #11-A, page 29; Research Interview #11-F, page 11; "Bold Banker: Wells Fargo Takeover

of Crocker Is Yielding Profit but Some Pain," *Wall Street Journal,* August 5, 1986, A1.

38. "Boot Camp for Bankers," *Forbes,* July 23, 1990, 273.
39. Research Interview #11-H, pages 10–11.
40. Chris Jones and Duane Duffy, "Layoffs Analysis" (unpublished), *Good to Great* research project, summers 1998 and 1999.
41. "Wells Buys Crocker in Biggest U.S. Bank Merger," *American Banker,* February 10, 1986, 39; "Wells Fargo Takeover of Crocker Is Yielding Profit but Some Pain," *Wall Street Journal,* August 5, 1986, A1; "A California Bank That Is Anything but Laid Back," *Business Week,* April 2, 1990, 95.
42. Chris Jones and Duane Duffy, "Layoffs Analysis" (unpublished), *Good to Great* research project, summers 1998 and 1999.
43. Research Interview #2-A, pages 1, 11.
44. "Industry Fragmentation Spells Opportunity for Appliance Retailer," *Investment Dealers' Digest,* October 12, 1971, 23.
45. "Circuit City: Paying Close Attention to Its People," *Consumer Electronics,* June 1988, 36.
46. Research Interview #2-D, pages 1–2.
47. "Dixons Makes $384 Million U.S. Bid," *Financial Times,* February 18, 1987, 1; "UK Electronics Chain Maps US Strategy; Dixons Moving to Acquire Silo," *HFD—the Weekly Home Furnishing Newspaper,* March 2, 1987; "Dixons Tightens Grip on Silo," *HFD—the Weekly Home Furnishings Newspaper,* February 3, 1992, 77.
48. Eric Hagen, "Executive Churn Analysis" (unpublished), *Good to Great* research project, summer 1999.
49. "Gillette: The Patient Honing of Gillette," *Forbes,* February 16, 1981, 83–87.
50. "When Marketing Takes Over at R. J. Reynolds," *Business Week,* November 13, 1978, 82; "Tar Wars," *Forbes,* November 10, 1980, 190; Bryan Burrough and John Helyar, *Barbarians at the Gate* (New York: HarperCollins, 1991), 51.
51. Research Interview #8-D, page 7.
52. "The George Weissman Road Show," *Forbes,* November 10, 1980, 179.
53. Joseph F. Cullman 3d, *I'm a Lucky Guy* (Joseph F. Cullman 3d, 1998), 120.
54. Research Interview #5-B, page 8.
55. Research Interview #5-A, page 7.
56. "How Do Tobacco Executives Live with Themselves?" *New York Times Magazine,* March 20, 1994, 40.
57. Research Interview #8-B, page 5.
58. Gordon McKibben, *Cutting Edge: Gillette's Journey to Global Leadership* (Boston: Harvard Business School Press, 1998), 256.
59. Joseph F. Cullman 3d, *I'm a Lucky Guy* (Joseph F. Cullman 3d, 1998), 149.
60. Research Interview #5-A, page 10.

CHAPTER 4

1. Winston S. Churchill, *The Hinge of Fate* (Boston: Houghton Mifflin, 1950), 61.
2. "Hermit Kingdom," *Wall Street Journal*, December 12, 1958, A1; William I. Walsh, *The Rise and Decline of the Great Atlantic and Pacific Tea Company* (New Jersey: Lyle Stuart, Inc., 1986), 74. Walsh states that A&P had sales of $3.2 billion in 1950 and was the largest privately owned company and the largest retail organization in the world. Its sales volume exceeded that of U.S. Steel and Standard Oil and was second only to General Motors in total sales volume for corporations of any kind.
3. "Hermit Kingdom," *Wall Street Journal*, December 12, 1958, A1.
4. "We Should Have Moved a Lot Sooner," *Forbes*, May 15, 1976, 99.
5. William I. Walsh, *The Rise and Decline of the Great Atlantic and Pacific Tea Company* (Lyle Stuart, Inc., 1986), 78–80; *Fortune*, March 1963, 105.
6. "We Should Have Moved a Lot Sooner," *Forbes*, May 15, 1976, 99; "A&P's Ploy: Cutting Prices to Turn a Profit," *Business Week*, May 20, 1972, 76; *Fortune*, March 1963, 105.
7. "Ailing A&P," *Wall Street Journal*, April 21, 1964, A1.
8. William I. Walsh, *The Rise and Decline of the Great Atlantic and Pacific Tea Company* (Lyle Stuart, Inc., 1986), 103–105.
9. "A&P's Ploy: Cutting Prices to Turn a Profit," *Business Week*, May 20, 1972, 76; "A&P's 'Price War' Bites Broadly and Deeply," *Business Week*, September 30, 1972, 56; "Banking Against A&P," *Time*, December 11, 1972, 108; "How A&P Got Creamed," *Fortune*, January 1973, 103; "A&P Counts the Cost of Its Pyrrhic Victory," *Business Week*, April 28, 1973, 117.
10. "Stumbling Giant," *Wall Street Journal*, January 10, 1978, A1.
11. "Shifting Gears: A&P's Price-Cutting Didn't Create Kroger's Problems . . ." *Forbes*, November 1, 1972, 29; "Superstores May Suit Customers to a T-shirt or a T-bone," *Wall Street Journal*, March 13, 1973, A1; "Plain and Fancy: Supermarket Boutiques Spur Kroger's Gains," *Barron's*, May 25, 1981, 37; "250,000 Unpaid Consultants," *Forbes*, September 14, 1981, 147.
12. Research Interview #6-C, page 6.
13. "Kroger and Fred Meyer Merge to Create No. 1 U.S. Grocery Biz," *Discount Store News*, May 3, 1999, 1.
14. "Trouble Stalks the Aisles at A&P," *Business Week*, September 23, 1991, 60.
15. "Pitney Bowes' Pep," *Financial World*, April 11, 1962, 22; "No Middle Ground," *Forbes*, January 1, 1961, 75.
16. *Moody's Industrial Manual 2000*.
17. "Roy Ash Is Having Fun at Addressogrief-Multigrief," *Fortune*, February 27, 1978, 46; "How Roy Ash Got Burned," *Fortune*, April 6, 1981, 71.

18. "Up from the Ashes," *Forbes*, April 16, 1979, 104; "AM International: The Cash Bind That Threatens a Turnaround," *Business Week*, August 18, 1980, 118; "Ash Forced out of Two AM Posts," *New York Times*, February 24, 1981, D1.
19. "Why Ash Was Ousted at AM International," *Business Week*, March 9, 1981, 32; "Roy Ash Resigns under Fire," *Fortune*, March 23, 1981, 16; "How Roy Ash Got Burned," *Fortune*, April 6, 1981, 71; "Up from the Ashes," *Forbes*, April 16, 1979, 104; "AM Files Chapter 11," *New York Times*, April 15, 1982, D1.
20. "When Technology Was Not Enough," *Business Week*, January 25, 1982, 62; "How Roy Ash Got Burned," *Fortune*, April 6, 1981, 71; "AM International: The Cash Bind That Threatens a Turnaround," *Business Week*, August 18, 1980, 118.
21. "When Technology Was Not Enough," *Business Week*, January 25, 1982, 62; "AM's Brightest Years Now Dim Memories," *New York Times*, April 15, 1982, D1.
22. "How Roy Ash Got Burned," *Fortune*, April 6, 1981, 71; "High-Technology Dream Turns into a Nightmare," *Financial Times*, March 2, 1982, 17.
23. "AM International: The Cash Bind That Threatens a Turnaround," *Business Week*, August 18, 1980, 118; "The Unflappable Roy Ash," *Forbes*, December 8, 1980, 38.
24. "AM International: The Cash Bind That Threatens a Turnaround," *Business Week*, August 18, 1980, 118; "Ash Forced Out of Two AM Posts," *New York Times*, February 24, 1981, D1; "When Technology Was Not Enough," *Business Week*, January 25, 1982, 62.
25. Research Interview #9-G, page 12.
26. Research Interview #9-E, page 11.
27. Research Interview #9-C, page 17.
28. Research Interview #9-G, page 12.
29. Research Interview #9-I, page 21.
30. Research Interview #9-C, page 20; #9-I, pages 21–22; #9-D, page 11.
31. Winston S. Churchill, *The Grand Alliance* (Boston: Houghton Mifflin, 1950), 371.
32. Churchill created this special unit and put a lot of weight on it. According to Martin Gilbert, Churchill frequently consulted his Statistical Office, which was headed by a civilian, Professor Lindemenn, before he made critical decisions. He directly and continuously asked them to "check facts" on such important topics as munitions production, imports and shipping losses, aircraft losses, and aircraft production. Martin Gilbert, *The Churchill War Papers*, vol. 2 (New York: W. W. Norton, 1995), xvii.
33. Winston S. Churchill, *The Gathering Storm* (Boston: Houghton Mifflin, 1948), 667.
34. Research Interview, #2-C, page 16.

35. "Man of Steel: Correnti Hopes to Take Nucor to No. 1," *Business Journal–Charlotte,* September 19, 1994, 3.
36. Standard & Poor's Industry Survey Database, Metals: Industrial, Iron and Steel, January 18, 2001, Leo J. Larkin, metals analyst.
37. Research Interview #7-C, page 13.
38. Research Interview #7-E, page 7; Jeffrey L. Rodengen, *The Legend of Nucor* (Fort Lauderdale, Fla.: Write Stuff, 1997), 45.
39. Jeffrey L. Rodengen, *The Legend of Nucor* (Fort Lauderdale, Fla.: Write Stuff, 1997), 39.
40. Research Interview #7-A, page 3.
41. Joseph F. Cullman 3d, *I'm a Lucky Guy* (Joseph F. Cullman 3d, 1998), 144; Richard Kluger, *Ashes to Ashes* (New York: Alfred A. Knopf. 1996), 485; "Beverage Management: Risky—but Straight Up 7UP," *Forbes,* April 12, 1982, 208; "Coke Peppers 7UP and Pepsi," *Advertising Age,* February 24, 1986, 2, 86.
42. Joseph F. Cullman 3d, *I'm a Lucky Guy* (Joseph F. Cullman 3d, 1998), 147.
43. John Strohmeyer, *Crisis in Bethlehem* (Pittsburgh: University of Pittsburgh Press, 1986), 72–73; "The Labors of Trautlein," *Forbes,* February 15, 1981, 36; "Bethlehem's Thin Slab Yawn," *American Metal Market,* November 17, 1989, 4; "Bethlehem Museum," National Public Radio transcript, July 5, 1998.
44. "Upjohn: Safety of Upjohn's Oral Antidiabetic Drug Doubted in Study; Firm Disputes Finding," *Wall Street Journal,* May 21, 1970, A6; "Upjohn: A Bitter Pill for Upjohn Shareholders (Drug Company Involved in Antibiotic Controversy)," *Financial World,* January 23, 1974, 28; "Upjohn: The Upjohn Company: Presentation by R. T. Parfet, Jr., Chairman of the Board and Chief Executive Officer, and L. C. Hoff, Vice President and General Manager, Pharmaceutical Division, to the Security Analysts of San Francisco, September 11, 1975," *Wall Street Transcript,* October 13, 1975, 41648–41650; "Upjohn: Hair-Raising Happenings at Upjohn (Testing a Cure for Baldness, the Company Squirms at the Unwelcome Clamor)," *Fortune,* April 6, 1981, 67–69; "Upjohn: FDA Says Upjohn Exaggerated Claims on Drug's Value in Treating Baldness," *Wall Street Journal,* June 18, 1986, A6; "Upjohn: Riptide: Can Upjohn Manage Its Way out of a Product Gap? If Not, It Could Be Swept into the Industry Merger Wave," *Financial World,* September 5, 1989, 26–28; "Upjohn: The Corporation: Strategies: Will This Formula Cure What Ails Upjohn? As the Sharks Circle, It's Spending Big on R&D and Marketing," *Business Week,* September 18, 1989, 65; "Upjohn: Technology and Medicine: Upjohn Sleep Drug Being Investigated for Safety by FDA," *Wall Street Journal,* September 20, 1984, B4; "Upjohn: Medicine: Halcion Takes Another Hit: Tainted Data Played a Key Role in FDA Approval," *Newsweek,* February 17, 1992, 58; "Upjohn: Medicine: Fuel-

ing the Fire over Halcion: Upjohn's Own Staff Has Raised Safety Concerns," *Newsweek,* May 25, 1992, 84; "Upjohn: Top of the News: Successions: At Upjohn, a Grim Changing of the Guard: Ley Smith Inherits the Problem-Plagued Drugmaker at a Critical Juncture," *Business Week,* May 3, 1993, 36.

45. Research Interview #11-B, page 7.
46. "No-Longer-So-Great Scott," *Forbes,* August 1, 1972, 25.
47. "Scott Paper Back on Its Feet," *Forbes,* December 15, 1976, 69–70.
48. "Scott Isn't Lumbering Anymore," *Fortune,* September 30, 1985, 48–55.
49. "Scott Paper: Back on the Attack," *Financial World,* August 1, 1979, 22–23; "A Paper Tiger Grows Claws," *Business Week,* August 23, 1969, 100–102; "Outlook for 1970—Year-End Statement," *Paper Trade Journal,* December 22, 1969, 33; "Profits Peak for Scott Paper," *Financial World,* April 22, 1970, 13, 28; "No-Longer-So-Great Scott," *Forbes,* August 1, 1972, 25.
50. Research Interview #5-F, page 2.
51. Research Interview #5-E, page 22.
52. Research Interview #6-A, page 19.
53. Ann Kaiser Stearns, *Coming Back: Rebuilding Lives after Crisis and Loss* (New York: Ballantine, 1988), 294. In her work, Stearns describes the findings of these studies, which we believe provide a scientific basis for understanding the effectiveness of the Stockdale Paradox. We were also influenced by the work of Mihaly Csikszentmihalyi. In his comprehensive investigation into the nature of happiness in the book *Flow,* Mihaly Csikszentmihalyi discusses the transformational potential of apparent tragedy, using as an example the studies of Professor Fausto Massimini of the University of Milan. In these studies, some paraplegics and other severely handicapped people asserted that their personal tragedies had actually resulted in a positive experience that led them to live fuller lives. (Mihaly Csikszentmihalyi, *Flow* [New York: HarperPerennial, 1990], 192–193.) For another viewpoint on this subject, also see the work of Dr. Al Siebert, who wrote *The Survivor Personality—How Life's Best Survivors Thrive in Difficult Situations and Convert Misfortune into Good Luck.*
54. Fannie Mae got 9.3 percent for its mortgage portfolio but had to pay 14.63 percent for the short-term debt it issued. "David Maxwell Takes Over Troubled Fannie Mae," *Washington Post,* May 21, 1981; "Fannie Mae Searches for Higher Ground," *Fortune,* July 13, 1981, 110.
55. "Fannie Mae Searches for Higher Ground," *Fortune,* July 13, 1981, 110.
56. "Fannie Mae Searches for Higher Ground," *Fortune,* July 13, 1981, 110.
57. Conversation with David Maxwell, November 14, 1997.
58. Tim Brooks and Earle Marsh, *The Complete Directory of Primetime Networks and Cable TV Shows* (New York: Ballantine, 1999), 929.
59. Jim and Sybil Stockdale, *In Love and War* (Maryland: Naval Institute Press, 1990); *Stockdale Triumphs,* video presentation—1994 Stanford Alumni Association (Stanford, Calif.).

CHAPTER 5

1. Plato attributed this pithy quote to the Scribes of Delphi in *The Protagoras,* 343B; *Plato: The Protagoras and Meno Translated by* W. K. C. *Guthrie* (New York and London: Penguin Classics, 1956), 77.
2. Isaiah Berlin, *The Hedgehog and the Fox* (Chicago: Elephant Paperbacks, 1993).
3. Conversation with Marvin Bressler, October 2000.
4. Research Interview #10-F, page 3.
5. Research Interview #10-D, page 22.
6. "Convenience with a Difference," *Forbes,* June 11, 1990.
7. Walgreens Annual Report 1998, 16.
8. "Turning In," *Forbes,* April 13, 1981, 96.
9. "Tandy Agrees to Buy Assets of Eckerd Unit," *Wall Street Journal,* July 5, 1985, A4.
10. *Moody's Industrial Subsidiary List* (Mergent FIS, 2000).
11. Lawrence A. Cunningham and Warren E. Buffett, *The Essays of Warren Buffett: Lessons for Corporate America* (Cunningham Group, Benjamin N. Cardozo School of Law, Yeshiva University 1998), 98.
12. "Warren Buffett's Favorite Banker," *Forbes,* October 18, 1993, 46.
13. "Wells Fargo Targets Southern California," *American Banker,* July 10, 1987, 1; "Wells Fargo to Cut Overseas Activities to Boost Its Profit," *Wall Street Journal,* May 3, 1985, A32; "Wells Fargo Trims Its Sails," *American Banker,* May 3, 1985, 2; "A Banker Even Keynes Might Love," *Forbes,* July 2, 1984, 42.
14. "BankAmerica Launches Probe," *Wall Street Journal,* January 28, 1985, A27; "More Than Mortgages Ails BankAmerica," *Fortune,* April 1, 1985, 50; "Big Quarterly Deficit Stuns BankAmerica," *Wall Street Journal,* July 18, 1985, A1; "Sam Armacost's Sea of Troubles," *Banker,* September 1, 1985, 18.
15. Research Interview #11-H, pages 5, 13.
16. Research Interview #11-F, pages 5, 11.
17. "Boot Camp for Bankers," *Forbes,* July 23, 1990, 273.
18. "Hospital Suppliers Strike Back," *New York Times,* March 31, 1985, C1; *The Abbott Almanac: 100 Years of Commitment to Quality Health Care* (Elmsford, N.Y.: Benjamin Company), 1987, 170, 210; "Abbott: Profiting from Products That Cut Costs," *Business Week,* June 18, 1984, 56; "In Medical Testing, Abbott Is the Name of the Game," *Business Week,* June 1, 1987, 90.
19. "Riptide: Can Upjohn Manage Its Way out of a Product Gap?" *Financial World,* September 5, 1989, 26; "Upjohn: The Corporation: Strategies: Will This Formula Cure What Ails Upjohn? As the Sharks Circle, It's Spending Big on R&D and Marketing," *Business Week,* September 18, 1989, 65.

20. "Riptide: Can Upjohn Manage Its Way out of a Product Gap?" *Financial World*, September 5, 1989, 26.
21. "Upjohn: Mergers: Upjohn Finally Makes It to the Big Leagues: How CEO Zabriskie Engineered the Pharmacia Merger," *Business Week*, September 4, 1995, 35.
22. 1960 and 1961 Abbott Annual Reports.
23. "Hasbro May Alter Bid to Appease Tonka Holders," *London Financial Times*, April 16, 1991, 26; "Tonka Says Yes to Hasbro," *London Financial Times*, April 19, 1991, 30.
24. "Tobacco: Profit Despite Attacks," *New York Times*, January 25, 1979, D1.
25. James C. Collins and Jerry I. Porras, *Built to Last* (New York: HarperCollins, 1997), 86.
26. Bryan Burrough and John Helyar, *Barbarians at the Gate* (New York: HarperCollins, 1991).
27. Research Interview #5-A, page 13.
28. "An Iconoclast in a Cutthroat World," *Chief Executive*, March 1996.
29. "Gillette Holds Its Edge by Endlessly Searching for a Better Shave," *Wall Street Journal*, December 10, 1992, A1.
30. Research Interview #3-G, page 7.
31. The comparison companies that displayed an obsession with growth were Bank of America, Addressograph-Multigraph, Eckerd, Great Western Financial, Silo, Upjohn, Warner-Lambert, Burroughs, Chrysler, Harris, Rubbermaid, and Teledyne.
32. "The Wall Street Transcript: Corporate Critics Confidential: Savings and Loan Industry," *Wall Street Journal*, June 12, 1989, 93,903.
33. "How Playing It Safe Worked for Great Western," *Business Week*, September 7, 1987, 70.
34. "The Wall Street Transcript: Remarks by James F. Montgomery to the Boston Security Analysts Society, October 8, 1985," *Wall Street Transcript*, December 23, 1985, 80245.
35. In a letter to Carl Seelig, Einstein wrote, "Between the conception of the idea of Special Relativity and the completion of the corresponding publication, there elapsed five or six weeks. But it would be hardly correct to consider this as a birthday, because earlier the arguments and building blocks were being prepared over a period of years. . . ." In a letter to R. S. Shankland in 1952, he estimated he "had worked for ten years" on the special theory. Ronald W. Clark, *Einstein: The Life and Times* (New York and Cleveland: The World Publishing Company, 1971), 74–85, 120.

CHAPTER 6

1. Viktor E. Frankl, *Man's Search for Meaning* (New York: Touchstone Books, 1984), 134.

2. Hoover's Online, *www.hoovers.com.*
3. Research Interview #1-E, page 11.
4. Bernard H. Semler, *Putting It All Together* (autobiography, draft version, 1998), 66.
5. Bernard H. Semler, "Measuring Operating Performance," 1. Article sent to the research team directly from Mr. Semler.
6. Research Interview #1-E, page 3.
7. "How 'Dr.' Ledder Cured Abbott Labs: Abbott Labs Was a Sick Company . . ." *Forbes,* August 1, 1975, 26; "Abbott Shapes Up," *Chemical Week,* October 20, 1976, 20; "Abbott Labs: Adding Hospital Supplies to Bolster Drug Operations," *Business Week,* July 23, 1979, 177; "Earnings Per Share for First Nine Months of 1980," *PR Newswire,* September 17, 1980; "Robert A. Schoellhorn Report on Company at Annual Shareholders Meeting," *Business Wire,* April 13, 1984; "Abbott: Profiting from Products That Cut Costs," *Business Week,* June 18, 1984, 56.
8. Research Interview #1-G, page 23.
9. Research Interview #2-E, page 1.
10. Research Interview #2-F, page 3.
11. "Managing: Carl E. Reichardt, Chairman, Wells Fargo & Co.," *Fortune,* February 27, 1989, 42.
12. Research Interview #11-H, pages 5, 9.
13. "Bold Banker: Wells Fargo Takeover of Crocker Is Yielding Profit but Some Pain," *Wall Street Journal,* August 5, 1986, A1.
14. Research Interview #11-H, pages 5, 9, 16.
15. Research Interview #11-H, pages 5, 9.
16. Research Interview #11-H, page 10.
17. "Managing: Carl E. Reichardt, Chairman, Wells Fargo & Co.," *Fortune,* February 27, 1989, 42; "A Banker Even Keynes Might Love," *Forbes,* July 2, 1984, 40; "Bold Banker: Wells Fargo Takeover of Crocker Is Yielding Profit but Some Pain," *Wall Street Journal,* August 5, 1986, A1.
18. Gary Hector, *Breaking the Bank: The Decline of BankAmerica* (Little, Brown & Company, 1988), 72.
19. Author experience in the early 1980s.
20. "Asset or Liability?" *Barron's,* October 20, 1986, 13; "BankAmerica Reports a Small Profit," *Wall Street Journal,* January 22, 1988, C4.
21. "Another Bout of Anxiety over Bank of America," *Business Week,* August 19, 1985, 33.
22. "Things Are Adding Up Again at Burroughs," *Business Week,* March 11, 1967, 192; "Anatomy of a Turnaround," *Forbes,* November 1, 1968, 25; "How Ray MacDonald's Growth Theory Created IBM's Toughest Competitor," *Fortune,* January 1977, 94.
23. "Things Are Adding Up Again at Burroughs," *Business Week,* March 11, 1967, 192; "The Burroughs Syndrome," *Business Week,* November 12, 1979, 82.
24. "The Burroughs Syndrome," *Business Week,* November 12, 1979, 82.

25. "Rubbermaid: TWST Names Award Winners Home Products: TWST Names Stanley C. Gault, Chairman and CEO, Rubbermaid Inc., for Gold Award, Home Products," *Wall Street Transcript*, April 18, 1988, 89116.
26. "Rubbermaid: Features: Marketing: The Billion-Dollar Dustpan," *Industry Week*, August 1, 1988, 46; "Quality of Products," *Fortune*, January 29, 1990, 42.
27. "Rubbermaid: Rubbermaid's Impact: New Stick Items Plentiful as Vendors 'Spruce Up' Household Cleaning Utensils," *Housewares*, January 1, 1990, 78.
28. "Chrysler's Next Generation," *Business Week*, December 19, 1988, 52.
29. Lee Iacocca with William Novak, *Iacocca: An Autobiography* (New York: Bantam, 1984), 161.
30. Lee Iacocca with William Novak, *Iacocca: An Autobiography* (New York: Bantam, 1984), 162, 163, 170, 199.
31. Lee Iacocca with William Novak, *Iacocca: An Autobiography* (New York: Bantam, 1984), 196.
32. "Iacocca Hands Over the Keys to Chrysler," *Investor's Business Daily*, January 4, 1993, 1.
33. "Mea Culpa," *Wall Street Journal*, September 17, 1990, A1.
34. "Chrysler to Buy Aircraft Maker," *Wall Street Journal*, June 20, 1985, A12.
35. "How Chrysler's $30,000 Sports Car Got Sideswiped," *Business Week*, January 23, 1989, 68.
36. "The Game's Not Over," *Forbes*, April 30, 1990, 76.
37. "Into a Skid," *The Economist*, June 16, 1990, 70; "After the Departure," *Fortune*, July 2, 1990, 55; "Can Iacocca Fix Chrysler Again?" *Fortune*, April 8, 1991, 50.
38. Robert A. Lutz, *Guts: The Seven Laws of Business That Made Chrysler the World's Hottest Car Company* (New York: John Wiley & Sons, Inc., 1998), 27.
39. "The Studied Gamble of Pitney Bowes," *Dun's Review*, February 1967, 30.
40. "Tough Choice," *Forbes*, May 15, 1965, 18.
41. "Tough Choice," *Forbes*, May 15, 1965, 18.
42. "Tough Choice," *Forbes*, May 15, 1965, 18.
43. "Fancy Footwork: Manager's Handbook," *Sales and Marketing Management*, July 1994, 41.
44. "Pitney Bowes: Jumping Ahead by Going High Tech," *Fortune*, October 19, 1992, 113; "Changes in Tax Law and Its Effects on Leasing Equipment," *Advantage*, July 1988, 28.
45. "Old-Line Selling for New Smokes Wins for Reynolds," *Business Week*, February 20, 1960, 74; *International Directory of Company Histories* (Chicago: St. James Press, 1991), 410.
46. "Voyage into the Unknown," *Forbes*, December 1, 1971, 30; Bryan Burrough and John Helyar, *Barbarians at the Gate* (New York: HarperCollins, 1991), 51.

47. "Voyage into the Unknown," *Forbes*, December 1, 1971, 30; Bryan Burrough and John Helyar, *Barbarians at the Gate* (New York: HarperCollins, 1991), 51.
48. "When Marketing Takes Over at R. J. Reynolds," *Business Week*, November 13, 1978, 82; "Voyage into the Unknown," *Forbes*, December 1, 1971, 30. RJR purchased McLean Industries in 1969 and Aminoil less than a year later. The article cited above ("When Marketing Takes . . .") states that in 1978 RJR committed a further $580 million on top of the $1.5 billion they spent in "earlier years." Thus, over approximately ten years, they poured over $2 billion into Sea-Land. Net stockholders' equity in 1978 was $2,657,900,000 according to the 1979 *Moody's* Report.
49. Bryan Burrough and John Helyar, *Barbarians at the Gate* (New York: HarperCollins, 1991), 62; "Cigarette Conglomerate," *Financial World*, February 5, 1969, 4; "New Fields for Reynolds Tobacco," *Financial World*, May 6, 1970, 13; "The Two-Tier Market Still Lives . . ." *Forbes*, March 1, 1974, 25; "R. J. Reynolds Stops a Slide in Market Share," *Business Week*, January 26, 1976, 92.
50. "Voyage into the Unknown," *Forbes*, December 1, 1971, 36.
51. Ken Iverson, *Plain Talk* (New York: John Wiley & Sons, 1998), 54–59.
52. "The Nucor Story," page 5 (document obtained from the Nucor Corporation)—chairman/vice chairman/president, vice president/general manager, department manager, supervisory/professional, hourly employee.
53. Richard Preston, *American Steel* (New York: Avon, 1991), 4–5.
54. Jeffrey L. Rodengen, *The Legend of Nucor Corporation* (Fort Lauderdale, Fla.: Write Stuff, 1997), 73–74; "The Nucor Story" (Nucor Web site)/Egalitarian Benefits, August 22, 1997.
55. Research Interview #7-G, page 4.
56. "Maverick Remakes Old-Line Steel: Nucor's Ken Iverson . . ." *Industry Week*, January 21, 1991, 26.
57. Ken Iverson, *Plain Talk* (New York: John Wiley & Sons, 1998), 14.
58. Richard Preston, *American Steel* (New York: Avon, 1991), 5.
59. "Hot Steel and Good Common Sense," *Management Review*, August 1992, 25.
60. John Strohmeyer, *Crisis in Bethlehem* (Pittsburgh: University of Pittsburgh Press, 1986), 34.
61. John Strohmeyer, *Crisis in Bethlehem* (Pittsburgh: University of Pittsburgh Press, 1986), 30–35, 86.
62. *Hoover's* Online.
63. *Hoover's* Online.
64. Jeffrey L. Rodengen, *The Legend of Nucor Corporation* (Fort Lauderdale, Fla.: Write Stuff, 1997), 101.
65. "Report of Darwin E. Smith to the Stockholders and the Men and Women of Kimberly-Clark Corporation," February 28, 1972.
66. Research Interview #5-E, page 10.

67. "Rae Takes On Paper Industry's Tough Lone Wolf," *Globe and Mail,* July 20, 1991, B1.

CHAPTER 7

1. "First Inaugural Address, March 4, 1933," Gorton Carruth and Eugene Ehrlich, *The Harper Book of American Quotations* (New York: Harper & Row, 1988), 230.
2. Drugstore.com 10K report filed February 28, 2000, page 28. "We incurred net losses of $123.9 million from the period from inception through January 2, 2000. We believe that we will continue to incur operating and net losses for at least the next four years (and possibly longer) and that the rate at which we will incur such losses will increase significantly from current levels. We intend to increase our operating expenses substantially as we: Increase our sales and marketing activities, particularly advertising efforts. . . ."
3. "There's No Business Like No Business," *Industry Standard,* August 7, 2000, 43.
4. "The Reluctant Webster," *Forbes,* October 18, 1999, 80.
5. "The Reluctant Webster," *Forbes,* October 18, 1999, 78.
6. "Struggling drugstore.com Cuts Staff: Online Retailer Fires 60 Employees—10 Percent of Workforce," *Seattle Post-Intelligencer,* October 21, 2000.
7. *Drug Topics,* February 3, 1997, 90; "Fleet-Footed Pharmacy," *Uplink Magazine,* a publication of Hughes Communications, Fall 1996.
8. "Walgreen—Pharmacy Chain of the Year, 1990," *Drug Topics,* April 23, 1990, 12.
9. "Walgreen—Pharmacy Chain of the Year, 1990," *Drug Topics,* April 23, 1990, 12.
10. "Walgreens Special Report: First in Pharmacy," *Drug Store News,* October 16, 1995, 27, 30.
11. Data taken directly from annual reports and 10K reports, 1971–1999.
12. "Plain and Fancy: Supermarket Boutiques Spur Kroger's Gains," *Barron's,* May 25, 1981, 37; "There's a Lot of Life Left in the Kroger Recap," *Business Week,* December 5, 1988, 164; "How Borrowing Bought Kroger More Than Time," *Business Week,* February 26, 1990, 71.
13. "Gillette Knows Shaving—and How to Turn Out Hot New Products," *Fortune,* October 14, 1996.
14. "Gillette: Gillette Sensor: A Case History," corporate paper, January 17, 1991, 9; "Gillette: How a $4 Razor Ends Up Costing $300 Million," *Business Week,* January 29, 1990, 62.
15. "Gillette: At Gillette, Disposable Is a Dirty Word," *Business Week,* May 29, 1989, 58.
16. Research Interview #3-E, page 13.

17. Research Interview #3-E, page 13.
18. Research Interview #3-F, page 5.
19. Research Interview #3-E, page 13.
20. Prominent physicists of the time had already developed similar theories, bolstered by remarkably good experimental evidence, that were mathematically consistent and equivalent to Einstein's exposition of relativity theory. All they lacked was the clear statement of a fundamental principle to start the chain of thinking that resulted in a clear picture of relativity theory and its consequences. In *Understanding Relativity*, by Stanley Goldberg (Boston: Birkhauser, 1984), the author points out, "There was not complete satisfaction with the theory that Lorentz and Poincaré produced in 1904, although that theory was *formally identical* to the theory that Einstein introduced a year later" (page 324). (Emphasis added.)
21. "Who Mattered and Why," *Time*, December 31, 1999, 48–58.
22. Richard Preston, *American Steel* (New York: Avon, 1991), 75.
23. Research Interview #7-E, pages 2–3.
24. "Nucor Corporation: Corporate Profile," *Wall Street Corporate Reporter*, September 9–15, 1996, 19.
25. Clayton M. Christensen, *The Innovator's Dilemma* (Boston: Harvard Business School Press, 1997), 88.
26. "Daniel S. Bricklin," *CIO*, December 15, 1999, 140.
27. "As Easy as Lotus 1-2-3," *Computerworld*, August 30, 1999, 71.
28. "Everyday Necessities, the Building Blocks," *InfoWorld*, October 26, 1998, 9; "IBM and Lotus Get Closer," *InformationWeek*, July 28, 1997, 73–80.
29. "Bigger Isn't Better: The Evolution of Portables," *InfoWorld*, October 26, 1998, 8–9.
30. Thomas J. Watson Jr. and Peter Petre, *Father, Son & Co.*: (New York: Bantam, 2001), 229.
31. Robert J. Serling, *Legend and Legacy* (New York: St. Martin's Press, 1992), 126.
32. *Centennial Review*, Internal Westinghouse Document, 1986.
33. "The Rise of Personal Digital Assistants," *Systems*, September 1992, 70–72; "Users Mourn Newton," *Computerworld*, March 9, 1998, 61–64.
34. Kara Swisher, *aol.com* (New York: Random House, 1998), 64.
35. Research Interview #9-D, page 11.
36. Research Interview #5-E, page 5.

CHAPTER 8

1. Quoted by Lorin Maazel, music director, New York Philharmonic, "Maazel Is to Lead Philharmonic," *New York Times*, January 30, 2001, A1.
2. "Some People Don't Like to Haggle," *Forbes*, August 27, 1984, 46.

3. Carl M. Brauer, "Circuit City Stores: Customer Satisfaction, Never Self-Satisfaction" (draft, April 1998), 6-1.
4. Total number of articles on good-to-great companies, pretransition decade = 176, posttransition decade = 423. Total number of *feature* articles on good-to-great companies, pretransition decade = 21, posttransition decade = 67.
5. Jeffrey L. Rodengen, *The Legend of Nucor* (Fort Lauderdale, Fla.: Write Stuff, 1997), 63, 70, 82.
6. Research Interview #5-B, page 5.
7. Research Interview #5-C, page 2.
8. "The Battle of the Bottoms," *Forbes*, March 24, 1997, 98.
9. Research Interview #1-C, page 7.
10. Research Interview #1-E, page 9.
11. Conversation between the author and Alan Wurtzel.
12. Research Interview #3-B, page 13.
13. Research Interview #4-D, page 3. The interviewee in this case was responding to the question, "Did the company make a conscious decision to initiate a major change or transition at some point during that time frame?"
14. Research Interview #5-A, page 7.
15. Research Interview #6-A, page 12.
16. Research Interview #7-A, page 3.
17. Research Interview #8-C, page 6.
18. Research Interview #9-F, page 25.
19. Research Interview #10-F, page 7.
20. Research Interview #11-G, page 6.
21. John Wooden and Jack Tobin, *They Call Me Coach* (Chicago: Contemporary, 1988), 244.
22. Research Interview #3-I, page 21.
23. Research Interview #1-G, page 31; Research Interview #1-A, page 14.
24. "Upjohn: The Upjohn Company: Remarks by C. H. Ludlow, Vice President and Treasurer, and L. C. Hoff, Vice President, before the Washington Society of Investment Analysts," February 20, 1974, *Wall Street Transcript*, March 11, 1974, 36246–36247.
25. Research Interview #6-C, pages 16–17.
26. Research Interview #7-F, page 11.
27. Fortune 1000 rankings, from Fortune.com Web site, February 9, 2001.
28. "Turning W-L into a Marketing Conglomerate," *Business Week*, March 5, 1979, 60; "Warner-Lambert," *Wall Street Transcript*, January 7, 1980, 56636.
29. "Chasing after Merck," *Forbes*, November 10, 1980, 36.
30. "Warner-Lambert Company," *Wall Street Transcript*, December 21, 1981, 64122.
31. "Warner-Lambert," *Financial World*, September 5, 1989, 24.
32. "On the Mend," *Barron's*, January 2, 1995, 19.

33. "W-L to Acquire IMED at Cost of $465 Million," *New York Times*, June 8, 1982, D4; "W-L Plan to Buy Imed Corp. Draws Cool Reaction by Analysts Due to Cost, Timing," *Wall Street Journal*, June 14, 1982, A41; "W-L to Dump Imed," *San Diego Business Journal*, December 2, 1985, 1.
34. The Warner-Lambert Web site no longer exists and you are automatically directed to the Pfizer site. Furthermore, the site includes information on how Warner-Lambert stockholders can exchange their shares for Pfizer stock.
35. Peter F. Drucker, *Managing for the Future* (New York: Truman Talley Books/Dutton, 1992), 160.
36. "In the News," *Fortune*, July 3, 1978, 20.
37. "Harris Is Raising Its Bet on the Office of the Future," *Business Week*, July 18, 1983, 134.
38. "Harris Corp.'s Bold Strategy," *Forbes*, April 25, 1983, 96; "Harris Is Raising Its Bet on the Office of the Future," *Business Week*, July 18, 1983, 134.
39. "Merits of Harris Tie to Lanier Debated," *New York Times*, August 11, 1983, D5, plus annual financial statements drawn from *Moody's* reports.
40. "Harris Heads into the Office," *Computerworld*, October 12, 1983, 29.

CHAPTER 9

1. Michael Ray and Rochelle Myers, *Creativity in Business* (New York: Doubleday & Company, 1986), 113.
2. *Hoover's Online* and Standard & Poor's Corporation Records, January 2001.
3. Sam Walton with John Huey, *Sam Walton: Made in America* (New York: Doubleday & Company, 1992), 35.
4. Sandra S. Vance and Roy V. Scott, *Wal-Mart: A History of Sam Walton's Retail Phenomenon* (New York: Twayne, 1994) 169–171; Bob Ortega, *In Sam We Trust* (New York: Times Books, 1998).
5. Research done for the *Built to Last* study; original sources courtesy of Hewlett-Packard Company Archives.
6. Research done for the *Built to Last* study; original sources courtesy of Hewlett-Packard Company Archives.
7. Letter from Bernard M. Oliver to IEEE Awards Board, May 23, 1972, courtesy of Hewlett-Packard Company Archives.
8. "Packard Style," *Palo Alto Daily News*, March 27, 1996, 10.
9. According to Amy Chamberlain, of the David and Lucile Packard Foundation, the amount was $5.62 billion as of the date the funds were received.
10. James C. Collins and Jerry I. Porras, *Built to Last* (New York: HarperCollins, 1997), 1.
11. David Packard, Commencement Speech, Colorado College, June 1, 1964, courtesy of Hewlett-Packard Company Archives.

12. Merck & Company, Management Guide, Corporate Policy Statement, February 3, 1989, courtesy of Merck & Company; George W. Merck, "An Essential Partnership—the Chemical Industry and Medicine," speech presented to the Division of Medicinal Chemistry, American Chemical Society, April 22, 1935; 1991 Merck & Company Annual Report, inside cover; David Bollier and Kirk O. Hansen, *Merck & Co.* (A-D), Business Enterprise Trust Case, No. 90-013, case D, 3.
13. George W. Merck, Speech at the Medical College of Virginia at Richmond, December 1, 1950, courtesy of Merck & Company Archives.
14. Richard Schickel, *The Disney Version* (New York: Simon & Schuster, 1968), 310.
15. Harold Mansfield, *Vision: A Saga of the Sky* (New York: Madison Publishing Associates, 1986), 167–201.
16. Robert J. Serling, *Legend and Legacy* (New York: St. Martin's Press), 79.
17. Robert J. Serling, *Legend and Legacy* (New York: St. Martin's Press), 20–22, 132.
18. According to "How Boeing Bet the Company and Won," in *Audacity*, winter 1993, 52, and Robert J. Serling, the project would cost between $15 and $16 million. We verified the $15 million figure with Boeing's income statements and balance sheets for the period 1947–1951.
19. Robert J. Serling, *Legend and Legacy* (New York: St. Martin's Press), 159, 323, 400–405, 409.
20. Standard & Poor's Industry Surveys: Aerospace and Defense, February 15, 2001, Robert E. Friedman, CPA, Aerospace and Defense Analyst. Also, in 1999, Boeing had twice the revenues of Airbus in this segment of the industry ($38,409,000,000 versus $16,817,000,000) according to *Hoover's Online.*

APPENDIX 8.A

1. "Hermit Kingdom," *Wall Street Journal*, December 12, 1958, A6; "Remodeling the A&P," *Business Week*, March 23, 1963, 36; "Ailing A&P," *Wall Street Journal*, April 21, 1964, A6; "New Men for A&P's Top Rungs," *Business Week*, June 20, 1964, 32; "A&P Reorganization Is Announced; Move Takes Effect February 24,", *Wall Street Journal*, January 15, 1969, A4; "A&P—Awakening the Giant," *Financial World*, February 25, 1970, 5; "Great Expectations," *Barron's*, January 19, 1970, 5; "Renewing A&P," *Business Week*, February 20, 1971, 68; "How A&P Got Creamed," *Fortune*, January 1973, 103; "A&P Goes outside Ranks for First Time, Picks Scott to Assume Eventual Command," *Wall Street Journal*, December 11, 1974, A8.
2. "IBM's New Copier," *Business Week*, March 22, 1976, 52; "Addressograph Gets Ash and $2.7 Million," *Business Week*, October 4, 1976, 31; "How to Nip Away at the Xerox Market," *Business Week*, November 8,

1976, 68; "Roy Ash's Challenge," *Newsweek*, December 13, 1976, 90; "Roy Ash Is Having Fun at Addressogrief-Multigrief," *Fortune*, February 27, 1978, 46; "Coup at AM; Roy Ash Resigns Under Fire," *Time*, March 23, 1981, 71; "Curious Tale of Mr. Black," *London Financial Times*, February 27, 1982, 28; "AM Files Chapter 11 Petition," *New York Times*, April 15, 1982, D1.

3. Gary Hector, *Breaking the Bank: The Decline of BankAmerica* (Little, Brown & Company, 1988); "At BankAmerica a New Regime Strives to Reverse Declines," *Wall Street Journal*, May 20, 1982, A1; "The Cost to Armacost," *Economist*, February 16, 1985, 76; "Bank of America Rushes into the Information Age," *Business Week*, April 15, 1985, 110; "Sam Armacost's Sea of Troubles," *Banker*, September 1, 1985, 1; "Schwab Joins the Ranks of Bank of America Dropouts," *Business Week*, August 25, 1986, 37; "Add Security Pacific to Bank of America," *Wall Street Journal*, August 13, 1991, A1; "BankAmerica Finds It Got a Lot of Woe," *Wall Street Journal*, July 22, 1993, A1.
4. John Strohmeyer, *Crisis in Bethlehem* (Pittsburgh: University of Pittsburgh Press, 1994); "Bethlehem Steel," *Wall Street Journal*, May 13, 1977, A4; "Bethlehem Sets New Pay Reduction," *Wall Street Journal*, January 21, 1983, A5; "Bethlehem to Ask Probe," *Wall Street Journal*, January 24, 1984, A2; "Making Retirees Share the Pain," *Business Week*, April 16, 1984, 50; "Bethlehem Plans Further Cuts," *Wall Street Journal*, January 15, 1985, A2; "Is Bethlehem Investing in a Future It Doesn't Have?" *Business Week*, July 8 1985, 56; "Bethlehem Exits Freight Car Building," *Journal of Commerce*, November 1, 1991, B2; "Faded Glory," *Forbes*, March 16, 1992, 40.
5. "Tandy Agrees to Buy Assets of Eckerd Unit," *Wall Street Journal*, July 5, 1985, A4; "Diversification Appeals," *Chain Store Age Executive*, August 1, 1979, 81; "Video Follies," *Forbes*, November 5, 1984, 43–45; "Jack Eckerd Holders Will Receive All Cash in a $1.2 Billion Buyout," *Wall Street Journal*, April 21, 1986, A31; "J. C. Penney Gets Eckerd Shares," *Wall Street Journal*, December 18, 1996, B10.
6. "Great Western: Great Western Financial Corporation: Remarks by James F. Montgomery, President, to the Security Analysts of San Francisco, March 8, 1977," *Wall Street Transcript*, April 25, 1977, 46873–46874; "Great Western: Great Western Financial Corporation: Remarks by James F. Montgomery, Chairman and President, to the Security Analysts of San Francisco, November 9, 1981," *Wall Street Transcript*, December 21, 1981, 64131–64132; "Great Western: Great Western Financial Corporation (GWF): Remarks by James F. Montgomery, Chairman and Chief Executive Officer, to the Los Angeles Society of Financial Analysts, September 11, 1984," *Wall Street Transcript*, October 22, 1984, 75659–75660; "Great Western: The Corporation: Strategies: How Playing It Safe Worked for Great Western: It Waited until Regulations Eased to Go on a Buying Spree," *Business Week*, September 7,

1987, 70; "Great Western: Corporate Focus: Great Western Financial Seeks to Chart a Fresh Course: No. 2 U.S. Thrift Faces Burden of Soured Home Loans, Bloated Overhead," *Wall Street Journal*, May 17, 1993, B4.

7. Bryan Burrough and John Helyar, *Barbarians at the Gate* (New York: HarperCollins, 1991); "Cigarette Conglomerate," *Financial World*, February 5, 1969, 4; "Voyage into the Unkown," *Forbes*, December 1, 1971, 30; "When Marketing Takes Over at R. J. Reynolds," *Business Week*, November 13, 1978, 82.
8. "A Paper Tiger Grows Claws," *Business Week*, August 23, 1969, 100–102; "No-Longer-So-Great Scott," *Forbes*, August 1, 1972, 25; "Now an Outsider Will Run Scott Paper," *Business Week*, April 23, 1979, 39, 42; "Scott a Paper Tiger," *Advertising Age*, November 3, 1980, 96; "Scott Paper's New Chief," *Business Week*, November 30, 1981, 62; "Scott Isn't Lumbering Anymore," *Fortune*, September 30, 1985, 48–55; "Bermuda Triangle," *Forbes*, January 6, 1992, 284; "Al Dunlap: An Insider's View," *Navigator*, December 1997; "Did CEO Dunlap Save Scott Paper—or Just Pretty It Up? The Shredder," *Business Week*, January 15,1996.
9. "Silo, Discount Appliance Chain, Enjoys Payoff from Hard Sell," *Barron's*, March 29, 1971, 35; "An Appliance Dealer with Real Clout," *Business Week*, November 6, 1971, 76; "Cyclops Acquires Silo," *Wall Street Journal*, October 16, 1979, A5; "Dixons Makes $384 Million U.S. Bid," *London Financial Times*, February 18, 1987, 1; "Silo-Dixons Power: How Far Can It Reach?" *Consumer Electronics*, November 1988, 14; "Dixons Strategic Move into Los Angeles Area," *London Financial Times*, November 12, 1989, 10; "Shake-up at Silo," *Discount Store News*, March 4, 1991, 1; "Dixons Tightens Grip on Silo," *HFD—the Weekly Home Furnishings Newspaper*, February 3, 1992, 77.
10. "Upjohn: Two Upjohn Antibiotics Barred from Sale; FDA–Drug Company Confrontation Is Seen," *Wall Street Journal*, May 15, 1969, A38; "Upjohn: Tweedle Dee: Upjohn Can't Ever Seem to Do Quite as Well in Ethical Drugs as Tweedle Dum, Its Corporate Lookalike, Eli Lilly, Which Is No Great Shakes Either," *Forbes*, March 1, 1970, 65–66; "Upjohn: Two Upjohn Drugs Linked to Thirty-two Deaths Needn't Be Banned, FDA Aide Testifies," *Wall Street Journal*, January 30, 1975, A14; "Upjohn: Hair-Raising Happenings at Upjohn (Testing a Cure for Baldness, the Company Squirms at the Unwelcome Clamor)," *Fortune*, April 6, 1981, 67–69; "Upjohn: R&D Scoreboard: Drugs," *Business Week*, June 22, 1987, 145; "Upjohn: Upjohn's Stock Falls on Study's Claim Its Anti-Baldness Drug Has Side Effects," *Wall Street Journal*, February 9, 1988, A2; "Upjohn: Law: Upjohn Settles Liability Suit over Halcion Sleeping Pill," *Wall Street Journal*, August 12, 1991, B2.
11. "Gillette President S. K. Hensley Resigns to Accept Presidency of Warner-Lambert," *Wall Street Journal*, June 21, 1967, A32; "Say Little, Do Much," *Forbes*, December 1, 1974, 52; "After the Diversification That Failed," *Business Week*, February 28, 1977, 58; "Turning W-L into a

Marketing Conglomerate," *Business Week*, March 5, 1979, 60; "Hagan Outlines Strategic Plan," *PR Newswire*, October 29, 1980; "Beating the Japanese in Japan," *Forbes*, April 27, 1981, 44; "W-L: Reversing Direction to Correct Neglect," *Business Week*, June 15, 1981, 65; "Hagan Outlines Strategic Actions," *PR Newswire*, December 2, 1981; "Hagan Announces IMED Purchase," *PR Newswire*, June 7, 1982; "Hagan Defends IMED Purchase," *PR Newswire*, July 12, 1982; "Did W-L Make a $468 Million Mistake?" *Business Week*, November 21, 1983, 123; "The Succession at Warner-Lambert," *Business Week*, September 17, 1984, 52.

12. "Things Are Adding Up Again at Burroughs," *Business Week*, March 11, 1967, 192; "How Ray MacDonald's Growth Theory Created IBM's Toughest Competitor," *Fortune*, January 1977, 94; "A Tough 'Street Kid' Steps in at Burroughs," *Business Week*, October 29, 1979, 50; "Will a Shake-up Revive Burroughs?" *Business Week*, May 4, 1981, 53; "Can Burroughs Catch Up Again?" *Forbes*, March 28, 1983, 78.
13. Robert A. Lutz, *Guts: The Seven Laws of Business That Made Chrysler the World's Hottest Car Company* (New York: John Wiley & Sons, 1998), 27; "President Iacocca," *Wall Street Journal*, June 28, 1982, A1; "Is There Life after Iacocca?" *Forbes*, April 8, 1985, 75; "Lee Iacocca's Time of Trouble," *Fortune*, March 14, 1988, 79; "Can Iacocca Fix Chrysler Again?" *Fortune*, April 8, 1991, 50; "After Lee," *The Economist*, March 21, 1992, 70; "How Chrysler Filled Detroit's Biggest Shoes," *Wall Street Journal*, September 7, 1994, B1; "Daimler-Benz Will Acquire Chrysler in $36 Billion Deal That Will Reshape Industry," *New York Times*, May 7, 1998, A6.
14. "Harris-Intertype, Radiation Inc. Directors Approve Merger Pact Valued at $39 Million," *Wall Street Journal*, April 3, 1967, 30; "Critical Mass?" *Forbes*, April 15, 1976, 86; "Technology Transfer's Master," *Business Week*, October 10, 1977, 120; "Harris Corp.'s Remarkable Metamorphosis," *Forbes*, May 26, 1980, 45; "Harris Corp.'s Bold Strategy," *Forbes*, April 25, 1983, 96; "Harris Is Raising Its Bet on the Office of the Future," *Business Week*, July 18, 1983, 134; "Harris Corp. Elects Hartley to Added Post of Chief," *Wall Street Journal*, April 1, 1986, A45; "New Harris President Prefers Growth to Downsizing," UPI, April 23, 1993.
15. "Hasbro: On a Roll: Toymaker Hasbro Continues String of 25% Yearly Growth," *Barron's*, July 19, 1982, 40; "Hasbro: Hasbro Toys Find Profits in Tradition," *Wall Street Journal*, December 12, 1983, A29; "Hasbro: News: Hasbro Gets Its Guns: Stephen Hassenfeld's Loading Up for Battle," *Industry Week*, April 30, 1984, 17–18; "Hasbro: Silver: A Play on Toys: Hasbro Bradley's Hassenfeld," *Financial World*, April 16, 1985, 29; "Hasbro: Merry Christmas: It Has Already Come for Hasbro, Biggest U.S. Toymaker," *Barron's*, December 23, 1985, 34; "Hasbro: The Corporation: Strategies: How Hasbro Became King of the Toymakers: With $1.2 Billion in Sales and $99 Million in Profits, It Is Now No. 1 Worldwide," *Business Week*, September 22, 1986, 90–92; "Hasbro: Marketing: Toys:

It's Kid Brother's Turn to Keep Hasbro Hot: Alan Hassenfeld Must Fill Big Shoes at the Toymaker," *Business Week,* June 26, 1989, 152–153.

16. "Rubbermaid: Sincere Tyranny (Why Has Stanley Gault Spent the Last Four Years Moving and Shaking at Rubbermaid? It Was a Case of Serious Problems Masked by Cheery Numbers)," *Forbes,* January 28, 1985, 54–55; "Rubbermaid: Rubbermaid Emerges a 'Clear' Winner; Food Storage Containers," *Chain Store Age—General Merchandise Trends,* October 1986, 67; "Why the Bounce at Rubbermaid? The Company Sells Humdrum Goods in a Mature Market, and Most of Its Competitors Undercut Its Prices. But It Has Doubled Sales and Tripled Earnings in the Past Six Years," *Fortune,* April 13, 1987, 77–78; "Rubbermaid: America's Most Admired Company," *Fortune,* Feburary 7, 1994, 50–54; "Rubbermaid: From the Most Admired to Just Acquired: How Rubbermaid Managed to Fail," *Fortune,* November 23, 1998, 32–33.
17. "Henry Singleton's Singular Conglomerate," *Forbes,* May 1, 1976, 38; "Two Ph.D.'s Turn Teledyne into a Cash Machine," *Business Week,* November 22, 1976, 133; "The Sphinx Speaks," *Forbes,* February 20, 1978, 33; "Teledyne's Winning Roster," *Forbes,* August 17, 1981, 35; "Parting with Henry Singleton: Such Sweet Sorrow for Teledyne?" *Business Week,* April 9, 1990, 81; "Teledyne to Pay $17.5 Million to Settle U.S. Criminal Charges," *Washington Post,* October 6, 1992, D6; "Teledyne Struggles to Recapture Magic of Yesterday," *Wall Street Journal,* November 22, 1993, B4; "Richard Simmons to Share Spotlight at Allegheny Teledyne, Sees 'Good' Fit," *Wall Street Journal,* April 3, 1996, B8.

INDEX

Page numbers in *italics* refer to figures and illustrations.

Built to Last

10th Anniversary Edition
with a new foreword by Jim Collins

Jim Collins & Jerry I. Porras

'*Good to Great* is about turning good results into great results; *Built to Last* is about turning great results into an enduring great company' Jim Collins

This is not a book about charismatic visionary leaders. It is not about visionary product concepts or visionary products or visionary market insights. Nor is it about just having a corporate vision. This is a book about something far more important, enduring, and substantial. This is a book about visionary companies.

Drawing upon a six-year research project at the Stanford University Graduate School of Business, Collins and Porras took eighteen truly exceptional and long-lasting companies and studied each company in direct comparison to one of its top competitors. They examined the companies from their very beginnings to the present day – as start-ups, as midsize companies and as large corporations. Throughout, the authors asked: 'What makes the truly exceptional companies different from other companies?'

Filled with hundreds of specific examples and organized into a coherent framework of practical concepts that can be applied by managers and entrepreneurs at all levels, *Built to Last* provides a master blueprint for building organizations that will prosper long into the twenty-first century and beyond.